Two Faces of a Serial Rapist

by Jack Mallard

Copyright © 2012 Jack Mallard
All Rights Reserved. No part of this publication may be reproduced or transmitted in any form or by any means, electronic or mechanical, including photocopy, recording, or any information storage and retrieval system now known or to become known, without permission in writing, except in the case of brief 'fair use' quotations or commentary.

ISBN: 1478213590
ISBN 13: 9781478213598

AUTHOR'S NOTES AND ACKNOWLEDGEMENTS:

The names of some victims have been changed to protect their privacy. The fictional names assumed and used are not intended to identify any other human being.

Italics and bold print are added for emphasis within the author's text and the trial testimony.

Grateful acknowledgement is given to Honorable Jay Stephenson, Cobb County Superior Court Clerk and his Office for use of the photographs from the archives of the trial of the State vs. Terry Greenway; and to the Georgia Department of Corrections for the current photograph of Inmate Terry Greenway, while in prison. My thanks also go to certain people for technical support during the writing and publishing of this book including my daughter-in-law, Dawn Mallard; son-in-law, Frank Neubert, both of Cumming, Georgia; and friends, Christie L. Davis, of Atlanta, Kimberly B. McCoy, Victim Advocate, Cobb County District Attorney's Office; Cobb County District Attorney Pat Head for access to the archived files from the trial of the Terry Greenway case; and to my friend, Debbie Clark, Gainesville, Georgia, for her editing support.

OTHER BOOKS BY THE AUTHOR:

The Atlanta Child Murders: the Night Stalker
Copyright © 2009 Jack Mallard

TWO FACES OF A SERIAL RAPIST

She awakened to the intruder's hand over her mouth, and with a knife, warning her: *Don't scream. I won't hurt you. I'll just be a minute, and I'll be gone.*

He lived two different lives: one by day, the other by night. By day, he was married with three teenage boys, worked two jobs, and was a pillar of the church and community, but at night he terrorized women in apartment buildings for years. He was a Jekyll and Hyde sexual predator.

⌘ ⌘ ⌘

"Rape" is the carnal knowledge of a female, forcibly and against her will. *Official Code of Georgia 16-6-1*.

DNA (deoxyribonucleic acid): The basic genetic material of our body which determines who we are—the blueprint or story of our body.

DEDICATION

I dedicate this book to the victims of violent crime; the Victim-Advocates in all Prosecution Offices, and particularly those of the Cobb County, Georgia, District Attorney's Office, all of whom are charged with the high responsibility of giving comfort, aid, and assistance to those victims during a time of recovery, and providing to the extent possible, support to their care while navigating the criminal justice system; and to those Police Officers and Detectives who investigate such crimes; and to those Prosecutors who vigorously seek justice on behalf of those victims. Likewise, I acknowledge and give thanks to all of those witnesses who testified in this prosecution on behalf of the State of Georgia—especially those *victims* who had the courage to come forward when called upon and to expose themselves to the invasion of their privacy and the lasting effect of a public prosecution upon their memories. May you have peace of mind!

JACK MALLARD
Prosecutor, retired (1967-2007)

TABLE OF CONTENTS

Chapter 1 – The Serial Rapist 7

Chapter 2 – The Arrest 15

Chapter 3 – Pre-Trial Proceedings 27

Chapter 4 – The Beginning to an End 39

Chapter 5 – The Crimes 53

    Cinnamon Ridge Apartments, January 7, 1990 53

    Woodlake Apartments, November 5, 1984 72

    Powers Ferry Apartments, August 26, 1987 82

    Concepts 21 Apartments, April 10, 1988 100

    Concepts 21 Apartments, July 15, 1988 115

    Concepts 21 Apartments, October 15, 1988 132

    Woodknoll Apartments, March 23, 1989 165

    Concepts 21 Apartments, August 10, 1989 176

Chapter 6 – The DNA Evidence 193

Chapter 7 – The Defense Evidence 239

Chapter 8 – The Jury, Verdict and Sentence 263

Chapter 9 – The Epilogue 269

Rape – the Crime 269

The Victims – in their words 271

Inmate Terry Greenway – in his own words 283

The Parole Board - the unspoken words 289

FOREWORD

Victims of crime suffer emotionally, physically, and financially from the acts committed against them. Criminal acts committed both locally and nationwide result in millions of Americans being victimized each year. Criminal acts happen to those we know, those we love, those who are strangers, coworkers, neighbors ... and the list goes on ... because anyone can be a victim of crime at any time.

The affects and impact of victimization are as varied as is the crime for each individual victim. Because we are all different, have different backgrounds, different beliefs, and different coping skills, we all deal with our victimizations differently. Some victims experience long term trauma while others, more easily, deal with what's happened. Some victims are merely inconvenienced and some lives are forever altered. And let us not forget that it is not just the victim that is impacted—because crime has a ripple effect (imagine the old cliché of dropping a pebble in a pond and watching the ripple effect of one small pebble), the victim's family, friends, coworkers, acquaintances, and indeed, the entire community surrounding them are forever impacted by this crime as well.

Victims of rape may in fact suffer the most personal form of trauma known – the invasion of her body by someone, a stranger in the case described in this book, without her consent or willingness. Rape is an act of violence in which the sex act is used as a weapon. Rape is a crime of power and control. The rapist uses the sex act, sometimes with force, sometimes with manipulation, sometimes with threats, to gain and maintain power and control over his victim. While forcible rapes account for less than 10% of all violent crimes reported to law enforcement, the impact and effect on victims is life-altering.

It is somewhat ironic that the very act that many consider as showing affection, love, intimacy and trust in most relationships can come to mean the exact opposite in cases where women are raped. Forced sex acts against an unwilling person often results in mistrust, lack of trust, fear, rage, hopelessness, despair, depression and anxiety for victims.

In the case of the State of Georgia vs. Terry Thaddeus Greenway, all of the victims that he raped were minding their own business. In fact, most if not all of them, were asleep in their own homes when he chose to attack them. Now, if that's not a cowardly act to awaken someone and then rape them, I don't know what is. Greenway is the classic serial rapist: he is white; he is educated; he was in his 30's; he was married; he claimed to be religious; he used intoxication as an excuse; he attacked in or near the victim's home; and he used a weapon, in most cases. While he may not have been overly forcible with his victims, the fact alone that a strange man has entered your home, your place of safety and refuge, and awakened you from sleep is intimidating enough.

While it is devastating to be raped by someone known to you, it is equally as troublesome to be raped by a stranger. Imagine the questions:

- Why me?
- Why now?
- What did I do?
- What did I not do?

As a victim advocate, I advise victims that the "Why" questions can never really be answered. The offender, and the offender alone, is responsible for what choices he made and when he made those choices – not the victim. The victim is the innocent party in the crime of rape.

While I had no personal involvement with the original prosecution of the Greenway trial, I was asked by Jack (Mr. Mallard) to contact the victims to discuss with them the fact that he was writing this book. At the same time, I researched when Greenway would be eligible for parole consideration. Upon calling a victim in an older case such as this one, I want to be prepared to answer any possible question since it is likely that the victim has had no contact with our office in quite some time. In reality, based on the evolution of the field of victim advocacy, it is unlikely that the victims had a full-time advocate available to them during the prosecution of this case and even less likely that they are aware of what resources exist today which did not exist in the late 1980's/ early 1990's.

During this research, I did in fact learn that Greenway would be considered for parole in February 2013. This does not mean he will get an early release, just that by law he must be considered within this time frame. I needed to ensure that the victims were registered, if they chose, with the State Board of Pardons and Paroles Office of Victim Services so that they themselves could be notified of potential parole decisions.

I remember clearly making the intrusive phone calls to each victim. Imagine hearing from the prosecutor's office, some of them for the first time since approximately 20 years after they've testified …. Needless to say, most of them were surprised, obviously, to hear from me. As you may imagine, the reactions were as diverse as the victims themselves….

I recall one victim, upon learning who I was, asking "Is he out?" Another victim shared with me that "this" [the rape] had a major impact on her life, and she is still affected by it. She expressed fear and concern over retaliation against her from the defendant and/or his friends and family. One victim said she wanted nothing even remotely "out there" that he could find that would identify where she currently lives. One victim was adamant that she wanted nothing to do with me, this office, the case at all and was, while not hostile to me, obviously upset at the phone call. One victim's husband shared with me that, on most days, the victim seemed to be getting along and moving on, but on other days, something would happen that would trigger her and she would have a bad day – but even after all this time, she is still sensitive to this [talking about the case]. Yet another victim expressed that, with the support of her husband, she has moved on and is doing well with her life – but did tell me that her children do not know and will never know of her victimization. This same victim said that, while she had moved on, this was devastating enough that it still can affect her after all these years; because of her range of emotions, anxiety, crying, distressed and disturbed, I encouraged her to return to counseling to get her through this unexpected reminder of the traumatic event in her life. She agreed that this would be a good idea.

Not uncommonly, most of the victims have moved out of the county, some even out of State in order to remove themselves from this area and possible reminders, or triggers, from their lives.

Yes, rape is a crime that impacts the lives of victims, often times for many years after the incident. And while we know that rape is the most under-reported crime in America (ncvc.org), it is shocking to realize that someone in this country is sexually assaulted every two minutes. For victims, it is difficult to emotionally overcome the trauma inflicted by this violent crime.

If you are a victim or survivor of rape, I encourage you to take good care of yourself while reading this book. Your experience and your reactions to it are your own, no one else's. Do not blame yourself for what happened – the offender is to blame. Give yourself permission to grieve your loss and to experience a wide range of and variety of emotions. Know your limits… know your abilities… some of you can survive on your own, but some of you will need help to establish a 'new normal' in your life. Seeking, asking for help is courageous, not weakness!

If you know someone who has been a victim of rape, believe her! Know and understand that she will experience a variety of emotions and feelings. Know that every survivor is different and will have different reactions and will therefore have different needs. Accept the survivors' decisions on how they cope/deal with the situation – this may be the one thing the survivor can control. Help the survivor find support if that is her choice, but don't take it personally if the victim will not accept your help or support. Know what resources are available if/when the victim wants/needs help. Mostly, just be there for the victim, not blaming or judging her, but just being there for support.

NATIONAL RESOURCES:
National Sexual Assault Hotline: 1-800-656-HOPE (4673)
Rape, Abuse, & Incest National Network: RAINN.org

Kimberly B. McCoy
Victim Advocate

I

THE SERIAL RAPIST

She awoke to a shadowy figure standing beside her bed, demanding: "Don't scream. I won't hurt you. Just do what I tell you and you won't be hurt. I won't be here but just a minute and I'll be gone."

The words, that he wouldn't hurt her, were not very comforting to the woman who had just been awakened by a masked intruder with a knife in his hand. She would, however, comply with his every wish. It was a matter of life or death, she feared. She would do whatever it took to live for another day, another time, in order to avoid a worse fate. Perhaps, justice would eventually prevail if she could live. Live to identify him. Live to testify against him. Hopefully, she could live to see him in handcuffs and leg-irons as he would be taken from the courtroom to state prison—never to harm anyone again.

When he was finished with her, the intruder left as he entered—silently in the night to prey on other women for several years under similar circumstances. You see, he was a serial rapist. He enjoyed the hunt and the excitement of taking what he wanted, although he was married with a family.

Nay, not only that, he was a man of the Church, and a man of two lives: one by day with two jobs, a pillar of the church and community, married with three teen-age boys, while at night roaming apartment complexes near I-75 North of Atlanta in Cobb County, peeping in windows until he found what he wanted: a young female who was alone in a ground level apartment and hopefully asleep. She would be his victim.

The serial rapist so mimicked his crimes, the modus operandi was akin to leaving his fingerprints. There was no doubt that once he was caught, he would be implicated in many assaults, but how many victims would there be before he was caught?

⌘ ⌘ ⌘

In law, Modus Operandi means a method of operating as in how a recidivist criminal repetitively commits his crimes. In some cases, the different crimes are so similar or alike that it's like leaving his signature. In other words, whoever committed one crime, committed all of them. Other cases may not be so obviously alike but show some unusual characteristics which are relevant to identifying the offender's style of work.

What causes anyone to commit a crime, much less the rape of a female? Most crimes have an obvious motive such as the need or desire for monetary gain, jealousy, or an array of domestic violence—some being *just plain meanness*. With rapists, they generally do not just get up one morning and decide they are going out to rape for the first time in their lives. From my experience as a prosecutor, stranger-to-stranger rapists start off at a young age, usually with minor crimes such as prowling, loitering, peeping, exposing themselves, and possession of pornographic material. Some (of them) tend to gradually move up to more serious offenses such as break-ins, assaults, and, at times, theft of women's undergarments—before they graduate to the "big-time" with burglaries and rapes.

Empirical studies will bear this out, and as any long-time prosecutor or judge will confirm, there is a correlation between the rapist and certain other minor offenses. No such correlation with such prior offenses will necessarily be found for the "murderer" or the "thief" who may commit their first such crime at any age, but I have seen first-hand, cases where the rapist possessed pornography or committed certain minor offenses, as a precursor to a rape, some ultimately ending with the murder of the victim. That, however, should be no surprise to those in law enforcement. I view such other offenses as having a strong correlation with sexual offenses.

It's worth noting that there are empirical studies showing that about one-third of normal men (male college students) have a proclivity to rape if they could be sure they would not be caught. *Rape Proclivity Among Males*, Neil M. Malamuth, Journal of Social Issues, Vol. 37, Issue 4, Fall 1981, published online April 14, 2010. Nevertheless, I can say that a small percentage of males commit the vast majority of stranger-to-stranger rapes. They are committed by serial rapists.

If one is curious about the motive for rape, it should be obvious: lust. To some, it is unrestrained, perhaps uncontrollable sexual desires—that which may cause him to leave his home, wife and children, and seek that which will excite him to the point of fulfilling his craving, and his need to sexually control another.

⌘ ⌘ ⌘

The term "Gentle Rapist" is misleading, an oxymoron. There is no such adjective for rape as "gentle" but I use it because, apparently, this rapist considers it less offensive and more acceptable if he assures his victim, in so many words, to "just relax, I won't hurt you, I'll be gone in a minute." From his view, being considerate, and conveying the message that he won't hurt them is mitigating and will give the victim a way out through submission and avoidance. The victim's fear and torment in those minutes, seemingly like an eternity, followed by years or a lifetime of psychological injury does not enter into the rapist's consideration.

"Gentle" is described in part: "considerate or kindly in disposition; amiable; not harsh, severe, or violent; easily managed or handled; docile." *The American Heritage Dictionary, 2nd College Ed.*

"Rape" is described in pertinent part: "carnal knowledge of a female, forcibly and against her will." *Official Code of Georgia 16-6-1*. The Courts have interpreted the law that the only force necessary to constitute the crime of rape is threats or intimidation: that consent through fear is no consent at all, and no positive resistance is necessary to constitute rape.

The law of Georgia was not always as supportive of the rape victim. For years during the early part of my career, I prosecuted rape cases when it was harder to convict in instances where the victim "gave in" or "submitted" under circumstances that now would constitute forcible rape. The Georgia Supreme Court in **1897** in the *Mathews v. State* decision said in part:

> *"In order that the offense might constitute rape, she must have resisted with all her power and kept up that resistance as long as she had strength. Opposition to the sexual act by mere words is not sufficient. Any consent of the woman, however reluctant, is fatal to a conviction for rape. The passive policy will not do. There must be the utmost reluctance and resistance."*

That legal principle remained the law until **1976** when the Court in the *Curtis v. The State* decision in revisiting the "force" issue in a rape case stated:

> *"We expressly disapprove and will not in the future apply this and similar language used in these and other cases, because such language is on its face plainly inconsistent with the principle that lack of resistance, induced by fear, is not legally cognizable consent but is force. Moreover, such language, literally applied, would strip a rape victim of the right to ask the law to redress her wrongs, if, in meeting the criminal threat posed, she had decided that it would be unwise or dangerous to have resisted. . .[this attacker] with all her power and [keep]. . . up that resistance as long as she had strength."*

This was the evolution of the law in Georgia by court interpretation and decisions in real cases.

I have been a prosecutor most of my adult life—40 years—now retired. I have prosecuted many rape cases, as well as murder following the rape, and I can tell you that without doubt many rape victims survive through submission and avoidance, while many die from resisting and fighting. Anyone can understand why it is best to live and fight another day on different terms. A case in point:

> I prosecuted one young man for murder and arson after he had scaled the outside of his apartment complex building to the upper level from his ground level apartment, where he then entered the female's apartment from her balcony while she slept. In attacking her, she resisted while fighting for her life as he slashed her throat with a kitchen knife. With her dying efforts, unable to speak, she dialed 911 for help—leaving only her last horrendous "death-rattles" on the recording, to be later played for the jury. The apartment building was set afire by the perpetrator in his ground level apartment while the Police Response Team was inside the victim's apartment as they began the crime scene investigation. To save themselves, the CSI team had to evacuate the building—leaving the body, knife, and other evidence to burn. The perpetrator was seen fleeing from his apartment with flames "licking at his heels." A follow-up investigation determined that the perpetrator had started the fire in three places in his apartment, including one in his bed. The apartment and his bed contained a large amount of pornographic material—some of which did not entirely burn.

The Rule of Law

I am dedicated to the proposition that those charged with a criminal offense are entitled to counsel for their defense and any defenses available to them. As the Prosecutor, I am an adversary as is the attorney on the other side. We do have separate and distinct responsibilities. The Defense Attorney is responsible for seeing that his client receives a "fair trial" though some take it that means "getting him/her off." While the Prosecutor is charged with seeing that justice is done above all else, the trial is, nevertheless, an adversarial process whereby both counsel will test the evidence through examination, cross-examination, and legal objections to the admissibility of the evidence offered by either side. The judge is like the referee. If either attorney "goes easy" for whatever reason, then he or she may overlook a weakness in the other side's presentation and an injustice may result. After all, the Prosecution is also entitled to a fair trial.

Thus, when we enter the courtroom, it is like entering the arena in battle—under the rules of evidence as laid out by the Legislative and Judicial Branches of Government. Justice will prevail because it must. The Judge and Jury will see that it does because they are the arbiter of the truth. With the burden on the Prosecution (State) to prove all the material allegations of each charge and the elements of each charged offense beyond any reasonable doubt, I must believe the truth will prevail if I have done my duty in charging the offenses correctly and preparing myself to present the evidence in a convincing manner to the court and jury.

The charged defendant is not required to prove anything. He may sit quietly through the trial without opening his mouth, or he may testify and present evidence if he chooses—even if he had previously admitted his guilt to police or shouted it to the high heavens in the middle of the park across the street from the courthouse while it was being videotaped. He has that right to be judged by his peers.

I have prosecuted many cases where the accused had confessed his guilt—yet he/she wanted a jury trial. People ask me all the time, "Why is such a defendant entitled to be tried for days or weeks in court, wasting the resources of the State, if he has confessed—if he has admitted his guilt?" Now you know.

I am motivated with all my might to see that justice is done for the victims while upholding the Rule of Law. Defense Counsel will see that I do my job by doing his job. The "Rule" is more important than all of us. If the Rule is not paramount—then none of us are safe. It is the Rule of Law or "Mob Rule." Thus, it is most important that a trial is seen to be conducted pursuant to the law with the evidence thoroughly tested by counsel for both sides.

II

THE ARREST

05:11 a.m., January 7, 1990. It was still dark except for the light outside the door of Apartment H-4. Jeannine McClean was sleeping. She awoke to her seven-year-old Himalayan cat, Precious, responding to a noise at the front door.

Jeannine's heart was pounding as she listened for a sound; then she heard a screeching sound outside her front door. She was alone, in her ground-level apartment, and fearful for her safety. She knew of rapes having been reported in the area. Her heart was now racing. Was someone lurking in the shadows, peeping in windows? Someone she knew, a friend, or neighbor? Many things went through her mind. She finally got out of bed, wanting to disbelieve the worst, and went over to the door. She looked out the window and saw a man's arm in a brown corduroy jacket with a white glove unscrewing the light globe at her front door. Now, she was really upset.

There was silence except for the screeching of the globe as it was being twisted very slowly—a little at a time—as if the perpetrator was trying to keep the globe from making a noise. Jeannine was so fearful she didn't immediately remember the emergency dial 911 number, but she did call the apartment manager because she knew that number. Jeannine was told to call 911 while the manager called police. She dialed the number and reported her disturbance. Now, seconds were like minutes, as the clock ticked ... the wait was painful. Would police arrive in time to save her? She stayed on the phone with the 911 Operator until a police officer was at the door, telling her he caught the man outside trying to break in through her front door. Jeannine then put aside the large butcher knife she was holding while waiting for police to respond. She would later credit Precious with saving her from being another statistic of a horrible attack. That cat would certainly enjoy many good meals ... and living to the ripe old age of 21, and passing away in April, 2004.

Earlier, Officer J.S. Biggers, Marietta Police Department, was in the vicinity and took the 911 call. He arrived in two minutes, parked behind the apartment building, and quietly walked around the corner of the building in an effort to catch the intruder in the act. As he rounded the corner, Officer Biggers saw a man at the door of apartment H-4 as the light flickered and went out. As the officer identified himself, the intruder had a screwdriver aimed at the doorknob.

Seeing the officer, the intruder ran and officer Biggers caught him at the corner of the building. The intruder had removed the light globe and bulb to the light. The globe had been placed on the ground. The light bulb was recovered from the intruder's jacket pocket. The man also had the "tools of his trade" with him: A knife, flashlight, gloves, and the screwdriver. They were seized as evidence—tools commonly used in burglaries and rapes. The white male with salt and pepper hair who would give no name and had no identification on his person was arrested and booked under a "John

Doe" alias. His vehicle was later located by police in a nearby parking area in the apartment complex with keys in the ignition, for a fast getaway if necessary, and his wallet was found on the floor of the car. The "John Doe" didn't take the chance of losing his car keys or wallet during his crimes. The plan was well thought out, and no doubt had been planned and carried out before—except for the arrest.

"John Doe" was charged with minor felonies: criminal attempt to commit burglary and possession of tools to commit a crime, and a misdemeanor, prowling, which would normally have ended with a minimum sentence, perhaps a probated sentence. However, at Police Headquarters, a young Detective, Scott Smith, who had recently been moved from Uniform Division to Detectives, remembered that he had recently taken an unsolved rape and burglary report at another nearby building, which prompted him to question whether this arrest was related to the rapes in other apartment buildings.

During questioning at Police Headquarters, "John Doe" gave an incoherent and implausible explanation for his conduct, saying he was drunk and didn't know what he was doing, or how he got there; notwithstanding, his car was later found nearby with keys in the ignition. Detective Smith retrieved the rape report he had taken from the young female victim in 1989 at the Concepts 21 Apartments, near the scene of this arrest. The wheels started turning and the adrenalin started flowing. The instinct, the gut feeling, prodded the young Detective on. ...

Meanwhile, "John Doe's" identity had been verified (through fingerprints) to be Terry Thaddeus Greenway, married with three teenage boys. He was released on a bond for the minor charges for which he was arrested. After he was identified by one rape victim, Greenway was rearrested and held in jail pending trial, while other similar cases were being investigated.

On March 19, 1990, after the arrest of Greenway, Detective Smith came to my office with reports of several reported burglaries and rapes in apartment complexes in the general area contiguous to I-75 through Cobb County going back several years in instances where females were alone, usually asleep at night, and unlawful entry was made through a window or door.

The rapist, a cloth over his face in some incidents, would surprise his victim—at times with a pocket knife—telling them in substance, *"Just relax. Do what I tell you. I won't hurt you, I'll be finished in a minute and I'll be gone."* At times, the rapist would have trouble getting an erection and would masturbate himself before the rape.

Detective Smith and I discussed leads and possible investigative efforts to clear some of the unsolved rapes and burglaries in the area. A new and recent genetic breakthrough had been developed which was useful in violent crime prosecutions. "DNA (Dioxyribonucleic Acid) profiling" was a novel scientific technology enabling a match or identification of a person through comparison of a sample of a suspect's known DNA to a specimen of DNA extracted from a vaginal swab from a rape victim.

DNA profiling, or fingerprinting as it was initially called, was begun in England in the mid-1980s by Dr. Alec Jeffreys. In conducting genetic testing of a family group he discovered that the pattern of inheritance from the father and mother were equally shared. It was found that the testing of genetic material in blood or semen in very small amounts could be matched to the donor to the exclusion of any other person, except that of an identical twin. Jeffreys' technology was used with success in criminal cases in England.

Authorities in this country immediately noted the significance to this newfound miracle in genetic testing which could be applied to forensics and crime-solving techniques analogous to traditional fingerprinting of the past. The evolution of DNA testing in this country began in the late 1980s with prosecutors in a few states, including Florida, New York, Pennsylvania, Virginia, and Georgia, using DNA testing to free the innocent and convict the guilty. All of the problems were dealt with as they arose with defense attorneys and civil rights groups in the mix—some advocating for and some against its use. The problems were dealt with as they emerged, including degradation of evidence, population genetics (the power of the match and databases of testing laboratories), as well as the lack of national standards in testing.

> At the time of this arrest in 1990, DNA testing was in its infancy. The only prior DNA prosecution in Georgia was the *James Robert Caldwell* arrest the previous year in 1989 in Cobb County. In that case, James R. Caldwell was arrested and prosecuted for the rape and murder of his 13 year-old-daughter. Semen at the crime scene was linked to Caldwell through DNA testing. Lifecodes, an independent laboratory in New York, one of two of its kind in the country at that time, did the testing in *Caldwell* which ended with a landmark decision in Georgia, setting the legal precedent and paving the way for admissibility of DNA testing in Georgia. DNA testing in the *Caldwell* case was upheld by the Georgia Supreme Court on July 3, 1990, albeit the conservative power of identity of one in 250,000 was allowed, rather than one in 24,000,000 as claimed by Lifecodes in that case. The *Caldwell* decision was handed down during the period of activities following the "John Doe" arrest in the

present case. The decision in the *Caldwell* case followed extensive and protracted pre-trial hearings before Trial Judge Robert Flournoy over a period of five months with expert witnesses testifying: six experts for the State and four for the Defense. The hearings ended with the Trial Judge ruling in favor of admissibility of the DNA evidence. Following those hearings and appeal to the Georgia Supreme Court, the actual trial of *Caldwell* occurred in 1991 before a jury on a change of venue to Columbus, Georgia. The trial ended with a conviction for rape and murder with life sentences imposed.

Now that DNA profiling was admissible in criminal prosecutions in Georgia and that State Laboratories, including Georgia, were beginning to set up their own DNA sections, I knew this was the way to go. While it was expensive and time-consuming for independent labs to do the work, the FBI laboratory was now available for testing if they would agree to do it. In contacting them, I found they would accept the case, it being a serial rape case, and that they would do the testing and make their testing witness available to the State for trial at no cost to the prosecution. What a deal!

Routine procedures for rape investigations involve an examination of the rape victim at a local medical facility with the treating physician obtaining a vaginal swab of any secretions left by the attacker, along with a "pubic combing" for any foreign hair or trace evidence. These samples compile a "rape kit" and are generally maintained by the crime laboratory for further investigation or until a possible suspect is identified for comparison.

In years before DNA, the rape kit was routinely prepared by medical personnel for testing in order to determine if sperm was, indeed, found, to prove penetration and to corroborate the complaint that there was, in fact, intercourse—an element of rape, for routine serology blood typing, and for possible hair comparison. DNA testing results may now be used, if the evidence was handled correctly without contamination and the testing protocols were followed. I learned from the experts in the previous DNA prosecution of *Caldwell* that the scientific community, the experts generally, would agree that DNA technology was capable of identifying an individual to the exclusion of all others, except an identical twin, and that the technology had reached a scientific stage of verifiable certainty, the legal threshold for admission in a criminal trial.

The rape kits from unsolved rapes in Cobb County, Georgia, for the past several years had been piling up at the crime laboratory.

Would the FBI be able to extract clean DNA from the samples and identify our suspect? Would the profiling be possible with samples which had been stored for several years? Had the samples been contaminated? Would the DNA testing cause the removal of a serial rapist from the streets? Would the victims ever receive justice? Justice is a fleeting word—hard to comprehend by some—and, unless you have been a victim, you would not know the full impact of a suffering victim of a horrible rape years after the traumatic experience. They commonly move their residence and jobs, sometimes to other states. Would the victims still be cooperative in coming forward to testify if there is a match? Some victims suffer tremendous psychological impact after such experiences and refuse to voluntarily testify, having to relive their traumatic experience. All of these questions needed answering, and many questions remained unanswered.

It was worth a try. Several of the major burglary and rape cases from the same general area were selected for review from the unsolved cold case files, along with several other attempted rapes, assaults, and burglaries which seemed worth pursuing. I approved four of the unsolved rape cases for which semen (swabs) from rape kits were available to be sent to the FBI for DNA testing. At my written request on March 20, 1990, those samples were prepared and forwarded by the Georgia Bureau of Investigation to the FBI Laboratory along with samples of blood from our suspect, Terry Greenway, and the rape victims. Related burglaries and assaults would be considered for prosecution where provable, while still other offenses which had the similar modus operandi but no DNA were not included for lack of sufficient evidence.

Because of a backlog of pending DNA cases, the samples sent to the FBI for testing remained dormant until November, 1990, when the testing was completed and matched to our suspect, Terry Greenway. During this time frame, before individual states were able to establish their own laboratories, the FBI and the few private laboratories were swamped with requests from around the country by prosecutors in attempts to clear cold cases of violent crimes which would probably never have been cleared with arrests, except for the advent and evolution of DNA testing in this country.

I anticipated that DNA (genetic) profiling would play a major role in this prosecution, particularly in those charges for which there was little else identifying the defendant as the rapist. There was other supporting circumstantial evidence, including other cases and similar transactions supporting each other. *Thus, showing Greenway to be a serial rapist was important to a true and fair verdict.*

Genetic profiling is based on the principle that every human being has a distinctive makeup with a unique combination of more than three million chemical rungs on the twisted ladder-like molecule of DNA. Experts generally agree that this technique will identify a human being, sometimes to odds of billions to one. Therefore, it is commonly said that where a good sample of DNA is matched, the odds are to the exclusion of every other human on earth, there being no identical twin. This is strong stuff! However, will the testing by the FBI Laboratory result in positive findings? Will the power of a match be substantial? Only through a review of the expert testimony under oath in a court of law would we know how powerful it is in each case.

That Jailhouse Religion

As a prosecutor, I saw it! All prosecutors and judges see it! It is common to see a prisoner in jail awaiting trial to "get it," that is, the "jailhouse religion." Is it a "con" or is it real? There are plenty of people who will say some or even most are con jobs, especially in major crimes, when prisoners are awaiting trial, hoping it will come to their aid in consideration of sentence, or in preparation of their defense at trial. Of course, I approve and believe that one charged with an offense against the law should have a right to utilize his good reputation in the community as a defense upon his trial. That is the law, and what good is a lifetime of good character and reputation in the community in which he/she lives or works, if it will not come to his or her aid in a time of need?

In preparing for a defense, either in mitigation at a sentence hearing or having character witnesses from the church to testify in their defense at trial, it is not uncommon to see the church members come to court and support their brethren in his/her time of need. It is to be expected. Church members are much more likely than the average acquaintance or neighbor to support their members who are in trouble, with moral as well as financial support. I have no statistical basis for this statement—just my observation over the years in actual cases I or other prosecutors have seen. I certainly am not critical of this as I believe in and see the church as an instrument to help those in need, not just when they may be innocent, but also when they are guilty. There is also the family of the guilty defendant who needs the support of the church, as does the family of the victim. The families suffer!

An attorney with the opportunity to have God-fearing members of a congregation or co-workers in support of his client has a valuable piece of evidence to tell the jury what good things a defendant has done in support of a "good character" defense. The jury will be authorized to give it whatever weight and credit the jury wishes. It may even raise a reasonable doubt of the defendant's guilt of the charge for which he is on trial.

However, in presenting a good character defense, it is a double-edged sword. It may help the accused in presenting his good side, but it also allows the prosecutor to investigate and present any evidence to the contrary. In such cases, the defendant opens up his past to be brought to the jury in the form of bad character in rebuttal, which may actually be more damaging than the good character is helpful. I have many times rebutted the good character witnesses with much evidence of bad acts and general bad character of the accused, though I would not have been allowed to do so had the defendant not elected to present evidence of good character.

In cases where the jury is presented with testimony of good character, the prosecutor is confronted with how to handle such witnesses on cross-examination. Such witnesses are usually friends, co-workers, or church members, who are good people who have been asked to testify before the jury about a defendant's reputation in the community. The prosecutor may concede the issue and decide to ask no questions and argue to the jury in closing that it, meaning the good character element, had nothing to do with whether the accused committed the crime—thus, the jury should convict notwithstanding evidence of good character. My experience, however, tells me that I should penetrate the veil of the testimony and see from where it derived. Did the accused for the first time decide to seek the divine intervention after being arrested and while in jail awaiting his fate? Many do! Or does the accused have a background in church participation and good work product, and just, for once, got caught up in something beyond the comprehension? Or does he have a track record?

We must see how this plays out with Greenway in his defense.

A thorough examination of the good character witness by the prosecutor armed with the background of the accused may reveal whether it is a con or for real. It may reveal that we have a Jekyll and Hyde character with two faces: one for the church family and another when in another environment.

That's how I viewed our serial rapist—one with two faces: a Jekyll and Hyde!

While awaiting trial and incarcerated in the Cobb County Adult Detention Center, inmate Greenway was housed with about 900 other felony inmates. They had access to a chapel at the jail and volunteer preachers of different denominations; they had regular worship services, sometimes with singers, just like back home. It is common for inmates to utilize this opportunity for them to continue their service to God; others use it as an opportunity to mix and mingle with fellow inmates. Some will admit that they got away from God and the church when they got involved with some bad people, or did some "backsliding."

I have heard all the stories!

Most noticeably, many defendants in major cases I have prosecuted—especially those facing a life or death sentence—appear in court carrying a Bible. Some will sit at counsel table with the Bible prominently displayed in front of them for the judge and jury's benefit.

On February 27, 1990, inmate Greenway was brought to court before [then] Magistrate Judge, James Bodiford, seeking a bond pending trial. When brought into the courtroom for the hearing, Greenway brought with him a black Bible which he maintained during the hearing.

While in county jail awaiting trial, Greenway was interviewed by a reporter for the Atlanta Journal/Constitution, Maria Odum. Inmate Greenway was quoted to say:

> "If it weren't for the worship services, I wouldn't make it ... The devil was putting thoughts in my head and told me to commit suicide. I twisted my sheet and tied it around my neck ... but the Lord got to talking to me, and I just decided to give my life back to Jesus."

Reporter Odum quoted other prisoners, chaplains, supervisory and custodial workers in various local jails to find the answer to her quest. One prisoner said, "Coming to jail has been the best thing to happen to me. I could have gotten out on [$50,000] bond, but I wanted to stay here and grow in the grace and love of God." Another inmate with a lengthy record reportedly said that "A lot of [inmates] have that jailhouse religion [...]. Most go back to doing what they normally did before they went in. Only a few keep it when they come out." One Chaplain observed that "as their trial comes closer, the inmates demonstrate a closer proximity with religion." One inmate charged with murdering his 14-month-old daughter reportedly said, "You can't con God." A Chaplain estimated that about 20 percent of the 876 inmates at the Cobb facility attend worship service, and that those who are convicted seem to remain religious more so than those who are acquitted, while those facing lengthy sentences are more likely to latch on to God.

PRE-TRIAL PROCEEDINGS

The arrest is just the beginning of a long series of events in the criminal justice process which is intended to ensure that the right person is on trial and that the case for the prosecution is not resting on "shifting sand" but rather on a rock-solid foundation: one that will stand firm in the blistering attack by the defense and a protracted series of appeals following a jury trial and conviction. Obtaining a conviction, but losing the case on appeal to a higher court, is not something to be envied when the only recourse may be to put the witnesses and participants through a second trial, or dismiss the case.

Following the arrest of Terry Greenway, a motion for bond was filed, and granted, over the objection of the prosecutor and police due to Greenway being a suspect in other crimes. Police and Prosecutors were working the "cold cases" in an effort to determine if they could be tied to our suspected rapist.

One rape and burglary victim did identify Greenway, and he was rearrested and jailed without bond pending further action in pursuing other reported cases. [Then] Chief Magistrate Judge James Bodiford, in denying bail, agreed that Greenway posed a significant risk of fleeing the jurisdiction.

Another motion for bond was filed on May 24, 1990, and denied after Assistant District Attorney Barrie Laux, who handled bond hearings, argued that the State was still awaiting results of the DNA testing of four rape cases for which Greenway was suspected. Finally, Judge Bodiford was required to set a bond by operation of law, since the case could not be indicted by the Grand Jury within 90 days of arrest. Judge Bodiford set a bond of $500,000 on each of two cases. Greenway could not post the bail and remained in jail pending trial.

Inmate Greenway's wife, Shermanda "Mandy" Greenway, on November 16, 1990, wrote Judge Watson White a two-page typewritten letter wherein she made a memorable, coherent, and cogent plea for her husband's release from jail on bond, pending trial. This was a very unusual thing for a wife to do, especially in cases where the accused is represented by counsel. Counsel is the "mouthpiece" for an accused, and makes the decisions about how the defense is to be handled, including statements of facts, motions, and all matters concerning the accused and how he is defended. However, one would only hope that *their* wife would be as passionate about defending them as *this* wife. She would remain faithful to this position before, during and after her husband's trial in expressing her belief in his innocence; but for how long after conviction and appeal would this last, I wondered.

Mrs. Greenway presented her written plea to Judge White in part by saying: *"I humbly request you to read this letter, as I know of no other proper manner to reach you. I am writing you on behalf of my husband,*

Terry T. Greenway, who has been held in the Cobb County Adult Detention Center continuously since February 27, 1990. We have three teenage sons, age 17, 14 and 13. We have been married almost 20 years." She goes on to say they have extended family in Georgia, and asks for the charges to be dropped or a reasonable bond set. She says her goal is to see the case solved by the arrest of the guilty party; that many people are praying for Terry and that they know he will be proven innocent.

Further, she wrote: *"My husband was arrested for one count of rape on February 7, and held in jail awaiting a probable cause and bond hearing until February 20 (our 19th wedding anniversary)[....] I was able to arrange with family members to go on a property bond and he was released on February 21. Then, on Friday, February 23, at 5:00 P.M., my husband was portrayed on TV as a 'serial rapist.' The story was on all 4 channels on Friday evening, Saturday noon, Saturday evening, Sunday noon, Sunday evening, Monday noon, six and eleven. After all this was on TV and new[s] paper headlines for 3 days was when he was accused by a second woman."*

Mrs. Greenway continued, writing that Terry is "tenderhearted" and even in jail has helped other inmates. She pointed out that he had worked two jobs prior to his arrest and had gone to a bar after work where he got something to drink, was unable to drive home, and got off the expressway, finding himself in an apartment complex two and one-half miles away from the expressway. She claims he was only guilty of "loitering" and that he did not do the other things. She further related that on the few occasions that he did drink too much, he was always very childlike and docile. Mrs. Greenway furthers her plea that other similar rapes were going on since Terry had been in jail, and that another man had been arrested.

Mrs. Greenway concluded her plea with the following: *"My husband has helped many men in jail [but] talking with them and trying to* *help them find an alternative to crime. I have received many letters and some phone calls telling me what a blessing my husband has been to them and how he has helped them change their lives around. My husband is a loving father and husband and a gentle and caring man. Please consider our request for a reasonable bond so my husband can come home and be with us throughout the holidays. No matter what information the district attorney may insinuate, my husband, Terry Greenway is <u>innocent</u>. I know God will help us prove that in His own time. People all over Georgia are praying for Terry and for us and for you and the others involved in this case. Whatever your religious convictions are, please pray also, before you consider this case on November 29. Thank you for 'listening.' May God bless you."* It was signed "Mrs. Mandy Greenway."

The court, subsequently, filed the letter as a matter of record, but it did not become an issue during the trial. **Not often have I seen such a well presented argument for a bond—even from attorneys.** However, judges cannot make decisions from such improper and informal contacts by persons or parties from either side of the case. Such motions and arguments must be made and filed in court with both parties present and responding.

This activity by this wife turned out to be not uncommon for her. On November 8, 1990, Ms. Audrey Lynch, the DNA testing expert for the FBI, advised me that Mrs. Greenway had called her earlier in the week, inquiring of the status of the DNA testing in his case. Ms. Lynch told me, "never had this happened before," that is, the inquiry from a defendant's wife. No information was divulged, and Mrs. Greenway was told she should deal with her husband's attorney.

Another noteworthy intervention by this defendant's wife involved a member of my own family, a sister who lived in Brunswick, Georgia. During my pre-trial preparations for the upcoming trial of Greenway, I received a communication from my older sister, Gracie Johnson, who along with her husband, Hinton, were members of the Church of God of Prophecy in Brunswick, the same denomination as the

Greenways' Church in the Cartersville area, over 300 miles away. Gracie informed me that she knew Mrs. Shermanda Greenway, the wife of the accused rapist, from a statewide church convention where they met in Macon, Georgia.

Gracie told me that Mrs. Greenway recently called her and requested a private meeting at Gracie's home. Subsequently, Mrs. Greenway appeared at Gracie's home in Brunswick where Gracie learned about Terry Greenway's arrest and pending charges, and that I was the prosecutor assigned to the case. It was unclear how Mrs. Greenway knew that Gracie was my sister; however, Mrs. Greenway's parents lived in nearby Manor, Georgia. Mrs. Greenway emphatically expressed to Gracie that "he didn't do it" and that he was not guilty of the charges, and specifically requested that Gracie ask me to take another look at the case. Gracie told Mrs. Greenway that "it wouldn't help" but she would communicate the request to me, which she did. I told Gracie it wasn't as simple as Mrs. Greenway had suggested, and that I had given the case many reviews, that the case was going to trial, and that I intended to seek the maximum sentences upon conviction.

I cannot recall such an effort in any other case over a period of 40 years on behalf of a loved one. Their efforts usually came through an attorney. Though I did not appreciate Ms. Greenway involving my family member, the contact played no role in my decisions in the case. I understood that a wife with three children was doing everything in her power in her husband's behalf. I would expect nothing else, though unorthodox in the channel she selected.

This will not be the last effort she will make on her husband's behalf.

⌘ ⌘ ⌘

Once the FBI had completed the DNA testing of the samples from the four rape victims and submitted their findings in official reports to the District Attorney's Office, I was ready to go to the Grand Jury. The Grand Jury was a body of between 16 and 23 citizens who were called upon to hear evidence in certain cases to determine whether there was sufficient evidence for probable cause to exist that the accused committed the offenses charged. If so, it took only 12 votes from the panel for a true bill of indictment, meaning the case should go forward to trial.

On November 29, 1990, I presented the case to the Cobb County Grand Jury against Terry Thaddeus Greenway wherein he was charged with 14 Felony Counts: Four rapes, six burglaries, criminal attempt to commit burglary, aggravated sodomy, aggravated assault, and possession of tools to commit a crime.

It was a routine proceeding, except that the rape charges being predicated partly on a novel scientific technique—DNA profiling—aroused some interest of the jurors in the process. A true bill of indictment was returned, filed, and routinely assigned to Superior Court Judge G. Grant Brantley. Following that, Terry Greenway was brought before Judge Brantley wherein Defense Counsel Marc Cella, who had been appointed to represent him, waived formal arraignment, and entered a "Not Guilty" plea to all charges. I served a copy of the indictment upon Mr. Cella, and the case was continued for pre-trial motions to be filed and heard.

Knowing the opposing counsel and the trial judge and their legal inclinations are important in anticipating what I should expect to be confronted with during the trial. I knew Judge Brantley would allow my evidence, including the DNA evidence, the identifications by the victims, and the defendant's prior "similar transaction" of being a peeping tom, if I could convince him with *legal precedent* that the case would be on sound legal footing and would not be overturned by the appellate courts. That is fair to the State and to the Defense. I would expect nothing more or less. I knew Judge Brantley was one who would hold both myself and Mr. Cella to strict rules of the Court, and keep the case moving without unnecessary delays.

Dozens of motions were filed by Mr. Cella, including Discovery (seeking to learn all they could from the State about the case), a Motion in Limine to Suppress Unreliable Scientific Opinion Evidence (DNA), a Motion in Limine to Suppress Evidence of Similar Acts (a prior peeping tom case in Hall County in 1984), a Motion to Suppress Testimony and reference to witnesses' photographic lineup and voice identifications of the defendant, as well as a Motion for Funds.

As expected, the defense was trying to suppress and keep from the trial all the DNA evidence, the identifications of defendant by some of the witnesses through photo lineups and voice identifications, as well as restrict the jury from hearing about Greenway's prior criminal history of being a peeping tom, which the State was offering as a "Similar Transaction" to show his propensity for committing crime. Such evidence may show a person's modus operandi, intent, and state of mind, which is authorized if a Judge holds a hearing and finds that such evidence would be admissible for such purpose, notwithstanding [he] had already been prosecuted, convicted, and sentenced in another county for that offense.

Another motion, Motion for Severance of Offenses for trial, was filed. If the Judge grants this motion, it will devastate the prosecution, in that, if granted, it will prevent the State from prosecuting all the offenses in one trial before one jury. In such event, the crimes would then be separated for separate trials, at least insofar as the crimes associated with each victim would have to be tried separately from other victims, requiring about a half-dozen trials. It would not only financially strap the State, but it could (possibly) affect the evidence each jury would be able to hear, including the evidence of the other cases.

Mr. Cella is just doing his job. I expected as much. I also had confidence that Judge Brantley would do his job as well: give the Defense a fair hearing, and rule for the State. I was on solid ground, legally.

The foregoing presents the *first battle* in the criminal justice process whereas the Defense is attempting to strip the State of its evidence, and the State is attempting to keep its evidence together in a trial before one jury.

I complied with the law requiring certain disclosure and discovery of materials to the Defense, including certain scientific publications concerning the DNA testing which I had obtained during the prior Caldwell DNA prosecution:

"Modifications to Improve the Effectiveness of Restriction Fragment Length Polymorphism Typing," HAE III – A suitable Restriction Endonuclease for Restriction Fragment Length Polymorphism Analysis of Biological Evidence Samples," "Applying Highly Polymorphic VNTR Loci Genetic Markers to Identity Testing," "Validation with Regard to Environmental Insults of the RFLP Procedure for Forensic Purposes," "DNA Analysis by Restriction Fragment Length Polymorphisms of Blood and Other Body Fluid Stains Subjected to Contamination and Environmental Insults," and "Semi-automated Analysis of DNA Autoradiograms."

This would give Mr. Cella many long hours and nights of reading material, if he indeed wished to do so. This was Cella's first DNA trial and my second. So we, along with all other Georgia attorneys, were novices at understanding how the process of DNA testing works; thus, we had to learn as we went along. That applied to Judge Brantley as well, since this was his first foray into the DNA world.

Though not required to do so at that time in Georgia, I opened the prosecution file to Mr. Cella to review in full. I wanted to be cautious of any claim of non-disclosure to the defense as I knew the law to be in transition, especially in regard to scientific reports.

On March 13, 1991, the defense motion for funds for an Investigator was granted in the amount of $1500.00, subject to providing the court a resume and for an accounting of funds. Another motion for bail was made on March 25, 1991—this time before the trial judge—with Mrs. Greenway testifying that ... "He's a gentleman," and that he wouldn't run, or hurt people. I elicited on cross-examination that she was aware that her husband had frequented bars at night, had a former girl-friend over in Douglas County, and in 1984 had been arrested in Hall County for peeping tom charges on two separate occasions.

Bond was again denied!

A Motion for Severance of Offenses was heard and denied on April 5, 1991. A major victory for the State: one trial on all charges!

On July 3, 1991, the Defense was granted an order to have access to a Lexis Terminal to conduct research with the Circuit Defender's Office bearing the expense. With all the research necessary in this novel scientific DNA case, this was helpful to Mr. Cella. Also, he was granted funds for an expert witness, authorizing $100 per hour for an expert to review the evidence, conduct research, discuss such findings with Mr. Cella, and for the generation of reports. The expert would receive $150 per hour for in-court testimony.

Defendant's Motion in Limine to Suppress Unreliable Scientific Opinion Evidence (DNA) was denied on June 21,

1991, after hearing testimony from the State's expert witness as well as the defense expert in a lengthy four-day hearing. In denying the motion, Judge Brantley issued an order holding that the [DNA] procedures are recognized as reliable, and had gained general acceptance in the scientific community, and further that the procedures and techniques being used by the FBI Laboratory were generally accepted in the scientific community and capable of producing reliable results. Therefore, the State was authorized to utilize these *novel but reliable* tests by the FBI Laboratory in this prosecution.

The State's motion, "Notice of State's Intent to Use Evidence of Similar Transactions" (prior similar transactions in Hall County in 1984) was argued, and Judge Brantley signed an order on September 25, 1991, granting the State's motion.

Some fine-tuning is always necessary before trial in order to eliminate anything which you don't need which may ultimately become a stumbling block to success. As most rapists, Greenway had a track record of arrests ... gradually escalating from minor stuff to being a serial rapist. During 1978-1979, he had three speeding convictions and a driving under the influence in 1983. None of those would be admissible or offered at trial, unless some unknown event would make them relevant. However, the two "Peeping Tom" arrests in 1984, for which he had been prosecuted, would be relevant—inasmuch as the circumstances of those arrests were quite similar to the present case arrest:

1) On April 2, 1984, at 00:30 hours, 31-year-old **Rhonda Lamphear** of the Woodlake Apartments in Gainesville reported she was in bed reading with the light on when she heard a commotion outside. She later learned that Greenway had been arrested

outside her apartment. The Gainesville arresting officer was working security at the apartment complex when he observed a subject prowling the area, and looked into a window of the victim's apartment. The officer called for backup as the prowler moved away, then returned and looked into the window a second time. Officer Barrett then stepped out of his vehicle and identified himself as a police officer, telling the subject to stay where he was. The subject fled the scene. Other officers arrived, and Greenway was arrested in the complex. He was wearing no shoes, only socks. When asked his purpose for being there, Greenway advised he was visiting a friend, but could not advise the friend's apartment number or name. Upon searching the area, the subject's vehicle was located in the last space in a nearby parking area of the complex. The subject's shoes were found in the front driver's side floorboard. The officer was watching the buildings due to several similar incidents which had occurred before that night.

Despite this strong case for conviction, Greenway elected to go to trial by jury. It was the right decision for him because he was acquitted. Upon revisiting this case for possible use at trial, I had my investigator, Merritt Cowart, locate and interview this victim. On February 14, 1991, Ms. Lamphear remembered the case well, and told the investigator that, prior to trial, the defendant's wife, Mrs. Greenway approached her and told her that they had four or five children and wanted her

(Ms. Lamphear) to drop the charges. Ms. Lamphear informed Mrs. Greenway that it was the police who brought the charges, not her. She later saw Mrs. Greenway in the courtroom at trial where he was acquitted.

2) On November 5, 1984, at 00:32 hours, Terry Greenway returned to the Woodlake Apartments in Gainesville, where he again was arrested for peeping tom and loitering and prowling. Police responded to a prowler call and report by Ms. **Geraldine Sertain,** a resident of apartment I-9, that she saw a certain described male approach and look into her window. The subject was found nearby at a telephone booth and arrested. After being given his Miranda rights, he told officers that he didn't know anything about it, that he was calling his wife to come and get him. Other officers who checked the area found a 1975 Chevrolet Impala which was registered to his wife, Shermanda Greenway. The keys were still in the vehicle, and papers were found inside with Greenway's name. He finally admitted the keys were his, and he wanted the vehicle left where it was. This jury didn't fall for his story this time, and he received a 1st Offender probated sentence.

Although both incidents are so alike and relevant to the present arrest in Marietta as showing the same modus operandi, the fact that Greenway was *acquitted* in the first case raises an issue which I don't need to fight, and therefore will not offer that case to the jury. I will only present the later similar case where he was convicted.

IV

THE BEGINNING TO AN END

It was February 12, 1992. The day of reckoning! I was crossing the street from the Cobb County District's Office to the Courthouse—the arena where combatants meet. I was in deep mental reflections. My heart was pumping in high gear. My mind was like a runaway train with no brakes as I was doing my mental "check-off" of things which were necessary for me to gain a conviction by utilizing DNA evidence which had only been used once before in Georgia. Am I prepared? Is everything in place? Witnesses were subpoenaed. Would all respond to court?

Out-of-state witnesses were necessary, and the compulsory process for obtaining witnesses from outside the state had been filed and approved by the courts of each state (Georgia and the State where the witness is located). However, once in a major high profile case—the prosecution of Attorney Fred Tokars for the murder of his wife—a hostile witness from California had still refused to board the plane after being ordered to do so by a judge in California, and follow-up assistance was necessary by the Los Angeles District Attorney's Office to have her put on the plane.

The physical evidence and exhibits were located and pre-marked, ready for court. All legal issues expected to arise had been researched. All pre-trial motions had been heard. Would there be some unexpected last-minute motions by the Defense at the call of the case for trial? There usually is! My plan for orchestrating the entire trial had been fine-tuned. My "trial plan" was a three-ring notebook, three inches thick, outlining the entire trial as I envisioned it. The entire trial was choreographed to the extent possible, everything over which I had control, which was most of the trial—as the burden was upon me. Several boxes of files made up my case-file and would be ready when the jury is selected.

Although I am up tight in approaching such an important case (even after 25 years as a prosecutor), when I arise upon being addressed by the Judge to proceed with the State's opening presentation, calm will overtake me. Once the ice is broken, everything will fall in place and the case will proceed as a well-oiled machine. The anxiety, the exhilaration, the contemplations preceding the trial will disappear as the trial begins. There will be no turning back. It's like that runaway train! The only thing to stop it will be a verdict, mistrial, or mistake!

The Prosecutor is the one who makes the case go. The Defense Attorney has no burden to present any evidence, and only needs to sit back and watch, wait, listen, and determine if there is reason to object to something the prosecutor does. Only if the prosecutor makes out a case sufficient to overcome a Motion for Directed Verdict will it be necessary for the Defense Attorney to decide if he will present a defense or rely upon his "brilliant" closing argument. Thus, the pressure is upon the prosecutor.

Any Defense Attorney will disagree with that assessment, saying they, too, must investigate and prepare as the prosecutor does, or put themselves in the predicament of being accused by the client (as a last resort) of being unprepared, and exposed to being held to be ineffective by the courts. Thus, any good attorney will admit he/she must fully prepare and defend even an obviously guilty client to cover their own "behind" from an accusation of ineffective assistance of counsel from the next set of lawyers who handle the appeal.

If I do my job as I have planned and prepared, there should be a conviction, but everything depends on me to see that every facet of the case goes as I have planned. If I falter or make a misstep, the case could suffer and *a rapist may go free*. I must know the procedural and substantive law supporting my position on all issues. Then, there is this new technology—genetic profiling—which is being used. Will the Jury understand it, or accept it as evidence in which to convict? The previous year the *Caldwell* jury *did* convict.

I have good vibes about how my opponent, Defense Attorney Marc Cella, defend cases. His client is charged with 14 felony counts, including 4 rape charges each of which could net his client a life sentence. Thus, much was at stake for both sides.

It is most important to know your opponent, how he acts and reacts in the arena, how he selects a jury, how he attacks the State's case, how he presents the defendant to a jury, and whether he will put up evidence or just attack the State's case and rely upon the presumption of innocence. I knew, and still know, Marc Cella to be an excellent lawyer with great legal skills. In fact, at this writing, Marc has now been an Assistant District Attorney in the office (where I was) for several years—doing what I was doing before retiring. He will attack my case with zeal. He will elicit contradictions of witnesses in an effort to impeach them. After all, some witnesses' events go back over five years before trial. Marc will 'nit-pick' the least (apparent) minor inconsistencies in witnesses' testimonies. Their memory will be fuzzy, perhaps, especially about minor details. He will attack the identifications by the victims. He will attack the DNA evidence by vigorous cross-examination and by calling an expert witness of his own.

This trial will involve over 30 witnesses, and some will be recalled. This is considered a somewhat lengthy case and will take probably two weeks (including jury selection) to complete. There will also be some extensive expert testimony regarding the DNA part of the case. I prepared the case by familiarizing myself with every witness, every detail of the case and will have no "back-up" if I get sick. A fellow prosecutor, Barrie Laux, who was involved in the early proceedings involving bond, was going to be my back-up and assist in the trial; however, he became sick the day of trial, and I will, therefore, be alone in presenting the case. I always worry in lengthy cases of becoming sick just before or during trial if there is no prepared co-counsel available to take over.

This is the concern in all major cases—that you will be remiss in some detail and let down the other components of the Criminal Justice System, especially the victims who have gone through so much in revealing the most intricate details of their lives in reporting the crimes, giving statements to police, and testifying at preliminary hearings or Grand Jury. The biggest event is about to happen to them: having to relive those traumatic experiences with the world watching and reading of it as they give live testimony in a court of law—open to the public.

⌘ ⌘ ⌘

Three years henceforth, that very fear would come true ... of being sick. I was one of three prosecutors in a major death penalty prosecution involving the trigger-man in a case where I would have to remove myself from the case on the eve of trial and undergo open-heart surgery with six heart by-passes performed. At age 59, I could only attribute the pressures of the job, the stress factor, to putting me in the hospital. In that case, the "trigger-man" who had voluntarily given a tape-recorded confession was put on trial in my absence. The killer had murdered Sara Tokars with a shotgun to the back of the head in the presence of her two small boys. Attorney Fred Tokars, former prosecutor in Atlanta and part-time judge, had "hired the hit" on his wife and would later stand trial and be convicted. [The same case referred to earlier.]

The trigger-man, Curtis Rower, went to trial and was granted a "mistrial" when a lone "holdout" juror refused to vote for conviction, notwithstanding a taped confession to the crime as well as other strong evidence of guilt. I was out of the hospital after three days at Christmas, 1994. While recuperating, I was able to attend the court proceeding when the jury was brought into the courtroom and announced they could not reach a verdict. I had a good laugh on my two fellow prosecutors, District Attorney Tom Charron and Assistant District Attorney Russ Parker, telling them they could not get a conviction with a tape-recorded confession *without me*. Seriously, it was a sad day for all of us! The family of Sara Ambrusko Tokars was in attendance and was devastated that one lone juror could cause a mistrial under such a pile of solid evidence, a confession included. However, this is the way it works in our imperfect system of justice, and, those people who would ask me why a confessed killer is entitled to a jury trial would be appalled at our criminal justice system. The accused trigger-man subsequently pled guilty in open court (following the capital trial of Fred Tokars and imposition of a life sentence) and was sentenced to life without parole. All three defendants (including the middle-man) are still serving life sentences as I write this.

⌘ ⌘ ⌘

Opening Statements
A jury having been selected, promptly at 09:00 a.m., Honorable G. Grant Brantley, Judge, Cobb Superior Court, called the case to trial, saying:

"Okay. We are ready to proceed with opening statements."

At that, Defense Attorney Marc Cella did not surprise me in saying:

"Well, I'd like to take up one matter before we bring the jury out, [asking] that there be a hearing conducted on the admissibility of the prior similar acts which involve peeping tom allegations from 1984, and I've asked that there be no mention made of these prior acts until the hearing is held. And I don't know if the D.A. had intended to mention this in his opening statements or not, but if he does, we object to it, and we'd like to have a hearing before that evidence is brought out in front of a jury." He overlooks nothing!

He correctly pointed out that the appellate courts had recently issued mandates on trial judges requiring a three-prong finding for such prior offenses to be used, and that the judge's order as (originally) issued did not provide for such findings. A technicality! I anticipated that Marc Cella would have read the recent court decision, and would be bringing this to the court's attention.

I responded that I did, in fact, intend to mention the prior similar "peeping tom" in my opening to the jury; that the pre-trial hearing on this issue a year before in response to the state's motion and the judge's second order issued a month before trial complying with the Appellate Court's mandate was sufficient without further evidentiary hearing.

Defense Counsel wanted to throw up a temporary roadblock or bump in the road as we call it, but it told me that Mark Cella was just doing his job as I expected of him.

After short oral arguments from both counsel, Judge Brantley ruled from the bench that the state had complied with the requirements of law, and he denied Mr. Cella's oral motion. The Judge called the jurors into the Courtroom and apologized for their having to wait in the jury-room for half-an-hour while a matter was taken care of. He proceeded to instruct the jurors for a few minutes about their conduct in taking notes, if they wished during the trial, and made pads and pencils available to them for "note-taking."

Finally! Now, hopefully, before someone can think of something further to delay the trial, Judge Brantley will call upon me to begin my opening when he said:

"At this time, I present to you Mr. Jack Mallard, who will make the opening statement on behalf of the State."

MR. MALLARD: "Thank you, Your Honor. Ladies and gentlemen, thank you for agreeing to serve voluntarily in this case. That's said a little facetiously, but as you, I'm sure, all know we sometimes have to do things we don't want to do and don't like to and would rather someone else do it. That's human nature. We sometimes do things here that we don't like to, and so, at any rate, we certainly appreciate the sacrifice that you're going to give to the citizens of Cobb County and the State of Georgia in the next several days or approximately perhaps another week.

"I do assure you that we'll move along as much as we can, but the nature of these proceedings being what they are, there are certain things we have to do that you may think, well, my goodness, that is insignificant. But there is a reason for it. We are going to call approximately 30 some odd witnesses. Some will be very short, but there will be a reason for their being on the stand. Others will be lengthy, and, of course, you will see why. So bear with us, and we'll get you out of here as soon as possible.

"I know that you're hurting in some regards in your profession, you're losing money, but if we are going to have the system that we have, that is, trial by jury of our peers, then we are going to have to have citizens sacrifice. It's a necessity.

"I'd like to introduce at the table with me on the far end Lynn Martin, who is chief investigator in the D.A.'s office, who will be in and out, will be lining up witnesses, bringing in evidence, facilitating, hopefully, the case moving along. So when he gets up and goes out or comes in, you will understand there is a reason for it, and so I'll call on him from time to time.

"Next to him in the middle is Officer Scott Smith with the Marietta Police Department. He is the case agent in this case. He likewise will come and go from time to time. I will use him several times in the case rather than one time at the end of the trial, as we do sometimes with a case agent, because I hope that by doing it that way, it will come together better, and you'll understand why, I think, as the case unravels, because he was involved in several of the incidents. I'd rather put him up at the proper time, go through that, and then subsequently, any other cases that he was involved in, he'll be recalled for that purpose. So we'll try to keep it in some kind of semblance of order.

"There will be a couple of witnesses that we will, from necessity, need to assist them because of vacation, two short witnesses, at least, that we'll probably put up out of order. I don't like to do that, but with these witnesses, it probably won't matter that much.

So if for some reason you see that a witness maybe doesn't seem to fit in right here, there is a reason for it.

"I'd like to tell you exactly when we'll finish, but all we can do is estimate, and with that many witnesses and knowing that interruptions do occur, there will be hurry-up-and-waits for you from time to time. But when that happens, there will be other matters that [are] taken up with the court concerning the case, perhaps, that you will not be required to be there. So just bear with us, if you will."

For the next 30-40 minutes, I proceeded to outline what I knew the evidence would be, in story form, to leave the jurors with an image of events which would help them in following the testimony as each witness testifies, including an orientation of the history of DNA profiling and its role in this case.

⌘ ⌘ ⌘

THE COURT: "Ladies and gentlemen, at this time I'll present to you attorney Marc Cella, who will make the opening statement on behalf of the defense.

"MR. CELLA: May it please the court, ladies and gentlemen of the jury, this is Terry Thaddeus Greenway. Mr. Greenway has been wrongfully charged in these cases. This is a case of mistaken identity.

"Terry Thaddeus Greenway is a former citizen of Gainesville, Georgia. He grew up there, spent most of his life in Gainesville. He was born in South Carolina. When he was six months old, his family moved to Gainesville.

"Terry was born to Dillard Greenway and Lillian Greenway. I believe Lillian is present in court, and her husband is deceased now.

Dillard and Lillian Greenway had four children. Terry Greenway is the third of those four children. He had an older sister, Reba Morgan, and an older brother, Clayton, and Terry also had a younger brother, Mitchell Greenway, who is deceased. Terry went through the 10th grade at Gainesville High School. He dropped out to go to work. He did later obtain his General Equivalency Degree.

"Terry, since the age of seven years old, has been very active in the Church of God of Prophesy. He's attended the Church of God of Prophesy at Gainesville, and also in Braselton where his family moved briefly, and then in Cartersville in his adult life.

"On February 20th of 1971, Mr. Greenway married the former Shermanda Minter, and Mandy Greenway is also present in court this morning. They had three children, Sean, 18 years of age, Jason, 16 years of age, and Mark, who's 14 years of age. They're all here in court also this morning.

"At the time of his arrest on January 7, 1990, Mr. Greenway was employed with Bickerstaff Clay Products Company, where he'd been working full-time since June of 1985. He was hired to supervise what is called the forge department over there at Bickerstaff, and you'll be hearing more about that as we get through the trial.

"Now, beginning in the spring of 1988, Mr. Greenway took a second job, too, because of the financial pressures that come down on a family when you're raising three boys. His second job, he worked for a place called Alert Security.

"Alert Security was the contractor to provide security at an office complex over on Roswell Road. It's called River Ridge Office Complex, and as I say, beginning in spring of 1988, Mr. Greenway had this second job. It was mostly weekend work. It called on him to serve what they call the third shift.

"Third shift is from midnight, approximately midnight. 10:00 p.m. to 6:00 a.m. is what they call the third shift. Mr. Greenway would be on duty by himself. He'd be the only security officer in the complex. Part of his job responsibilities there were to escort women to their cars so that they didn't have to be concerned for their safety. The people who hired him are going to describe for you his work performance in that regard.

"Now, on January 7th, Mr. Greenway bonded out of jail on that prowling charge that Mr. Mallard was talking about. His book-in sheet at that time describes him as being 6 feet tall and weighing 185 pounds."

With that introduction, a great effort to *humanize* an accused serial rapist, Mr. Cella continued for about the same period as I took, with his attempt to tear down the State's case by attacking the similarities between the crimes, the reliability of the identifications by victims, inconsistency of the descriptions, and suggesting that some of the rapes were by others involved in a crime-wave during that period using a pass-key. He further asserted that DNA was not yet reliable, and he would be presenting a DNA expert of his own to contradict the opinions of State experts.

Finally, Mr. Cella finished his opening statement, and Judge Brantley gave the jury a short break.

We have been hearing two contradicting versions—to say the least. I was beginning to wonder if I was hearing about the same case from Mr. Cella as the one I was prosecuting, but Marc just lived up to his reputation of throwing it all in, whether it would be proven or not, so the jury will be confused. Not a bad tactic for the Defense. I could have objected to some of it being argumentative and beyond the scope of the evidence, but seldom will a judge sustain an objection to an opening statement since he does not know what evidence will be forthcoming. The Judge will also instruct the jury that opening statements are not evidence in the case, but only what each attorney expects the evidence will be. Of course, I will remind the jury in closing argument when the defense fails to prove what Mr. Cella said they would prove.

Every attorney has his or her own style about opening statement to the Jury. I try not to tell the jury anything I am not sure will come out during the trial—details of what witnesses may say, but may not, or evidence which, if objected to, will not be revealed to the jury. I think it's important to have credibility with the jury by not saying something I may not be able to prove. Thus, I will be conservative in opening statement about questionable testimony and let the Jury hear it from the witness, under oath, and draw their own inferences. In opening, I like to paint a picture for the jury and give them a roadmap—to take them where I want them to go. Defense attorneys commonly do as Mr. Cella, and 'throw it all on the wall' hoping something will stick and give rise to a hung jury if only one juror has a hang-up about what was proven. This is good strategy for the Defense in an effort to get one or more jurors on his side. A 'hung' jury is always favorable to the defense—only one juror is all the defendant needs. The State needs all 12 jurors for a verdict.

⌘ ⌘ ⌘

Rather than start my lineup of cases with the oldest first, I will begin presenting the most recent offense—the arrest of Greenway at the victim's door—followed by regressing eight years before (to 1984) and present a prior similar arrest and conviction for peeping tom; then, I will begin with the oldest case for which he is now on trial, and come forward. Hopefully, the jury will get the full impact of Greenway being caught in the act of attempted burglary, and of having been convicted under prior similar circumstances of peeping tom. Following that, I will present all the other major crimes occurring between those two events. I like my first witness to be a great witness, unshakeable, and the facts indefensible in order to make a good impression with the court and jury. The image and memory of such event will carry forward with the jurors through the trial.

THE CRIMES

Cinnamon Ridge Apartments, January 7, 1990—Attempted Burglary; Possession of Burglary Tools

I called my first witness, Jeannine McClean to the stand:
DIRECT EXAMINATION
BY JACK MALLARD:
"State your name, please, ma'am."
"Jeanine McClean."
"Ms. McClean, are you single or married?"
"Single."
"Were you single (back) on January 7, 1990?"
"Yes, sir."
She proceeded to testify that she was a long-distance operator, a cashier, and a full-time student in interior design at the American College for the Applied Arts.

I then directed her attention to January 7, 1990, at Cinnamon Ridge apartments on Franklin Road, Apartment H-4 where she lived at the time. She described the complex of "probably 200 units" as being West of I-75 between Delk Road and the 120 Loop.

"When did you move from there?"

"February the 2nd, as soon as I could get out."

I directed her to 05:11 a.m., and asked her if anything unusual occurred.

"Yes, sir. My cat woke me up, and I heard a noise outside my bedroom window."

"Were you alone?"

"Yes. ..."

She continued: "I heard a noise outside my window, a squeaking type noise, and first I thought it was a puppy whining, but I realized later that it wasn't."

"What did you do then?"

"I tried to be rational and tell myself it was a puppy, and I finally got up and peeked out the window, and I saw a man's, I saw a brown corduroy jacket and a white glove unscrewing the globe off of the light at the front door by my bedroom window ..."

She then explained for the jury exactly where the front door and light were in reference to her bedroom window, and said that she had left the porch light on that night. She could clearly see the man's arm reaching up towards the light, which she could see as well.

"I could see that he was unscrewing the globe," she responded.

"What transpired after that?"

"Well, I put my robe on, and I started to go; I was actually looking for my mace, and I [scatterbrained] and couldn't find it, and I started to go to the kitchen for a knife. And I got out into the living room, and I thought, wake up. You're dreaming, and, you know, it's not happening. And I went to the front door, and I put my hand on the lock until the lock couldn't be turned, and I looked out the peephole, and at that time I saw a man's face, a blue shirt, and a corduroy jacket, and the light went out."

"What did you do then?"

"I ran to the kitchen, and I called, I couldn't think of 911, but I had a friend that worked at the complex office, and I knew the office number by heart, and I called it real quick, and we have an answering service there. I told them what was happening, and they called 911 and then told me to call 911."

"They told you to call 911?"

"Right. They contact[ed] them first, and then they told me to call them myself."

"Meanwhile, during this time, were you terrified?"

"Yes, sir."

Ms. McClean then testified that she dialed 911, reported what was going on, and was instructed to remain on the line with the officer taking the call. She said she "stood there with my butcher knife in one hand and the phone in the other and waited."

"And did something happen then?"

"They told me that the police had apprehended the man at my door, and that they would be at my door shortly, and to remain on the line with them until they got to my door. And then there was a knock at the door, and they said, that's the police. Go answer your door."

"So the operator was telling you that's the police at your door?"

"Yes, sir."

The witness explained that she opened the door and found a police officer, at which time she hung up the phone. She talked to the officer, he left, and later "two more officers came back and went over it all again." The two officers went through the apartment. They checked all the windows and made sure that all were secure after which they explained what they were suspecting was about to take place if she hadn't called when she did. After police left, the complex security guard came over and sat with her until daylight when he left. She then went to the police station and identified some clothing (corduroy jacket and blue shirt) and a picture.

"All right. And did you get a look at the perpetrator outside your front door?"

"Yes. When I looked out the peephole, yes, sir."

"All right. And I ask you whether or not, looking around the courtroom, you see the person that you saw that night."

"Yes, sir. It's that man over there with the salt and pepper hair and the mustache."

She then pointed to the defendant sitting to the left of Mr. Cella, his attorney.

"Now, I ask you whether or not you ever knew or saw, to your knowledge, the person you identified in court here, the Defendant, before that night?"

"No, sir, not to my knowledge."

"Was he at your front door by invitation or with your authority?"

"Absolutely not."

"And this was your apartment H-4, Cinnamon Ridge Apartments?"

"Yes, sir."

"I ask you whether or not this event has caused you subsequently to change your lifestyle in any way?"

"MR. CELLA: Object to the relevance on that, Judge."

"THE COURT: Since the court, Mr. Mallard --

"MR. MALLARD: I don't insist on the question."

I anticipated Judge Brantley would probably sustain the objection, and I basically withdrew it as it would involve getting into questionable areas. However, victims in such cases are allowed to file and/or testify to Victim Impact Statements which are considered by the judge upon sentencing if the perpetrator is found guilty.

MALLARD: "I believe you said you moved February 2nd?"

"Yes, sir."

"After this event?"

"Yes, sir. That was the soonest that I could acquire enough money to get another apartment, to pay all the security deposits and everything, because I obviously lost all of mine when I said, I'm leaving here, and didn't give a notice and broke a lease, and I couldn't stay there."

Ms. McClean proceeded to recount that she was looking outside as the light went out; she later learned he had unscrewed the globe and the light bulb.

I then turned the witness over for cross-examination.

CROSS EXAMINATION
BY MR. CELLA:

"Ms. McClean, how long would you say that you had to observe this man's face at the time you were looking through the peephole?"

"15 seconds."

"And what was he doing during that 15 seconds that you had him under observation?"

"Staring at the door."

"How close to the door was he? I know that sometimes your view gets distorted looking through the peephole."

"He was right on the door, because he had his arm over here on the globe, and the globe was about 6 inches from the front door, so he was right at the door."

"Okay. And was it at this time that you say you saw him unscrewing the bulb?"

"No, sir, that was earlier. That was when I first looked out, and that's all I saw was the arm and the glove."

"At that time, you didn't see any face, then?"

"No, sir."

"At that time, you were looking out your bedroom window?"

"Yes, sir."

Mr. Cella continued by having the witness go over the details of her actions in calling for help.

CELLA: "Did you ever at any time hear any police officers yell anything out there?"

"After they told me that the police were there, and they had him."

"Okay. Tell us what you heard."

She repeated it.

"When you looked through your peephole, and you saw this man's face, did you notice anything about the color of his face?"

"I noticed he was a Caucasian."

"Okay. Do you recall anything about his eyes?"

"They were kind of squinty and [weaselly] looking." [Check his photo below.]

Cella continued with pounding questions as to the color of his eyes, whether droopy or bloodshot, which she didn't know, and that the man's time at the front door was close to three minutes before the police arrived. She said she didn't know what was going on outside the apartment by the police.

CELLA: "What about a screwdriver? Did you ever see a screwdriver in this man's hand with the corduroy coat?"

"No, sir. The only time I saw his hand was whenever I saw it on the globe."

"By the way, whatever happened to that globe?"

"The police officers had it, and then they brought it back."

"Brought it back to you, you mean?"

"They put it back up for me."

"They never took it away from the scene?"

"No. There would have been no fingerprints. He had a glove on. They took it away from my front door, but it didn't, to the best of my knowledge, it came back that night. I could not, I could be wrong on that, but I'm pretty sure it came back that night."

"Okay. Did you ever see the man with a handkerchief?"

"He had a handkerchief around his neck." She wasn't sure of the color. [Important, because previous rapes were by an individual with a cloth around the lower part of his face.]

CELLA: "Have you ever been shown a photo line-up?"

I had not gone into the photo identification, as I knew Cella would—not that it mattered; after all, there is no issue in that it was Greenway at her door; he was arrested there. And, the witness identified Greenway in the courtroom for the jury. The attack on her identification of him flies in the face of reality and an effort in futility.

THE WITNESS: "Yes, sir."

"Could you tell us when and where that was?"

"It was at the Marietta Police Station a few days after the incident."

"Okay. And do you remember who the police officer was that showed you the photo line-up?"

"Yes, sir. It was Detective Scott Smith."

"That's this gentlemen sitting here next to Mr. Mallard?"

"Yes, sir."

"How many photos were in that line-up?"

"Six."

"Was there a picture of Mr. Greenway in there?"

"Yes, sir."

"Could you describe it for us, the picture itself?"

"The picture itself, it looked just like the man, salt and pepper hair and a mustache, kind of scruffy looking but --

"Was it a black and white picture?" [Cella didn't like where the previous answer was going, so he cut her off.]

"I believe it was in color."

"Was it just of his head?"

"Head and shoulder shot."

"Could you tell where he was when the picture was taken?"

"No."

"Was it a Polaroid?"

"It was a picture. It wasn't a portrait."

"MR. CELLA: I think that's all, Your Honor."

The Court asks me if there is any redirect. I reply there is.

RE-DIRECT EXAMINATION
BY MR. MALLARD:

To the Clerk: "Mark that State's Exhibit 45. Ms. McClean, I show you what is marked State's Exhibit 45. Do you recognize the person in that photograph?"

"Yes, sir."

"Who is that?"

"That's Mr. Greenway. It's the man at my front door."

"Does that look like the squinty and [weaselly] eyes you described?" I asked.

"Yes, sir."

"MR. MALLARD: That's all."

RE-CROSS EXAMINATION
BY MR. CELLA:

"The salt and pepper description that you've given, are those words that came to your own mind, or did the police ask you if he had salt and pepper hair?"

"No, sir. The police didn't ask me that. That's a general, that's for someone with black and gray hair. That's a very normal description."

"Is that a phrase that you used formerly in your vocabulary?"

"Yes, sir."

With that, Mr. Cella finished. I excused the witness without her having been compromised, but withstood a grueling cross-examination.

I then called Marietta Police Officer J. S. Biggers, who on the evening of the 911 call was on patrol and responded to the incident location. He testified he had been employed for three years and nine months, and had answered many calls of break-ins, theft and burglaries. He responded that he received a signal of attempted break-in at Apartment H-4 Cinnamon Ridge Apartments about 05:11 a.m.

I asked him: "How did that come to your attention?"

Officer Biggers: "Response call from a person reporting a prowler attempting to gain entry to an apartment complex. I was in the vicinity. I was a backup officer, but I was closer than the initial officer that was supposed to respond to the call, so I proceeded immediately to Cinnamon Ridge Apartments."

He responded, he said, and was at the scene in about two minutes. There was no traffic whatsoever. *It was raining at the time,* he said, and he came in with no sound and no lights. He parked and came around the back of the victim's apartment to catch the prowler at the front.

He testified further: "As I came around the back side of the apartment, which would have been Ms. McClean's apartment, I observed a light that was flickering. Upon arrival at her door, front door, I observed the Defendant had removed the light bulb itself from the socket. The globe was already laying neatly on the patio. It's a concrete area in front of the door. It was laying neatly against a door there. At that point, I identified myself as a police officer. The Defendant whipped around immediately, observed I was in uniform, and he attempted to flee."

"Let' back up a little bit. You said you came up. You said the light was flickering?"

"Yes."

"Did it go out?"

"It went out."

"And after the light went out, and he had the bulb in his hand, is that when you identified yourself?"

"He had a screwdriver already aimed at the front doorknob. The light itself is right at the front door. He already had the screwdriver at that position at the doorknob while he was unscrewing the light bulb."

He continued: "He ran off to my right. Myself being quicker than he was, he was very alert, but I jumped ahead of him, caught him at the corner of the building. At that point, with him still having a screwdriver in his hand, I produced my weapon in a ready position and told him to stop."

"And did he stop?"

"He stopped immediately, dropped the screwdriver on the ground. I then ordered him to face his stomach and his head on the pavement there."

"And what did you do then?"

"I placed him under arrest, and at that point, I observed he had on two white cotton gloves."

"What about the light bulb?"

"It was in his right coat pocket. Since Ms. McClean was still upset about the incident, I figured it would be better if we had the light working properly, make her feel more comfortable."

At that point, Officer Biggers placed the subject under arrest, put him in the police car, and gave him the Miranda rights (against self-incrimination).

I had the officer read the rights he gave the subject again from the "Miranda card" for the benefit of the court and jury.

"And what did you next do?"

"I tried to find out, he didn't have any personal identification on him, no wallet. I tried to find out his name."

"And did you obtain his name?"

"No, sir. To this day, I still know him as 'John Doe.'"

"Well, did you ask him his name?"

"Yes, sir, many times."

"What was his response?"

"Oh, God, please. I didn't do anything wrong."

Officer Biggers testified that the subject was wet from it being rainy outside, and he had a strong perspiration of odor. An odor of alcohol was also detected. Biggers did not see a vehicle which he could say might belong to the subject. Other officers arrived on the scene. The screwdriver, flashlight, and a pocket knife were seized as evidence, as well as a white handkerchief was taken from the subject's right pocket. The flashlight was found in his right rear pants pocket with the handkerchief covering it. At that point, Biggers checked on Ms. McClean.

"What was the extent, as best of your opinion, of the Defendant's intoxication?"

"He was very alert. He may have had some alcohol in his system, but to my knowledge, it had not impaired him from what he was trying to accomplish."

I asked him what he did with the globe and light bulb which he had found.

"I took the globe and the light bulb back to my patrol vehicle where I talked with my supervisor about processing the crime scene. We came out take photographs. He, at that point, advised me since the Defendant had gloves on, there could be no fingerprints taken from the globe. The globe or the light bulb neither one was damaged, so for Ms. McClean's safety, I screwed the light bulb back in, and placed the globe back in its place so she could have light outside her door again."

The witness described the light fixture, and I asked him:

"In reattaching the globe, is there any screeching to it?"

"Yes, sir."

The officer then checked the whole apartment, under the beds, porch, and windows, and found no damage to them. Officer Biggers then took the "John Doe" to the station.

"And was he locked up on charges?"

"Yes, sir. At the book-in room at the Marietta Police Station, we have to fill out a book-in report. I again asked the Defendant his name. I had to guess on his physical appearance because he did not provide that for me, and that's when I talked to the magistrate's office, advised them the subject would not give me any of this information, and everything was booked in as 'John Doe.'"

The evidence, he testified, was then tagged, bagged and checked into the evidence room. The officer pointed out Defendant Terry Greenway, in the courtroom, as the person he arrested on January 7, 1990.

At this point, Judge Brantley announced we would take a noon recess, and return at 1:30. He then instructed and admonished the jurors about their conduct during recess: they could not discuss the case among themselves or with anyone else while away from court, and they should report any attempt by anyone who may try to discuss the case with them.

Upon returning to court after the noon recess, I continued.

"Officer Smith, let me show you what is marked State's Exhibit 37. Would you take that bag and open it and tell me if you've seen the contents before."

"Yes, sir."

"Would you describe what the contents of State's 37 is?"

"This item here is a screwdriver the Defendant had in his left hand when I first approached him, same evidence I took from the scene."

"All right."

"The flashlight that I found in his right rear pocket that was covered up by the white handkerchief."

"All right. And the third item?"

"The white gloves that he was wearing at the time of the incident."

"All right. Now, would you tell us, these three items that you just described, what would a burglar have use of those for in committing a burglary?"

"The screwdriver is used to make forced entry into a location, through doors, windows, any type of locked-type object that requires pressure being applied to that object to make it open. The flashlight, of course, is used at nighttime so the subject can see what he's doing, and gloves will be used to prevent the identity of himself being known through fingerprints."

"In other words, with gloves, you wouldn't leave fingerprints?"

"Right."

Such questions may sound trivial, but I qualified the officer initially as having some expertise in handling burglaries and thefts, and I needed to *make a record* for what these 'tools' are commonly used for: committing burglaries and other crimes, in order to satisfy the requirements of the law that the defendant was in possession of "burglary tools," a felony offense. It is obviously relevant testimony, and Mr. Cella never lodged an objection to it.

"I show you [now] what is marked State's Exhibit 36. If you would tell me the contents of that, please."

"This is a pocket knife that I retrieved from the Defendant's right front pants pocket."

"All right. Is that the same knife that you recovered from his pocket and turned in at property room as evidence in this case?"

"Yes, sir."

Two Faces of a Serial Rapist

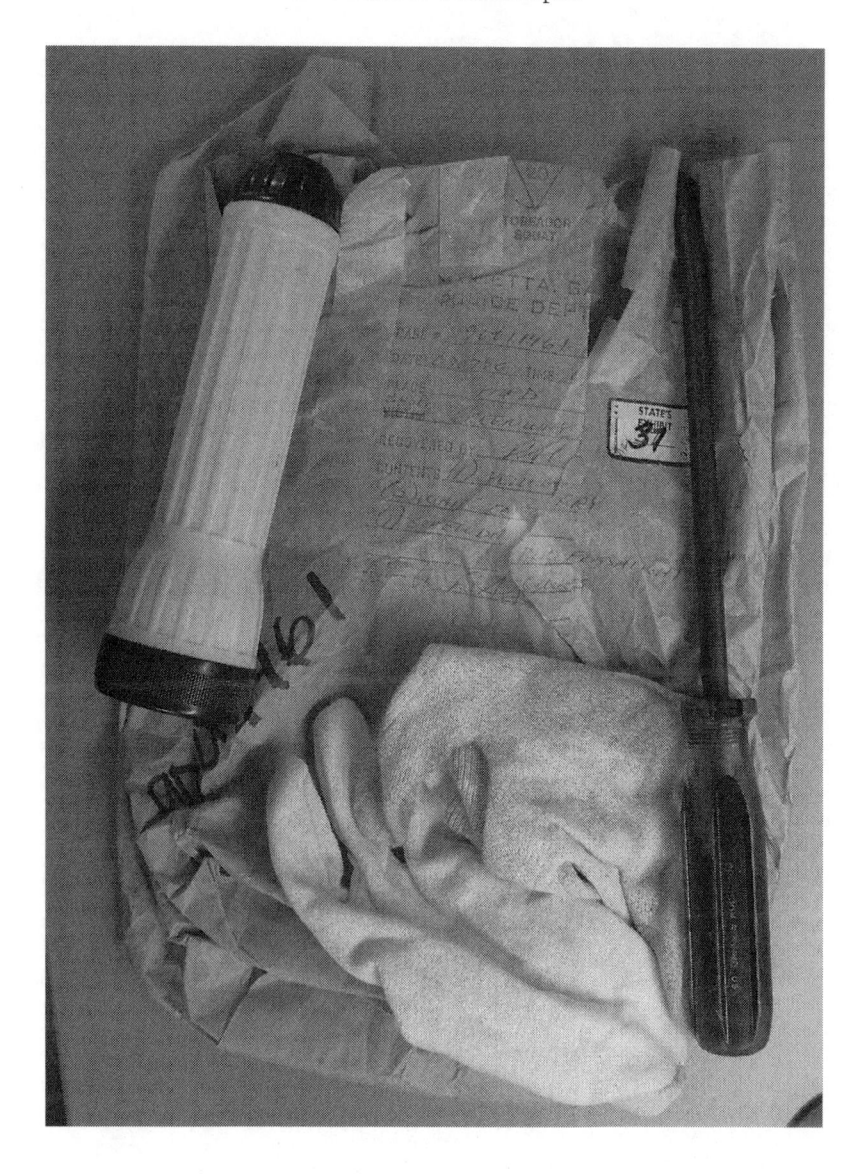

CROSS EXAMINATION BY MR. CELLA:

"What ever happened to the handkerchief?"

The witness explained that he turned it in to the property room as the defendant's personal property, which was later given back to the inmate when he was released on bond.

"You said that his handkerchief was covering up the flashlight. How was that?"

"It was wadded on top of the flashlight. This end of the flashlight was protruding from his right rear pants pocket. The handkerchief was on top of that inside his pants."

Cross-examination continued with minute details of where the property, including the clothing, had been since arrest, and the sealing and maintaining of the evidence in the evidence locker until delivered to court.

"Did Mr. Greenway have any money on him?"

"No, sir. He didn't have anything."

Cella kept peppering the witness with questions which I had asked about his arrival at the scene, removal of the light bulb, and flickering of the light as it was unscrewed.

"You're saying that the light bulb made noise?"

"The light bulb itself made noise whenever I screwed it back in."

"Are you sure you're not thinking about the globe that made the screeching sound and not the light bulb itself?"

"The socket itself has got a lot of deterioration due to humidity in the area. Wherever you screw a light bulb itself in, it also makes a screeching noise with the contact."

Cella continued to test the officer's memory about sequence of events, but the witness stood firm on what he saw and heard. As if this really attacks the main events which is that Greenway was arrested at the front door, trying to break into the woman's apartment.

Cella: "You said that you were faster than him?"

Witness: "Yes, sir."

"How many steps did he take in attempt to get away from you?"

"Approximately eight to ten steps to my right."

"And you said you drew your weapon at that point?"

"Yes, sir. I placed it in the ready position which is at a 45 degree angle. He still had the screwdriver in his hand, and that's when I told him to stop and drop the screwdriver."

Mr. Cella then questioned the extent of Greenway's intoxication.

"He had an odor of alcohol about his person, but his body odor was more evident. He didn't appear to be intoxicated to where he couldn't carry on a normal conversation or normal actions without appearing to be severely intoxicated."

Cross examination continued on the question of intoxication for some time as to Greenway's speech, unsteadiness, watery eyes, body odor, and the rainy weather conditions. Further cross involved repeating the officer's testimony about why he didn't attempt to take prints from the items, how long he was on the scene, placing Greenway in the police car and other insignificant matters, without finding any loophole in the witness's testimony.

"When Detective Smith arrived, had you already taken your warrant out?"

"I believe so. Immediately after the Defendant was booked in and held at Marietta Police Station, that's when I obtained a warrant, and after I got the warrant, that's when I was doing my report, and that's when I made contact with Detective Smith."

"So I thought you told us that there was no evidence that anybody had ever broken the seal (on the evidence bag)?"

"Not through evidence, no, sir."

"No?"

"To my knowledge, no, sir."

"You got me totally confused now. Can you tell from looking at that bag whether the knife has ever been taken out of it or not?"

"No, sir."

"You can't tell?"

"I can't tell."

"Okay. You can't tell if any of those things are, in fact, what you put in the bag, can you?"

"No, sir."

"MR. CELLA: Okay. I think that's all, Judge."

[A good lawyer will attempt to stop his cross-examination at a high note where he has seemingly made a point about an issue, here chain of custody.]

"THE COURT: Any redirect?"

"BY MR. MALLARD:

"I believe you indicated the knife was in the one bag which is State's Exhibit 36. Does that knife appear to be the knife you took off the Defendant the morning of January 7, 1990?"

"Yes, sir."

"Do these three items you just identified appear to be the three items you took off of him the same morning?"

"Yes, sir."

"MR. MALLARD: Thank you. Offer into evidence State's Exhibit 36 and 37."

Before the court could rule, Mr. Cella wasn't satisfied and directed further re-cross-examination:

BY MR. CELLA:

"Patrolman Biggers, was this envelope, State's 36, did you take that out of here? I didn't really see you do that."

"The knife came out of that envelope there."

"And this envelope was in here or not?"

"No, sir."

"It wasn't in here?"

Cella continues for two more pages of cross-examination about the items and their presence in the bag, and how they got there.

"And you don't know how the knife got taken out of there?"

"No, sir."

"But this looks like the same knife?"

"Yes, sir."

"And you're saying that based on your recollection from two years ago?"

"Yes, sir."

"Is there anything unusual about the appearance of this knife that makes you feel confident that it was the same knife?"

"It was a black, plastic handle, small blade, which is the same thing I noted on my evidence sheet."

[Now, one can see the extent of which a vigorous cross-examination may take you, whether important or not—in the hopes of finding a jewel.]

At that point, Cella completed his cross-examination, and excused the witness. The court asked if Cella had any objection to State's Exhibits 36 and 37.

"MR. CELLA: Yes, sir. We object on chain of custody grounds that has not been proven."

"MR. MALLARD: These are not fungible items. They're physical items that can be identified by appearance. It's not required he have everybody who's ever touched it." [It is not necessary for each person in the chain of custody to testify.]

"THE COURT: The objection is overruled. The exhibits are admitted. Please call your next witness."

The charges for which Greenway was arrested, Criminal Attempt to Commit Burglary and Possessing Tools to Commit a Crime, have now been proven prima facie to the jury.

Woodlake Apartments, November 5, 1984— Similar Offense

I called Ms. Geraldine Sertain as a witness. She was sworn.
[This witness will testify to a similar transaction by Defendant Greenway of peeping tom in Hall County, where he was arrested in 1984, and convicted.]

The witness testified that on November 5, 1984, she lived in a ground level apartment in Gainesville, Georgia, with her daughter and two grandchildren; it was her daughter's apartment and she was out on a date. It was about midnight!

"Okay. Now, when did you ever see him look into the bedroom window?" I asked.

"He just walked up like I'm facing you, like you're the window. He didn't get up against it, he just looked up against it, and you couldn't see through the curtains, you know."

"And what location of the apartment building was this window?"

"Well, I would call it the side, because we had like a wooden door. You come in our front room door, then we had the glass doors in the living room, but I would call it the side doors because that's where my window was, on the side. ..."

She further testified: "And I said, who you hunting, sir? And he never give me no answer, and I told my little granddaughter, she was deaf, I said, get grandma the gun, then he took off and left. And then I called 911 and the Gainesville police came, and just a few minutes after, and they had found him up there in a phone booth, and they took me up to the car to identify him."

"Okay. When you saw him in the custody of the police, did you identify him for them?"

"Yes, sir. They told me, said I didn't have to get too close, and I looked, and I knew him from where he was sitting."

The witness then testified to the man having come back to see her before the court date when Mr. Cella objected, and I pointed out that it went to identity. Judge Brantley overruled the objection.

"You indicated that before you went to Court, that this man you saw looking in your window came back to your apartment?"

"Yes, sir."

"And would you tell us what he said?"

"Well, he came to the door. He was nice dressed, and I don't remember exactly what he said it was, but when he got into the house, he said, 'I'm Mr. Greenway, and I want to talk to you about what happened.' And we sat there and talked. And he said, '*I advise you not to go to court in the best of your interest.*' Then he asked me, he said, '*Do you love your kids, your grandkids?*'" [Sounds like intimidating the witness/victim.]

"And I said, 'Yes, sir.'"

"He said, 'Well, I've got children I love, too.'"

"All right. Did you tell him whether you were going to court or not?"

"I told him, I said, I don't know. I'll have to talk to my daughter, because I was upset and didn't know what to do."

[Interesting, that in the first arrest of Greenway at this same apartment complex under similar circumstances six months earlier, where the jury later acquitted him, Greenway's wife had visited *that* victim before the court date, and made the same request: that the victim not go to court.]

"And did you end up going to court?"

"Yes, sir, I did."

"And did you testify against him in Hall County?"

"Yes, sir."

"And did you identify him in court up there?"

"Yes, sir."

"And did the jury convict him?"

"They told me that he would be punished for it, but I never heard no more from them."

"All right. And did you subsequently to that, about January of 1990, did you have an occasion to see the same man, Mr. Greenway, you referred to on TV?"

"I don't remember what month it was, but I [seen] Mr. Greenway on TV one night, yeah."

"And did you recognize him when you saw him on TV?"

"Yes, sir, I did."

"And what was the occasion that you saw him on TV?"

"I don't know. It just, it was the news, and it said something about him, and I just looked, and I don't remember what it said about him, but I remember seeing him on TV because I told my children that was the man."

I then turned the witness over for cross-examination. [What a witness she made. She was obviously intimidated, but she stood firm in her resolve to follow through with the prosecution in Hall County.] Now, let's see what Mr. Cella can do with her.

CROSS EXAMINATION

BY MR. CELLA:

"Do you see Mr. Greenway in the court today?"

"Sir, I can't see back that way now because my eyes has got cataracts on them, and I can't see that far."

"Okay. You said that he didn't get up against your window?"

"He wasn't up against the window, but he was on the dirt there beside the window."

"Is there a sidewalk that goes behind your apartment?"

"No, sir."

"How far away from your window was he, if you can give us —

"About like this, maybe a little farther, this to me."

"Okay."

"Because there wasn't no walkway or nothing, you know, a little bit of yard and the embankment over there."

The witness explained she was inside her apartment on the bed when she saw him; the kids had gone to bed, and she was just laying there expecting her daughter home any time. She looked through her bedroom window; the curtains were not completely closed.

"Well, I was laying just like this to the window, and I seen Mr. Greenway come up. He didn't look like he had been to the wooden door. He came up, and he looked like he was looking through the glass, sliding glass doors. Then he came on down to the bedroom window, and he stood there, and I asked my granddaughter, I asked him first I said, 'Who you hunting, sir?' or something like that. He did not answer. Then I told my granddaughter to get the gun, which my grand-daughter don't hear, and we didn't have any gun, but he turned and disappeared then."

The witness did not see him carrying anything or trying to break into the apartment, just standing outside the window—but she testified that her apartment was the "end" apartment, and the only way he could go was turn around and go back the way he came.

"And he came back, and you said he was well-dressed."

"He was well-dressed, and, you know, I'm the type preachers or something come to talk to me. I asked him in. He said he was Mr. Greenway, and he wanted to talk about the children."

"Was he polite to you?"

"He was nice, but he told me it would be to the best of my interest if I would not testify in court. And he said if I loved my grandchildren—"

"How long did you talk to him?"

"Maybe three or four minutes, just very shortly because I told him I said, it's time for my daughter to come home, and she told me not to open the door for nobody."

"But you did anyway?"

"Yes."

"You wouldn't have let him in if he was mean or threatening to you?"

"He looked altogether different. Like I said, he could have been the preacher come to talk to me, but when he came back, he was nice dressed like you, you know, you come to me and tell me I ..."

"Did he try to explain to you about why he was out there that night?"

"No, sir. He told me that him and his wife was separated, and he's trying to get back, and said he'd been to this apartment before since we live here."

Mr. Cella asked the witness whether it appeared Greenway was drinking, but it didn't appear that way to her.

I called Ronald Sharpley as a witness. He testified he was Assistant Principal at Mary Parsons High School in Forsyth County. In 1984, he worked for the Gainesville Police Department as a patrolman. He said he was working on the 11:00 to 7:00 shift on November 5, 1984, and responded to a call to Woodlake Apartments at 32 minutes after midnight where he met Ms. Sertain at apartment I-9.

I asked, "Is that the young lady who just left the stand and passed you going out?"

"Yes, sir, it was."

He proceeded to testify the lady made a complaint of a white male looking inside her window; he received a description and put it out on radio broadcast. Two officers saw the subject at a phone booth, some 100 to 200 yards away, where he was arrested and identified by Ms. Sertain. The subject was identified as Terry Greenway.

Mr. Sharpley continued to testify that Greenway was given his Miranda warnings and escorted to Police Headquarters where he was questioned.

"Once you advised him, did he give an account of his actions?"

"He stated that he was using the phone to call his wife because his vehicle had torn up."

"And did he indicate to you what kind of vehicle he had there?"

"He stated he had a Dodge."

"Were you ever able to find a Dodge?"

"No, sir, we were not."

"And so what was done with the Defendant then?"

"After reading him Miranda, then I asked him about some keys which were found."

"Where were they found?"

"In another vehicle."

"And what kind of vehicle was this?"

"It was a Chevrolet."

"A Chevrolet and not a Dodge?"

"Yes, correct."

"Where was it found?"

"It was found at Woodlake Apartments."

The witness further responded that two other officers found the Chevrolet vehicle with keys in the ignition. Mr. Greenway further requested the keys be turned over to him and the vehicle to be left in the parking lot; that his wife would pick it up.

"What was the condition of his (Greenway's) shoes and clothes, if you remember?"

"They were wet-looking with grass on them."

"All right. Did you subsequently testify in the case against Mr. Greenway that you've identified in court?"

"Yes, sir, I did."

"Was he convicted?"

"Yes, sir, he was."

I turned the witness over for cross-examination by Mr. Cella.

CROSS EXAMINATION
BY MR. CELLA:
For four pages, Mr. Cella questioned the witness about his having reviewed his police report in Gainesville, and that his fellow officer,

Commander Campbell, was in court to testify. Cella then used some time as to the exact location of the telephone booths where police found Greenway, which is at the adjoining property next to Woodlake Apartments.

The witness was taken back through his testimony about receiving the call, responding within 3-5 minutes to the scene, talking to the victim, and placing the lookout.

"Okay. Did the wet feet indicate to you that somebody had walked off the pavement? Is that why you said that he had wet feet?"

"And the grass stains. Yes, it indicated that someone had been off the [pavement]."

The witness testified there was nothing notable about Greenway's physical condition, no indication of alcohol, and he had no screwdriver, flashlight or knife on his person.

The witness was then excused, and I called the next witness, John Campbell.

The witness, John Campbell, testified he had been employed by the City of Gainesville as a police officer for 19 years, and that he was a Captain. He was on duty the night of November 5, 1984 after midnight. He was aware of a reported prowling, peeping tom call from the Woodlake Apartments, by Ms. Sertain.

Captain Campbell: "Officer Sharpley worked under me at that time. He responded to a call. I heard him place a subject into custody, and I was riding towards the area at that time."

Campbell further testified when he arrived at the apartments the subject had been taken to jail, and he assisted in trying to locate a Dodge vehicle when he found another vehicle.

Mallard: "What was that?"

"It was a Chevrolet Impala. Once after running the tag through the Georgia crime information center, it came back …"

"MR. CELLA: Objection. I think that record would speak for itself."

"MR. MALLARD: Yes, sir, it sure will." [I was ready for the objection. I had in my hand a certified copy of the registration.]

"I show you State's Exhibit 46. What is that, please, sir."

"It's a tag receipt."

"Is that the certified copy from the State of Georgia?"

"Yes, sir, it is."

"And is that the registration on the vehicle you were just testifying about?"

"Yes, sir."

"And who does it show it's registered to?"

"Shermanda M. Greenway."

"You know that to be the Defendant's wife?"

"Yes, sir."

The witness then identified the Defendant in the courtroom as Terry Thaddeus Greenway.

"Now, this vehicle that you just have spoken about, this sedan, where was it parked in the Woodlake Apartments?"

"It was several buildings down from the I building, close to the upper swimming pool area."

"So how many buildings or approximately how many yards away from Ms. Sertain's apartment would you estimate it was?"

"I guess it was about two buildings down from her, probably 200 or 300 yards."

"All right. Were any keys found?"

"Yes, sir."

"Where were the keys?"

"In the ignition."

Mr. Cella again objected unless the witness personally found the keys.

"Did you find the keys in the ignition of the vehicle?"

"Yes, sir, I did."

"And were any papers in the vehicle?"

"Yes, sir. I found some papers in there with Terry's name on them."

I turned the witness over for cross-examination.

CROSS EXAMINATION

BY MR. CELLA:

Mr. Cella went through the witness's testimony, learning that he was a Lieutenant at the time of the incident in 1984, and how long it took to locate the car in the dark. The car aroused suspicion because it was parked below the swimming pool where no one usually parks. The officer just happened to run a tag number on it. They found no burglary tools in the car, but they did not search the trunk.

Then, Cella asked a dangerous question of the witness.

"Any complaints from the residents of that apartment complex that indicated to you it might have been him they were complaining about?"

"No, sir. We had had some complaints before about prowling in that area."

"But he wasn't a suspect?"

"Yes, sir, he was."

"At the time that you were looking through his car, he wasn't a suspect of any prior incidents, was he?"

"Yes, sir, he was."

CELLA: "Why was that?"

THE WITNESS: "He was arrested one time before."

[A "Why" question can be dangerous. That's the potential fallout from being an aggressive cross-examiner—sometimes it's worth the effort, but sometimes you lose.]

"And even with that, you didn't find any evidence of burglar tools in his car?"

"No, sir."

At that, Cella finished and the witness was excused.

This completes my presentation of the "Similar Transaction" of peeping tom in Hall County in 1984 where he had been convicted and put on probation.

Before the next witness was called, the bailiff advised the court that there was a juror who wanted to be excused. The juror was brought into court where he was identified and told the judge that his superintendent had quit that morning and he had been filling in for him while serving on the jury. The juror worked for Williams Brothers Concrete Company where he was in charge of all commercial concrete mix designs and submittals on all contracts in Atlanta, and he was the only one who could do the work.

Although there were two alternate jurors, Mr. Cella told the Judge, before the juror was brought into court that he would not agree to excuse the juror. The juror conceded that he was working his job at nights to help his company. The juror was denied release from jury duty since Cella objected, as it may have resulted in an error upon appeal requiring a new trial. The safe thing to do was keep the juror on the jury.

Powers Ferry Apartments, August 26, 1987— Rape; Burglary

The victim, Linda Linnard, was called to the stand and sworn. I directed her attention to August 26, 1987. She stated she was married and they lived in a ground level apartment at Powers Ferry Station Apartments in Cobb County. They had only been living there about a month. They did not have complete furniture at the time. Her husband was working a security job on the evening shift and had left for work at about 10:00 p.m. She testified she went to bed after her husband left for work.

MR. MALLARD:

"Okay. And where were you sleeping?"

"I fixed me a pallet in the living room floor."

"Did you even have a bedroom suit at that time?"

"Not a full bedroom suit."

"Okay. And had you watched TV?"

"Yes, sir."

"And did anything unusual occur the morning hours, about 4:30 in the morning?"

"Yes, sir. I was awakened with a man standing over me."

"All right. And what is the first thing when you awoke that was said or done?"

"When I realized he was there, I started screaming, and he told me to stop screaming, and he wouldn't hurt me."

"What else did he say?"

"He told me to, [as I was], after I saw him there, I was screaming. He told me to stop, and he wouldn't hurt me. I was edging my way away from him, trying to get back off from him, and I started, he stopped me. He put his arm on me. He stopped me, and I started crying, and he grabbed my shirt. I said, please don't hurt me, and he says something to the effect of, well, I won't be here but just a few minutes."

"I won't be here for just a few minutes?" I repeated.

"Yes, sir."

"Did you see anything in his hand?"

"Yes, sir. At this point, when he stopped me, he held up his hand, and he had a knife."

"All right. Could you tell what kind of knife?"

"To me, it looked like a machete at the time, but in the end, I found out it was, you know, I guess probably a pocket knife."

"Okay. Did you say he raised it?"

"Yes, sir."

"Were you crying?"

"He raised it towards my face to make sure I saw it."

"Were you crying at that time?"

"Yes, sir. It kind of seemed like it agitated him a little bit, so I tried to get myself together."

"All right. Was it dark in the room where you were?"

"No, sir. I was a little apprehensive about staying at night by myself. That's the main reason for sleeping in the living room. So my TV was on, and my dining room light was on, which it was a living room/dining room combination, and I believe my porch light was on."

"You have a porch light on the outside of the apartment?"

"Yes, sir, patio light. It was on when I went to sleep, because I turned it on. I did not notice at that point whether it was still on or not."

"Did the subject have anything over his face?"

"He had a blue bandanna."

"And would you tell us how far up the bandanna came?"

"About right here, across the bridge of his nose."

"You're showing across the bridge of your nose?"

"Yes, sir."

"So the lower part of his face was covered by the bandanna?"

"Yes, sir."

"What did he do then?"

"He put his arm up here and told me to lay back on the pallet, and I laid down. I was wearing a pair of shorts and like a hospital-type shirt that people wear, and he took off my shorts and my underwear. And he, at this point, was on his knees in front of me, and he unzipped his pants, and he started, I'm not sure I remember the order of events here, you know. He started playing with himself, and then he started rubbing it on my chest and up on my mouth, and I turned my head at this point, and he rubbed it for a few minutes, and he inserted his penis in me."

"And you say he rubbed it on your face, and so were you talking about his penis?"

"Yes, sir, I am."

"You mentioned he had [a] looked like a pocket knife to you. Do you remember telling Officer Tallman later that it was a small, folding-type knife?"

"Yes, sir."

"Okay. And I might ask you a few questions here. Did the subject proceed to have sexual intercourse with you?"

"Yes, sir."

"And was that with or without your consent?"

"Without."

"And did you know this person?"

"No, sir."

"Let me ask you specifically. Was there penetration of your vagina by his male organ?"

"Yes, sir."

"And was that forcibly and against your will?"

"Yes, sir."

"Prior to this, you indicated he was playing with himself. Did he, in fact, masturbate?"

"No, sir."

"When you say, playing with himself, what do you mean?"

"Fondling his penis like he was trying to get an erection."

"Did he have trouble with an erection?"

"It seemed like."

"Did he keep the knife in his hand during the time that he was having sexual intercourse with you?"

"Yes, sir. Like I said, my head was turned, but the last time I noticed, he was knelt on the floor with the knife in his hand."

"All right. Could you tell whether or not he ejaculated in you?"

"At that time, I could not, but I did find our later, yes, sir."

"Afterwards, what did the subject do?"

"After he finished, he zipped up his pants, and he threw the blanket that I had made the pallet out of over me, and he told me to turn over where my back would be facing the wall. At this time, I saw him from the corner of my eyes kind of walk around to where I had my telephone set up, and at this point, I thought he was going to kill me, so I turned back around to see what he was doing. Later, I found out that he was cutting my phone cords. He went to my front door, he opened my front door and walked out."

"Ms. Linnard, you said he zipped up his pants. I take it, then, that he never removed his pants. He just unzipped his pants?"

"Correct. He did not remove his pants."

"All right. And what did you do then?"

"Ironically enough, during this time I had had a gun near me. It took me a second to kind of get myself together. I grabbed the gun. I went to the back bedroom where I also had a phone. I found that he had evidently been back there first and cut my phone cord. I went back to the living room. I hesitated for a few seconds. I was not sure if he was still out there, so I decided that I had the gun in my hand, and if he was there, I would just shoot him. So I walked out the door. I looked. He wasn't there. I went to my neighbor's house, knocked on the door, and we called the police."

"And when you went over to the neighbor, was that in the same apartment building?"

"Oh, yes, sir."

The witness went on to relate that 911 was called, the police responded and checked the spare bedroom window where they found the point of entry with the window open. She testified when she went to bed she had shut and locked the window. She further testified the intruder had a "country accent."

She said that Detective Rogers met with her, and they went to Kennestone Hospital where Dr. Malcom examined her.

Subsequently, she and her family moved across the state to Savannah, Georgia. On March 27, 1990, Detective Eddie Herman met her at the Chatham County Police Department for the purpose of drawing her blood for follow-up testing. [Subsequent to Greenway's arrest for purposes of DNA testing.]

I asked her if she had tried to black out the whole thing since it happened.

"Yes, sir. I've [went] through two years of therapy to try to forget this."

CROSS-EXAMINATION
BY MR. CELLA:

Mr. Cella had the witness describe the perpetrator as having dark, sandy blond hair, cut short, medium build and about six foot tall. She guessed his weight at "like 180."

"Did your attacker have anything with him other than the pocket knife that you described to us?"

"He had the pocket knife in his hand, and the bandanna across his face."

"And nothing else that you recall?"

"Not in his possession."

"Did this man ever use bad language to you?"

"He did not cuss at me, no, sir."

"Could you describe his hands?"

"He had large hands. By the time he was to the point where he was touching me, I was numb, so I wasn't really able to tell whether he had rough hands or dry hands or ..."

"Okay. In other words, it didn't hurt as he rubbed his hands over you like somebody with really rough hands might?"

"Then again, not that I recall. But there again, at this point, I was, I guess I was in shock. My body was numb. It was as if my body was on the floor, but myself was somewhere else, removed from the situation."

She was questioned about the subject's accent, and explained that "It was a southern, country accent." She described the clothing the subject was wearing as a pair of black, nylon-like pants, and no shirt; the bandanna was of a cotton material.

She was asked about the point of entry.

"Did the screen in the bedroom without the phone, did that window have a screen on it?"

"No, sir, it did not."

"Were you able to see any, I guess what the police would call, pry marks or any signs that the wood had been tampered with in any way on the window?"

"Where the latch hooks, you could see scratch marks."

"Do you feel like you might have left that window unlocked?"

"No, sir, I did not."

The witness explained that police tried to get fingerprints from the window, but they were smudged. She never looked at any photographs of a possible suspect.

"Could you describe this man's demeanor toward you? I mean would you characterize him as rough or gentle or somewhere in between as far as the way he treated you?"

"He didn't hit me or use bad language towards me. He wasn't ..."

"Would you call him aggressive?"

"He wasn't rough with me."

"Okay. I'm almost as embarrassed to ask this question as you probably will be answering it, but it has to do with a comment that you made to Detective Herman. Did you notice anything about the size of the man's penis?"

"I believe the statement you're referring to is he asked me if I could tell if he had ejaculated inside of me, and at this time, I told him that either he was, I couldn't tell. It was either he was very small-built or I was just so in a state of shock, I was numb and could not tell."

"Were you able to tell if the rapist was circumcised or not?"

"No, sir."

The witness was excused.

Detective Roy Rogers, Cobb County Police, Crimes Against Persons Unit, was called and testified:
BY MR. MALLARD:

"Sir, would you state your name, please."

"My name is Roy Rogers."

"You're not married to Dale Evans, are you?" [I just had to do it.]

"No , sir."

The witness testified to his history with the department going back to 1978, and was referred to the burglary and rape incident at the Powers Ferry Apartments on August 26, 1987. He was working the midnight shift and responded to the location, arriving shortly after the uniform officer. Detective Rogers interviewed both the victim and her husband, who had arrived home shortly after Rogers arrived. He described the crime scene and the point of entry.

"Were there discovered to be phone cords cut in the apartment?"

"Yes, sir, there was."

"And did you attempt to get any fingerprints from anything?"

"From the window itself as well as the window sill surrounding it."

"Were you able to?"

"No, sir, I was not."

"Did you attempt to get any prints anywhere else?"

"I talked with Ms. Linnard and her husband and asked if they could possibly go into a restroom in the apartment and try to get fingerprints from her skin, based on information I'd received about the incident."

"Were you unable or able to do anything else?"

"No, sir. I was not able to locate any prints. The method I used was a method that we use in the unit."

"All right. Is the skin a good place to remove prints in the first place?"

"Usually on a person who is deceased, it can be done. On a person who is still alive, it's very difficult to get prints from their skin."

"Did you seize any evidence that was subsequently sent to the crime lab from the area of the window sill?

"Yes, sir, I did."

"What was that?"

"It was a light-colored human hair, appeared to be a head hair."

"All right. Is that just a routine investigation? Do you have any reason to think the perpetrator left the hair there?"

"Well, the hair, when I found it, was on the window sill. It was where the window itself joins the base. The hair was not compressed as if it had been inside the window for a period of time. It appeared to be recently placed there, so I felt it needed to be collected and sent to the lab."

"All right. And subsequently, was there a subject by the name of Comstock that was investigated?" [Since the defense was pointing the finger at John Comstock, who had been arrested and investigated for break-ins, I decided to face it 'head-on' and show the police did a good job and eliminated other persons of interest.]

"Yes, sir, there was."

"And did you ever at any time consider him a serious suspect?"

"Not a serious, but serious enough that I felt I needed to obtain some samples from him just to clear him."

"And did you obtain pubic and head hairs from him with his consent?"

"Yes, sir, as well as blood and body fluids."

"You sent that to the crime lab with the hair you had cut?"

"Yes, sir."

"And as a result of that, was he released?"

"He was eliminated as a suspect."

"And was the crime lab able to indicate, in any way, whose hair it could be?"

"No, sir."

Det. Rogers completed the crime scene, and met the victim and her husband at Windy Hill Hospital, where the victim was examined by Dr. Malcom with Ms. Mainer, RN, assisting. Det. Rogers furnished a rape kit for the examination.

"After you turned the rape kit over to the doctor, when is the next time you saw it?"

"The next time I saw it was right after Dr. Malcom had completed his examination. He showed me everything that he had collected in the examination while he was placing it in the kit. The kit was then sealed in my presence by Ms. Mainer, and I received it from her at that time."

Detective Rogers explained that the rape kit included vaginal swabbings, which was sealed inside the kit where it remained in his possession. He transported the kit to police headquarters where he prepared all the paperwork and turned it over to Detective Steve Alexander for transport to the crime laboratory.

CROSS-EXAMINATION
BY MR. CELLA:

Mr. Cella's inquiry revealed that the victim's husband was at work at the time of the attack, and that the hair found on the window sill was creased. The witness said that he is trained in doing composites but did not do so in this instance. Cella went back over the investigation at the point of entry:

"Okay. Do you recall observing any damage on the outside of the window, Detective Rogers?"

"I don't recall seeing any major damage out there, no, sir. There might have been some scratches, but no major damage that I could see."

"Do you have an opinion about how entry was gained in this case?"

"The window was open definitely from the outside. It's possible that the lock could have been slit from the outside. It had a basic cheap latch on it. But the window was just pushed up. There was no screen covering the window. It was just pushed up, and entry was made."

Dr. George Edward Malcom was called, sworn, and testified that he was employed at Kennestone Hospital at Windy Hill on August 26, 1987, when he received a patient, Linda Linnard, as a reported rape victim. He saw her at 6:56 a.m. He testified:

"Well, I did a complete physical exam to make sure that there was no medical problems that needed to be attended to, and then I took samples from the vagina. I took pubic combings, known pubic hair, known head hair. I made swabs from the vagina. I made slides from the swabs, and I collected these and labeled them and put them in the appropriate kit that's provided by the police department."

"Did you see any sperm?"

"I made, and also made slides of our own, and I did see sperm on the slide that I examined."

He testified all items were labeled with the victims' name and placed in the rape kit, and was given to Detective Roy Rogers.

I had the witness identify State's Exhibit 2A as the vaginal swabs (Q-tips) labeled with the victim's name.

"Was any medication or instructions provided [to the victim]?"

"I gave her Ampicillin and Probenecid, and that was to help prevent any infection. Of course, like I explained, nothing absolutely would help prevent infection." "I gave her some Vistaril, which is just something to help calm your nerves down, very mild sedatives."

While on the stand, I referred Dr. Malcom to a second rape victim whom he had examined on October 15, 1988, at 5:41 a.m. by the name of Donna Hightower.

The witness conducted the examination in the same manner as the previous case, also finding sperm in the Hightower case. In this case, the rape kit was turned over to Detective Christopher of the Marietta Police Department. Dr. Malcom treated this victim in the same manner with antibiotics. He identified State's Exhibit 5A as containing the swabs from patient Hightower.

CROSS EXAMINATION
BY MR. CELLA:

"Dr. Malcom, what kind of a utensil is used for doing this pubic combing procedure that you have described?"

"Just a simple black comb."

"Okay. When you're doing a pubic combing procedure, is there a certain number of hairs that you try to get in your sample, or how does that work?"

"You try not to, obviously, hurt the patient, but you try to get some. I mean you like to get several, but if you get one you're happy. Sometimes you occasionally, you can't get any."

"Is that the way it works out in the real world, or do you almost always get some of the subject's pubic hairs mixed in, too?"

"I don't think you always get some of the pubic hairs from the subject mixed in, but you can."

"On the average, how many do you get from this procedure?"

"One to two."

"Okay. And even with that small a number, you don't count them and put in your reports, I got one pubic hair, or I got two?"

"No."

The witness was excused.

Detective Eddie Herman, Cobb County Crimes Against Persons Unit, was called to the stand. I presented this witness for a limited purpose and out-of-order to accommodate his itinerary—to be on vacation. He did some follow-up work on a reported burglary and rape complaint made to him on August 27, 1987, by the victim, Ms. Linda Linnard. During the follow-up investigation after Greenway's arrest, I had asked Detective Herman to personally obtain a vial of the victim's blood to be sent to the FBI laboratory for DNA testing and in order to eliminate the need for other long-distance witnesses in the chain of custody [technician extracting the blood, sealing, delivery, etc.], that he should personally witness the blood as it is extracted from the victim so he would be able to testify as an eye-witness.

Ms. Linnard was employed and living across the State in Savannah, and worked for the county Emergency Medical Service. The victim met Detective Herman at the Chatham County Police Department where the blood was drawn on March 28, 1990.

Detective Herman testified he was in his 12th year, and was an investigator in the crimes against persons unit on August 27, 1987, when the victim reported she was attacked in her home.

"And did you obtain a sample of Ms. Linnard's blood?"

"Yes, I did."

"How did you do that?"

"Chatham County E.M.S. workers met with us, and one of the E.M.T.'s drew the blood into viles, and it was handed over to me. I secured it and maintained it, and the next day transported it to the Georgia Crime Lab here in Atlanta."

"Were you present at the time the E.M.T. people drew the blood from Linda Linnard's arm?"

"Yes, I was."

"Did you watch the blood flow into the tubes?"

"Yes, I did."

"And did you see the tubes sealed in your presence?"

"Yes."

"And once they were sealed, did you take charge of the tubes of blood?"

"Yes, I did."

"And did you keep them until you delivered them to the State Crime Lab?"

"Yes."

"And was that the next day?"

"Yes, March 28, 1990."

"Where did you stay overnight?"

"The Knights Inn in Savannah."

"All right. And then returned here the next day?"

"The next morning, yes."

"And did you take the samples of the blood you just said that were drawn from Ms. Linnard's arm to the state crime lab?"

"Yes, I did."

"And what did you do with it there?"

"At the State Crime Lab, it was turned over to one of the evidence technicians, one of the serology technicians."

"Is this drawing and delivery of the blood sample routine handling?"

"Yes."

"And as far as to being obtained in your presence, is that routine?"

"Yes."

"From the time that you saw the blood drawn and put into the tubes until you turned it over to the technician at the state crime lab, had there been any changes, alterations in the blood samples?"

"No."

"Was it still sealed when you turned it over to the technician at the state crime lab?"

"Yes, it was."

"Were the tubes of blood properly labeled with the name of the victim, Linda Linnard?"

Yes, they were."

MR. MALLARD: Counsel may cross-examine.

The foregoing eye-witness account of ensuring the blood received at the laboratory was not altered, is sufficient foundation for the evidence to that point; subsequent testimony from the technician at the state crime lab, and finally the FBI expert who did the testing will ensure the integrity of the evidence at the time of testing. Chain of custody is necessary because the blood, like other fluids, is a soluble item (subject to easily change) whereas the burglary tools were physical items subject to identification by sight.

I was waiting to see how Mr. Cella would handle this. Normally, the technician drawing the blood would be called as a witness. What normally would be a short terse cross-examination to try to interrupt or question the chain of custody turned out to be an extensive 24-page cross-examination.

BY MR. CELLA:

"Detective Herman, are you qualified to draw blood yourself?"

"No."

"Why did y'all have somebody else do it?"

"A qualified E.M.T."

"How did you know that this person was an E.M.T.?"

"Well, they were working with Chatham County Emergency Medical Service."

"Do you remember the person's name that drew the blood?"

"I do not, no."

"Do you remember the person's name that you gave the viles to the next day?"

"No, I don't recall."

"Okay. Somebody that you see regularly in your trips to the crime lab?"

"I wouldn't describe it as regularly. I don't recall exactly which technician I handed the blood to."

"Could you describe what kind of paperwork is involved in this procedure, Detective Herman?"

"A property evidence form."

The witness was taken through the point by point procedure for the forms which are used to document the transmittal of evidentiary items to the crime laboratory.

MR. CELLA CONTINUES:

"Okay. Could you describe for us your involvement in Ms. Linnard's case from the beginning? We've kind of got you in the end so far, haven't we? How did you initially become involved in Ms. Linnard's case?"

[It appears Cella will be going into hearsay, to which I could object. If I do object, he will just re-call the witness to try to catch the victim in a contradiction; thus, I decide I will play *loose* with his cross, and handle it on re-direct.]

"The morning, several hours after the assault, I was briefed by Detective Rogers who had worked the crime scene at the time of the incident, and I consulted with him about some things that we were going to try to do and planning on how to go about, you know, a door-to-door canvass, checking with other agencies, teletypes, those kind of things. And at about 10:00 o-clock on the morning ..."

The witness goes on to explain how the interview was recorded, subsequent follow-ups with the victim, her description of the perpetrator, and that the attacker had a "southern accent" and possessed a knife. Mr. Cella was obviously eliciting all the details of the reported crimes in the hopes that some difference will be indicated from her testimony.

"Okay. Detective Herman, have you ever conversed with a suspect named John Comstock as a suspect?"

"Yes."

"How did y'all develop Mr. Comstock as a suspect?"

"Mr. Comstock was taken into custody on Terry Mill Road in an apartment complex, I believe Windcliff on Terrell Mill Road. I believe for, I don't recall, public indecency or peeping. Then Detective Rogers dealt, mainly dealt with Mr. Comstock."

"Okay. What was it that made y'all think that he might be connected to the attack of Ms. Linnard?"

"Well, there really wasn't any one thing. During the course of investigating Ms. Linnard's attack, we were interested in anyone that was apprehended at apartment complexes on foot during early morning hours, peeping or acting in a suspicious manner, and he was one of the individuals that were picked up for that."

"Did she (the victim) ever tell you that the assailant at one point in time tried to put his penis in her mouth?"

"Yes."

When Mr. Cella finished, I took the witness on re-direct examination.

BY MR. MALLARD:

[I decided I would elicit some of the victim's hearsay statements since Mr. Cella had 'opened it up' and would not now object to my doing the same.]

"... Of course, this is all of what the victim told you. It's hearsay to you, is that correct?"

"Yes."

"And did she say she was crying?" [When she was assaulted.]

"Yes."

"He raised a knife. Did you remember her telling you the perpetrator raised a knife at her?"

"Yes."

"Do you remember her telling you that he said he'd be here just a few minutes?"

"Yes."

"That he unzipped his pants, started playing with himself. Do you remember her telling you that?"

"Yes, sir."

"That he tried to force it in her mouth. Do you remember her telling you about that?"

"Yes, sir."

"Remember telling you she thought he was going to kill her?"

"Yes."

"That her phone cord was cut?"

"Yes, sir."

"Remember she said that he was trying to get an erection?"

"Yes, sir."

"Do you remember her telling you that 'If I would have thought, if I would quit screaming, he wouldn't hurt me if I quit screaming.' He said it a few times. Do you remember that?"

"Yes, sir."

I concluded my examination, and the witness was excused to go on vacation.

Concepts 21 Apartments, April 10, 1988— Rape; Burglary

Melissa Hilyard, the victim, was called and sworn as a witness.

She testified that on April 10, 1988, she lived at the Concepts 21 Apartments in Cobb County, but later moved to the State of Wisconsin with her family. At Concepts 21, she lived in a lower level apartment with a female friend. She said that sometime after 1:00 o'clock a.m. she was asleep when she was awakened by an unannounced intruder.

MR. MALLARD:

"And would you tell us what happened, how you awoke?"

"I don't know what made me wake up. There was a flashlight shining in my face, and I thought it was my roommate. And I recall saying, did the electricity go out? And I realized it wasn't my roommate."

"What was said to you?"

"Something like, I think I asked, what do you want, or who are you? And then this person said, just be quiet. I'm not going to hurt you. And I think I tried to like get out of bed, and then I was pushed back down. I had a water bed, so it was kind of wavy."

"And did he say anything else to you then?"

"Not that I recall."

"What did he then do?"

"He told me to take my underwear off, and I don't know if I said no or argued with him, and then he said pretty sharply, you have ten seconds, and so I took my underwear off."

"Were you afraid?"

"I was scared to death."

"All right. Did he unzip his pants?"

"Uh-huh."

"And what did he do then?"

"He fondled himself into an erection, and then he proceeded to rape me."

"Initially, did he have trouble getting an erection, Ms. Hilyard."

"Yeah. It took, I mean it seemed probably longer than what it took, but he didn't have an erection when he unzipped his pants."

"And did he then force himself on you?"

"Yes, he did."

"Did he have sexual intercourse with you against your will?"

"He certainly did not have my consent."

"And I need to ask you this. Did his male sex organ penetrate your female sex organ?"

"Yes, sir, it did."

"Do you know whether or not he ejaculated in you?"

"He did."

"All right. And what did he do afterwards?"

"He got up off me, pulled up his pants, zipped his zipper, and left."

"All right. Did he exit your apartment by any particular way that you noted?"

"The front door because it was locked, and it was unlocked when the police came."

"Did you determine later how entry may have been made?"

"Yeah. In our apartment, the roommate plan is there is two rooms at opposite ends of the apartment, and by the front door is the room to my roommate's, a window to her room. And that was how he got into the apartment, on the other side of the apartment."

"So your roommate is on the other side of the apartment?"

"Uh-huh. And he came through her window."

"Well, how do you know entry was through her window?"

"When the police came, that's when they said he went through this window."

"Okay. And I take it your roommate, then, was not home?"

"No, sir, she was not."

"After the subject left your apartment, what did you do immediately?"

"I sat there for a few minutes quietly, afraid that he was going to come back in because he closed my door on his way out. So I was sitting in the bedroom in the dark, and I picked up the phone and dialed 911."

The witness proceeded to testify that the police responded, took a report from her, and she was later taken to Kennestone Hospital where she was examined by a doctor and nurse. She was subsequently taken to the police station where a statement was taken. As soon as she could get a flight out, she returned home to her parents in Wisconsin.

Mallard: "Did you subsequently to that, several years later, March 19th of 1990, to be specific, did you [...] come to Marietta and meet with Officer Smith?"

"Yes, sir, I did."

"And what was the reason for that?"

"For more samples or something for DNA testing."

"All right. Did he take you to get a blood sample?"

"Yes, sir."

"And was the blood drawn in his presence?"

"Uh-huh."

"And did he also show you a photographic spread, that is, a spread of several photographs in an attempt to make an I.D.?"

"Yes, sir, he did."

"And were you able to say that anyone was the subject that interrupted you on the night in question?"

"I could not identify anyone."

"Did you ever think that you could?"

"With a flashlight in your eyes, I didn't really think I could."

"The apartment on Bentley Road, was this your apartment, this your home?"

"Uh-huh."

"And was the intruder there without your consent, on the premises?" [Burglary.]

"Yes, sir."

"Can you tell us any particular regional accent or anything you noted about the intruder as far as the voice?"

"Considering I'm from the north, he definitely had a southern accent. It was not a [northern accent]."

CROSS-EXAMINATION
BY MR. CELLA:
"Ms. Hilyard, my name is Marc Cella. *I need to ask you a few questions.* [But, his questions will last for 15 pages of court transcript.] I know this is a very emotional time for you. If you need to take a

break, just let me know, or if you need some water, we'll do that. Let me start at the beginning. You said you had a roommate who wasn't home that night?"

"Yes, sir."

"Was it a male or female roommate?" [This is common of defense counsel to repeat it, though she had told us earlier it was a female roommate.]

"I said it was female." [She gave him a *spunky* response.]

"And when had you last seen her?"

"In the morning, before we went to work."

"Okay. What time would that be? Did she leave the same time every morning?"

"I can't say for her if she leaves the same time every morning. We left at the same time in the morning."

"Okay. Approximately what time was that?"

"I would say, can't be approximate, this was a few years ago. If we had to be at work at 8:30, probably 8:00 o'clock in the morning."

"Okay. And then you didn't see her at all again before the, before you were woke up with the flashlight in your face?"

"No."

Cella continued to bear down regarding the roommate's schedule, how long the victim had lived there, and other mundane questions not important to the rape.

[Cella had told the jury in his opening statement that he did not question that these women were raped; that these women are real victims, he said, and that he was not going to cross-examine these women with intent of showing they were not raped, or about them being raped, or about how the women acted. ... None of these are issues, he stated. He made a point of saying he would be treating them gently. Well, let us see how he sticks to his promise.]

"After it happened, did you learn that there had been similar incidents?"

"Yes."

"Okay. Had you ever seen any composites posted around the property of suspects who had attacked other residents?"

"No."

Cella continued to go over what she had already testified to on direct about the point of entry, and whether she gave a physical description of the perpetrator. The witness was unsure as it had been a long time, and she did not recall what she had told the police about a description.

"Do you recall telling him (police) that your assailant had a receding hairline?"

"No."

"Okay. Do you recall telling (police) that the man had cologne on?"

"I don't recall."

"Okay. Do you recall whether the man had a screwdriver?"

"No, sir."

"He didn't have one?"

"Not that I saw."

"Okay."

"He could have. He could have had a toolbox on the floor."

"You never saw a screwdriver?"

"No."

"Was he wearing gloves?"

"No."

"Was he wearing a bandanna or a handkerchief or any kind of cloth over his face?"

"Not that I recall."

"Do you recall what happened to the flashlight during the time that, between when you first woke up and it was shining in your face and the time when the man walked out of your front door?"

"I believe it was laying on the bed like beside me or something, shining this way."

"Okay. So it was never turned off, but he did set it down?"

"He had to, yeah."

"Okay. Do you recall whether he turned it off or not?"

"No."

"Okay. He could have turned it off, or he could not have. You don't know one way or the other?"

"Well, it was laying on the bed during the rape with the light shining up this way. When he left, I have no idea what he did with the flashlight."

"But you know he didn't leave it behind, don't you?"

"No, he didn't."

"Okay. You said that when you first woke up and the flashlight was in your face, you started to get up out of bed and that you were pushed back down?"

"Uh-huh."

"Which arm did he push you back down with? Was it his right or his left?"

"I don't know. It was my left side. I don't know what arm."

"Were you laying on your back when you woke up?"

"Uh-huh."

"And was he off to your left?"

"Yeah."

Cella continued for some time asking which hand held the flashlight, which hand he pushed her back with, and whether he pushed her back on the bed.

"Okay. Do you recall struggling with him at all during this episode?"

"*After I was told I had ten seconds to remove my underwear, I cooperated. I was not going to fight. I didn't know what he was going to do. I thought he was going to kill me, so I figured ...* "

"Did you ever see a knife?"

"No, sir."

"Did he ever tell you he had a knife?"

"No."

"Okay. Were any other kind of weapons?"

"No."

"When he said, you've got ten seconds, I'm sure you interpreted that as a threat, but did he make any direct threats to you about what he would do to you?"

"No. It basically was pretty well, you have ten seconds, and I understood that as I had ten seconds, and I better do what I was told to do."

"And did you conclude that because of his tone of voice at that time?"

"I think just due to the situation, tone of voice or not, you have ten seconds sounds pretty threatening to me, and I just wasn't going to wait any longer."

"Okay. Well, I understand that no matter what tone of voice he said, it would have been intimidating, but I'd like you to tell us, if you can, how would you describe his voice at that point in time?"

"I wouldn't say he was yelling. I mean is this what you're, like volume? It was you have ten seconds."

"Okay."

"And did he seem impatient when he said that?"

"No. It was just pretty much, you have ten seconds. It wasn't, and it was kind of slow because southern people talk a little [more] slower than northern people so ... "

"Did he ever tell you to pull up your shirt?"

"Yes, sir."

"And did you do that, or did he do that?"

"I don't recall, but my shirt was up."

"Okay. Did he put his hands on you?"

"Actually, he inserted several fingers into my female parts."

"Okay. Which hand did he use to do that? Do you recall?"

"I do not recall."

"Okay. Was that when he, after he had put the flashlight down?"

"Yeah."

"Okay. Was that after you had, you told us that he had masturbated himself trying to get an erection."

"I don't know if that was before or after the fingers, but I do remember the fingers so …"

"Okay. Did he seem to be hiding one hand from you, or did you see both of his hands?"

"I don't recall."

"Okay. Do you recall his hands touching your skin to where you could have told something about the texture of his skin, whether he was an outdoor person who worked and had rough hands or … "

"No."

"You don't recall anything about that?"

"No. The only place he touched me was to insert his hand. He didn't rub me. He didn't caress me. He didn't touch my hair. So there is no way I could tell if he was an outdoor man or not."

"Okay. You told Mr. Mallard that he did ejaculate in you. Do you know that because you went to the hospital, and they found sperm, or could you feel it at the time that this was happening?"

"I could feel it at the time."

"All right. How would you describe his penis? Anything stand out as far as physical characteristics of it?"

"No, nothing stood out." [Where can it go from here?]

"Okay. It wasn't unusually small or unusually large?"

"Considering I had only been with one other person in my entire life, I don't think I have any room to compare." [Auucchhhh. This should change the subject.]

"Okay. Was anything missing from your apartment after this episode?"

"No, sir."

Cella continued asking whether any jewelry, accessories, etc. was missing, and whether police worked with her on a composite. She had worked with Officer Sides on a composite, but could not recall further details.

"Do you recall telling the police that your assailant did not require very much time to reach an orgasm?"

"It was brief."

"Okay. Did you wear glasses at the time of the incident?"

"I was sleeping."

Cella continued for some time on unimportant unrelated matters, and the witness was excused. The court took a recess. *In Georgia, the law permits extensive cross-examination.*

I called Kimberly Gaither, an RN at Kennestone Hospital, as a witness. She testified she had been employed for 12 years at the hospital, and was a trauma and emergency room specialist. She said she was on duty at 02:28 a.m. in the morning of April 10, 1988 when she saw a patient identified as Melissa Hilyard, a rape victim.

Ms. Gaither explained that when a rape victim is brought into the hospital, a nurse is present and works with the patient during a routine examination by a doctor—in this case, Dr. Spilker.

Ms. Gaither: "In this case, I was the nurse, because we don't, once you start working with a rape victim, you don't change. You have to build a rapport with that person. And then you take their vital signs, and you talk with them and get an idea of what happened to them, and that is usually done on a one-to-one. It was done with Melissa and I. It was done on a one-to-one.

"Then I had her get undressed, or you have the patient get undressed, and the nurse then does her preliminary examination in which you not only note the psychological effect of the patient, but also the physical status of the patient. You look for marks or for bruises, cuts, bite marks, anything like that, and then you obtain certain samples. The nurse obtains like hair samples, and then once the physician comes in with you, he obtains vaginal samples, or depending on different types of penetration, depends on which samples you obtain. And then your exam continues to whatever treatment you render to that person."

The witness testified that Ms. Hilyard was able to clearly respond to questions. There was no alcohol noted; a sample of the victim's head and pubic hairs were taken and placed in a specimen container. A white sheet was placed under the victim's buttock, and using a comb, Ms. Gaither gently combed through the pubic area for any loose hairs possibly left by the perpetrator. The witness said that Dr. Spilker, in her presence, did a vaginal examination.

"First of all, he just looks her over vaginally. He looks at the external vulva and all to see if there is any tears or abrasions, any markings. Then he uses a speculum and does an internal exam, where again, you look to the walls of the vagina to see if there is any tears or [abrasions], and you look to see if there is any discharge, any semen residue, anything like that that you would see actually inside the vaginal vault. And then he obtains swabbings from the vaginal area. I hand him the cotton tips, and I tell him what I want, and if I want swabbings, and he does the vaginal swabbings and hands them back to me."

"What did you do with them in this case?"

"In this case, you, they want them air dried, and you put them into a container like a little pouch container and you seal it and label it."

"And did Dr. Spilker, in your presence, do a vaginal swabbing of Melissa Hilyard?"

"Yes, sir."

The witness explained that she used a Q-tip for the swabbing, identified as State's Exhibit 3A, which she placed in a container, sealed and labeled by her. It was then placed in the rape kit along with the other evidence collected from the victim. She said she handed the completed rape kit to Detective Sides from whom she had received the empty kit.

CROSS-EXAMINATION
BY MR. CELLA:

Unusually, Mr. Cella only asked a few questions, going over things I had already asked.

Cella: "Okay. Now, you said that there are different things you do (the medical examination), depending on whether there is oral-genital act or anal-genital act."

"Yes, sir."

"Was there either one of those in Ms. Hilyard's case?"

"She denied it. She said there was just vaginal penetration."

The witness was excused.

Lieutenant David William Sides, Marietta Police Department, was called to the stand.

Lieutenant Sides testified he was now in charge of the traffic enforcement unit. On April 10, 1988, he met the victim, Melissa Hilyard, at Kennestone Hospital to investigate a rape. At the hospital, he also saw Dr. Spilker and a registered nurse, Ms. Gaither, while a rape examination was performed. Lt. Sides provided the rape kit. After the examination, the rape kit was returned to him sealed and labeled with the victim's name and information on it.

"Did you subsequently go with (the victim) back to her home or apartment?"

"Yes, sir."

"And what did you find there?"

"The purpose of returning was to determine method of access and processing of the crime scene. We, or I, was able to determine a possible point of access being a window in the roommate's bedroom."

"All right. Is that on the front, back, or side of the house?"

"It's on the side of the building."

"Did you examine the window and the locks on the window?"

"Yes, sir."

"And what did you find?"

"They were of a thumb-slide type, being metal windows. The only method of access that we could determine was by exerting pressure on the window and popping the locks."

"All right. And could that cause the window to open when you're carrying out this procedure?"

"Yes, sir."

CROSS-EXAMINATION
BY MR. CELLA:

Mr. Cella elicited from the witness that an incident report was initially made, as well as a video-taped interview, and a supplemental report was later completed with the victim. During the interim period since 1988, the videotape cassettes were (apparently) destroyed due to a police policy. Cella questions him for several pages about the missing tape cassettes, and the physical description given by the victim.

Lt. Sides: "She described her attacker as a white male, southern accent, hair around the ears, medium color, 30 to 40 years of age, described him as wearing cologne, having a blue Oxford button-down type shirt and twill pants."

Lt. Sides explained that Officer Moss, who was the initial responding officer who took the victim to the hospital, was now deceased. Cella attempted to penetrate Officer Moss's report through this witness, which the court would not allow. Cella then asked the witness to explain how a "composite kit" is prepared, which was done with the help of the victim.

"A composite kit that we use is manufactured by Smith and Wesson, the same large corporation that makes handguns. It is comprised of numerous different types of facial and hair features, and during the training you receive, you're taught how to work with someone in completing these prefabricated parts of faces and hair to try to build a [...] composite of a suspect or person."

"And in what way do you do that?"

"You basically just keep putting different combinations of faces and noses and hair, facial hair, if required, until you either A, realize you can't get something that the person agrees with, or B, until you get something that they say is similar."

After brief re-direct and re-cross examinations, the witness was excused.

Lieutenant W. B. Lunceford, Marietta Police Department, was next called to testify that the victim's rape kit was taken from the police evidence vault and was delivered to the State Crime Laboratory on April 29, 1988, sealed, where he gave it to a technician, "Connie (Pickens)," who signed for it.

In instances where the evidence is a soluble substance and easy to contaminate or alter, it is necessary to satisfy the court that the chain of custody was maintained from the point of origin to the final stage where the substance would be received and examined so that any test done would be valid and admissible. The blood and rape kits in these cases were so delivered to the State Crime Laboratory, and recorded with a chain of custody document showing each person in the chain who signed and dated them, and finally forwarded to the FBI Laboratory, sealed, via overnight express.

I turned the witness over to Mr. Cella for cross-examination, wherein he stated, "No questions" for the first time that I can remember.

I then called the detective, Scott Smith, who had pulled all the cases together after Greenway's arrest from which the charges were eventually filed.

He testified that he followed up on the complaint by victim Melissa Hilyard who had been raped at the Concepts 21 complex on April 10, 1988. He said that on March 19, 1990, after Greenway's arrest, he took the victim to Kennmed Hospital after she returned from out of state for the purpose of providing a sample of her hair and blood for DNA purposes. While the blood was drawn by a Registered Nurse, Smith witnessed the blood drawn in two vials, sealed, labeled, and turned over to him along with the hair samples for delivery to the Georgia Crime Laboratory.

Concepts 21 Apartments, July 15, 1988—Aggravated Sodomy; Burglary
Twila Pruitt, the victim, was called and sworn.

She said she had gotten married since the attack on July 15, 1988. At the time of the assault, she lived with another female roommate in a ground level apartment at the Concepts 21 Apartments in Cobb County, Georgia. It was a two-bed apartment with only a front entrance. She said she was home alone on the morning in question at about 6:19. She was taking a shower, and getting ready to go to work. It was still dark outside.

"And would you tell us what happened, the first thing you noticed someone that didn't belong there?"

"I was taking a shower, and when I got out, I turned off the water, and I heard a noise. It was, seemed like the blinds were rustling, and I was really frightened when I heard the noise, but I had no idea what it was. And I went in, or I locked the door immediately to the bathroom, and I sat in the bathroom for awhile and thought maybe whatever it was, I was just, it was all in my mind, and I was just scared for no reason. So I opened the door, and someone from behind the wall in the hallway grabbed me, and pushed me back."

"What happened then?"

"He pushed me back into the bathroom, and he made me sit on the toilet."

"All right. And what transpired at this point in time? Just relax. And had you ever seen, that's all right. Just take your time. Had you ever seen this person before?"

"No."

[I had to take my time with her. She was visibly upset, and it was hard for her to relate what she had experienced. I'll lead her with 'soft-ball' questions as much as possible and come back to the hard part.]

"Was he a white male?"

"Yes."

"And can you describe the person you saw?"

"He had looked like gray hair, kind of dark and salt-pepper type, and it was curly, short. He was probably about 5'10", 5'11". He had rough hands, and had a bandanna around his mouth and nose."

"All right. When you say a bandanna around his mouth and nose, was it across his nose, covering his face from here down approximately?"

"Yes."

"And were you close to that individual?"

"Yes."

And after he forced you to sit back on the toilet, did the subject unzip his pants?"

"Yes."

"Did he ever take his pants off?"

"No."

"And I'll ask you whether or not he masturbated until he was erect?"

"Yes, sir, but he never, he never got erect."

"All right. He never did?"

"No."

"Did he instruct you to do anything?"

"Yes, he did."

"Did he threaten you?"

"Yes."

"How did he threaten you?"

"He said he had a knife, and that he'd kill me."

"All right. Did you do what he made you do?"
"Yes."
"Were you afraid that he would kill you?"
"Yes."
"Let me just ask you whether or not he forced you to take his penis into your mouth?"
"Yes, sir."
"Was that against your will, Ms. Pruitt?"
"Yes."
"Did you comply only with a threat of death?"
"Yes."
"And after this, what did the subject do then?"
"He touched me."
"All right. Did he say anything further? Did he make you lie on the floor?"
"After he couldn't become erect, he told me to go out into the living room, and lie on the floor, and he pulled me with him walking out, and then said, 'it's not going to work', and he told me to get back into the bathroom and stay for ten minutes until he was gone."
"And what did he do then?"
"He left."

She said after he left she went into her bedroom and called 911. The police arrived. She reported what had happened to her. She said the intruder had a "slow southern accent." She went to the hospital and was examined.

She further testified that years later on February 7, 1990 (after the arrest of Greenway), she met Detective Smith at police headquarters, where she was shown a photographic line-up and listened to an audio tape interview between Detective Smith and another individual.

"Do you remember a photographic spread, something like State's Exhibit 48? Does that ring a bell?"

"Yes."

"Do you recall Officer Smith asking you to see if you could recognize anyone?"

"Yes."

"And were you able to identify anyone in the line-up?"

"Not any one person."

"Did you indicate that either No. 2 or No. 4 looked like the person?"

"Yes, sir."

"And did you indicate that more likely No. 2?" (Terry Greenway.)

"Yes."

"Now, you had previously been shown other line-ups without being able to identify anyone, is that correct?"

"Yes."

I asked her if she recognized the voice of the person Officer Smith was interviewing on the audiotape which he played for her.

"I did recognize it immediately."

"Can you tell us why the voice that you heard Detective Smith play for you on the tape interview, can you tell us why that voice rang a bell with you or why you recognized it?"

"It would be real hard to forget it."

"Why is that? Was it the same voice you had heard in your apartment?"

"Yes."

"Was it the same voice that commanded you to do what you said earlier?"

"Yes."

"The salt-pepper curly hair you are referring to, is there anything more that you can tell us about it?"

"It wasn't neatly combed."

"And was it similar to the hair that you see in State's 48, No. 2 photograph?"

"Yes."

I then turned the witness over for cross-examination by Mr. Cella, which would last about 50 pages of a vigorous cross-examination.

CROSS-EXAMINATION
BY MR. CELLA:

"Ms. Pruitt, my name is Marc Cella. I would like to ask you a few more questions [a few more?] about this. I'll try not to get you emotional again, but if you do get that way, we'll take a break and do whatever we need to get you calmed down again. Did you give the officers an approximate age of this man?"

"Yes."

"And was that approximately 45 years of age?"

"Yes."

"All right. Now, this tape recording that you said you listened to, how long did you listen to that tape?"

"Two or three minutes."

"Okay. And where did you listen to it?"

"In my attorney's office. [She identified him as Mr. Deville.]

"Was Mr. Deville present when you listened to that voice recording?"

"Yes, he was."

She further testified it was at the same meeting when she was shown the photographic line-up by Detective Smith. She had also seen a composite at police headquarters a few months after she was attacked. She said she had also been shown about 20 pictures during that period of time in several photo line-ups without identifying anyone.

"Okay. And then did the officer say anything to you before he turned the tape on?"

"He said that they had picked up someone a few nights ago, and there were several voices on the tape. Could I pick out one specific voice that might have sounded like what I heard that day."

"Okay. What were these voices saying on the tape recorder?"

"It was just an interview of …. [T]hey were asking him, you know, certain questions like what were you doing?"

"And what did he say he was doing?"

"I think he said he was drunk."

"Okay. Anything else you remember him saying?"

"He didn't know what he was doing. He was drunk. That was all."

"And did you listen to that tape all the way through?"

"No."

"How long did you listen to the tape?"

"A couple of minutes."

"Okay. Now, did somebody turn the tape recorder off before the tape recording was finished?"

"No. I had to leave the room."

"You left the room?"

"Yes."

"Okay. Why did you do that?" [It's always the "why" question that is dangerous.]

"I couldn't listen to it anymore."

"You listened to it for two minutes, but then after two minutes, you couldn't listen to it anymore?"

"No."

"Where did you go when you left the room?"

"Out in the hallway."

"Did either Mr. Deville or Officer Smith come out to talk to you at that time?"

"No. My husband was out there."

"Okay. Did you, at some point in time after you walked out of the room, go back and have any more conversation with Officer Smith?"

"I told him that's who I thought, I thought it was that man."

"You thought it was?"

"I told him that it sounded like him."

Cella continued for some time, then changes his direction.

"Now, you had an attorney in this case because you asked him to file a lawsuit against the Concepts 21 apartment complex, isn't that right?"

"Yes."

"Okay. And the Concepts 21 apartment complex lawyers filed a motion to add Mr. Greenway as a party to your lawsuit, and your lawyer told you about that, didn't he."

"Yes."

"And he asked you to come in and sign an affidavit in opposition to that motion, didn't he?"

"Yes."

"And do you recall what you said in that affidavit?"

"I believe they wanted him in the courtroom if it ever went to trial, and I did not want him in here."

"You said the reason you didn't want him in there is because that you have never positively identified him as the man who sodomized you, isn't that right?"

"Yes, other than the voice."

"Well, that's not what you said in your affidavit. You said you never positively identified, isn't that right?"

"Yes."

"You didn't say, other than the voice, in here, did you?"

"No."

"Why was that?"

"Well, he would be sitting in the courtroom. I wouldn't hear him."

"You also said right in the sentence before that, 'I was not able to identify him as the man who attacked me,' didn't you?"

"Yes." [But, that's not all that's in the affidavit. I'll wait and see if Mr. Cella introduces it into evidence. I'll have a 'shot' at it on re-direct examination.]

Mr. Cella continued attacking the witness as to her recollection of whether the attacker had a wedding ring on, whether he wore gloves, and whether she actually saw a knife. She did not see the knife, doesn't remember seeing gloves, but remembers seeing a wedding ring.

"Now, he used some rather vulgar language with you at times during this episode, didn't he?"

"Yes."

CELLA: "He said, 'suck my d[---]' to you, didn't he?"

WITNESS: "Yes."

"Okay. Now, this man was very rough and very aggressive with you in a physical sense, wasn't he?"

"Yes."

"In fact, he injured you pretty bad, didn't he, at one point in the attack?"

"No."

"Did he not push you back into the bathroom?"

"I had a bruise on my back."

"Which gave you back trouble for about two weeks, I think you said in your deposition, didn't you?"

"Yes, but I thought I was lucky."

"You don't remember that to be rough treatment?"

"Well, yes."

"Why did you say no when I asked you if he was rough with you?"

"Well, he could have been rougher."

"Okay. What color eyes did he have?"

"I don't remember."

Cella asked the witness if she wanted some water to which the Judge, said: "The bailiff will get it."

Cella questioned the witness about how the subject entered the apartment, and whether anyone had a key to the apartment, which was only her roommate. He went over the same questions again about her discovering the intruder and calling 911 after the perpetrator left. Then, Cella goes into her visit to the hospital where [they] performed an examination, using Q-tips.

"What did they do with those Q-tips?"

"They took samples."

"And where did they take the samples—was it from your mouth?"

"There."

"From any where else?"

"My vagina."

"Okay. I'm sorry. I know it's hard to say those words, but I can't say them for you. So they swabbed both places, then?"

"Yes."

"Okay. Now, was there ever any contact between this man's penis and your vagina?"

"Yes."

"And where did that take place?"

"In the bathroom."

"And at that point was where you said that he could not maintain an erection?"

"Yes."

"Actually, he couldn't even get one, right?"

"Yes, right."

"Now, do you recall if he ejaculated anywhere there while y'all were together?"

"Yes, he did."

"And could you tell us about that?"

"He played with himself until dribbles came out."

"And did any of them come out on you?"

"No."

"Where did they come out on?"

"On the floor."

"Did you have a carpet in the bathroom in there?"

"Yes."

"Is that what they came out on, or did they come out on the floor?"

"The carpet."

Cella continued, asking about the carpet, how it was installed, who installed it, though he initially said he had a "few questions."

"And at the time he ejaculated, then, he was doing himself, basically? You weren't having any contact with him at that time?"

"No." [No wonder that this witness didn't want to testify, didn't want to be in the same room with him.]

"Okay. When the police officers came, did you point out that area to them where he had dribbled on the carpet?"

"Yes."

"Could you still see traces of it at that time?"

"Yes."

Cella changed direction again to the rustling blinds she heard, the over-turned plant, the police dusting for fingerprints, and the witness checking the screen. The witness testified the police showed her where the intruder broke in, and where the screen was torn and removed. The other screens had holes poked in them. She remembers he wore polyester trousers of a dark color.

Mr. Cella finished and I asked for redirect examination.

REDIRECT EXAMINATION
BY MR. MALLARD:

"Just a few questions, Ms. Pruitt, on redirect. You, of course, didn't want to be down here testifying either, did you?"

"No."

"You said earlier that when the tape recording was played to you, you heard the voices on it, that you had to leave the room. You couldn't listen to it anymore. Why is it that you had to leave the room, that you couldn't listen to it?"

"It frightened me."

"And why did it frighten you?"

"It brought back memories."

"The time you heard that voice, were you as sure as you could be that the voice you heard on the tape was the same voice you heard in your apartment on the morning hours that you told us about?"

"Yes."

I decided to follow-up on the damaged window screen which had been found damaged, and laying outside the apartment.

"All right. Did it look as though, if an instrument like a long screwdriver was pryed in it and bent it? Could that account for the bend?" [Greenway had a long screwdriver when he was arrested.]

"Screwdriver could have made the holes in the, in each of the screens."

"Regarding the ejaculation on your carpet in your bathroom, did you later learn that the crime lab did not find anything?"

"I think I did."

I finished, and Cella decided to try again.

BY MR. CELLA:

"Ms. Pruitt, I'm handing you at this time Defendant's Exhibit No. 4, and asking you if that's not the affidavit that we just talked about a few minutes ago."

"Yes." [Now that he's identified it and going into the contents, we'll see what happens.]

"Okay. And would you flip the page over and tell us if that's your signature at the end of it?"

"Yes."

"And what did you say in Paragraph No. 3 there?"

"You want me to read it?"

"Yes, ma'am."

"I was shown a number of composite drawings of suspects by the Marietta Police Department, including the picture of Terry Greenway. I was not able to identify him as the man who attacked me and have never positively identified the man who sodomized me on 7-15-88."

"Okay. And what date did you swear to those facts?"

"The 19th of October, 1990."

"And that was after the point in time when you saw the pictures and listened to the audio tape with the voice on it, isn't it?"

"Yes."

"MR. CELLA: Thank you, ma'am. Nothing further." [He just scored a major point, but now I can go into the affidavit since he walked in that door.]

"MR. MALLARD: Are you offering in this exhibit?"

"MR. CELLA: I'm not tendering, Judge."

"MR. MALLARD: You're not? Okay. I want to go into it then."

REDIRECT EXAMINATION
BY MR. MALLARD:

"Did you also say in this affidavit, 'If Defendant's motion to join Terry Greenway, or John Doe, is granted, it would be emotionally and psychologically devastating to me to sit in the same courtroom with a rapist for the expected 30 days this trial will likely last'?" [Speaking of the civil trial lawsuit.]

"Yes."

"And was that the reason for this motion and this affidavit?"

"Yes."

"Could you sit in the courtroom in a civil case with Mr. Terry Greenway for 30 days?"

"MR. CELLA: I object. That's an irrelevant question."

"THE COURT: Mr. Mallard, do you wish to be heard on it?"

"MR. MALLARD: No, Your Honor. It's her statement here."

"THE COURT: I believe there is a rule if you go into it, he has a right to go over the rest of it. Do you wish to be heard further?"

"MR. CELLA: No, sir."

"THE COURT: I'll allow you to continue."

"MR. CELLA: But I don't abandon my objection, for the record."

"THE COURT: I gave you an opportunity to speak to the rule I just mentioned, and you chose not to. That's fine."

MALLARD: "My question was, Ms. Pruitt, could you sit in a trial for 30 days with the Defendant, Terry Greenway?"

"No."

"You were, were you not, objectionable to coming down here and testifying for a short period of time with him in the courtroom?"

"Yes, I did object."

"And is it not true that you did not want to even look at him?"

"Yes."

With that, I completed my re-direct on a high note, and Mr. Cella had no further questions. The witness was finally released after a lengthy, blistering cross-examination by Mr. Cella. Despite the weakness of this particular case—with no DNA from the attack, no positive photo identification, but a voice identification by the victim, I still whole-heartedly believed we had the right man. Whoever committed the rapes, also committed this attack, and the witness, I thought, held up well and was believable. I do realize the jury will have a hard time convicting based only upon the evidence of this witness alone, but with the underlying circumstantial evidence, I have a good chance for conviction.

The Court recessed the trial for the day, and asked counsel whether the trial was on schedule. After jury selection, Mr. Cella and I had told the Judge we thought the trial would last six to eight days to present the evidence. Judge Brantley was a stickler for punctuality and sticking to schedules, and would not hesitate in letting it be known if the lawyers fell behind a schedule.

"MR. MALLARD: I think we dropped behind, but we picked up, I think, today, where hopefully tomorrow night, we'll be where I had anticipated, which would hopefully be that we would start the DNA part next week, Monday."

Detective Scott Smith testified he met with victim Twila Pruitt on February 7, 1990, to determine if she could identify her attacker from the photo spread of six people, State's Exhibit

48, which he had shown other victims. She believed that number two (Terry Greenway) was her attacker. As a follow-up, Smith said he played a tape recording of the interview with Greenway after his arrest to determine if the victim could identify the voice when the tape was playing: "All I know is I just got drunk. I didn't even remember anything. I don't even ..." and at that time Ms. Pruitt was extremely shaken. Her hands were shaking. She began crying hysterically, and she stated to Detective Smith that "that's him. I recognize the southern accent," and she kept telling Smith to please turn it off.

A voice-identification, if believed by the jury, is sufficient to convict as a matter of law.

⌘ ⌘ ⌘

The reader (especially if he is an attorney) will quickly note that both state and defense attorneys are not objecting at every opportunity in the examination of witnesses by the other. Both of us are experienced trial attorneys, and we will know when it is important to keep out testimony hurtful to our case. There may be a good objection available, but you may want to rebut, or respond later, with a redirect examination of the witness, a later witness, or even in closing argument. Much consideration goes into the strategy of a trial by both sides. 'When do you object?' is one of those questions to be considered.

When the attorney keeps getting too far afield from the issues, the court will usually get him or her back on track, so you may have to allow the questioning to go awhile before making an objection which will be sustained. You want to have a reasonable chance of success in making the objection; otherwise, you will be seen as one who just wants to keep the jury from knowing what you are hiding, or wasting the court's time in jumping up and down. Both lawyers want to ingratiate themselves with the judge and jury, and that's just part of that battle: to gain the (jurors) recognition that you are on the righteous side of the case. In that effort, it may be seen as a game of chess or probing the defenses of the other side as in a boxing ring where the combatants 'jab' and 'probe' in an effort to find the other's weakness.

Another consideration in deciding whether to object is that there are rules, but then there are exceptions to those rules; at times, there appear to be more exceptions than rules, especially, when it comes to exceptions to hearsay. Thus, an objection to hearsay comes with it a consideration of whether the testimony would be admissible under any of the exceptions to the hearsay rule. You must consider whether it is worth objecting when the information may very well come in despite what appears to be a good objection.

New attorneys (as well as moot court law students) will, more likely than seasoned attorneys, liberally object to questions by opposing counsel. The former want to show their stuff. Often, judges will overrule their objections or comment "let's move along," meaning you are holding up the trial and wasting time with unimportant objections. The jurors may roll their eyes at the attorney with disgust. After all, jurors view the Judge to be legally "correct" and knowledgeable of the law, and will defer to his/her judgment. An attorney, who often objects on insignificant matter, will *not* be endeared in the eyes of the jurors when the objections are overruled.

I tend to use the common-sense or conservative approach to objecting for several reasons. First and foremost, judges tend to give wide latitude to counsel in trying the case, and if something is borderline admissible, the judge will allow it and overrule the objection. Unless I am pretty sure the judge will sustain my objection, I will not object to some issue which is not important to me, though it would be a good technical objection. Simply put, I do not like to lose my objection—allowing the jurors to believe I was wrong and the other attorney was right. However, in keeping out testimony which goes to important issues which would be detrimental to my case, I will, hopefully, have anticipated such issue with legal research supporting my position.

An important consideration in this respect is whether the witness can handle a vigorous cross-examination if I do not object. Many times, this will be the case when I know my witness can handle anything the attorney throws his/her way and will look good to the jury in doing so. I may even suspect the aggressive defense attorney will stumble into an area he regrets after the witness *has his lunch*.

Generally, professional and expert witnesses will be given full rein to handle the aggressive cross-examination without objection so long as he stays within the realm of his expertise for which he was qualified. Also, victims of crime, especially violent crime victims, will be protected within certain confines of law, and the attorney (in most cases) will treat them with respect knowing the jurors are watching. Not always, however.

One final consideration is that courts (especially in Georgia) tend to allow wide latitude in cross-examination of witnesses, including leading the witness in preliminary matters. I love to lead the witness, even on direct examination ... so long as there is no objection. It helps in moving the case along, and sometimes keeps the witness from blurting out something which becomes troublesome from a legal viewpoint.

Concepts 21 Apartments, October 15, 1988—Rape; Burglary

I called the victim, Donna Hightower, to the stand where she was sworn and testified.

DIRECT EXAMINATION
BY MR. MALLARD:

The witness identified herself to the court and Jury, and stated she had lived in Cobb County all her life. She lived in the Concepts 21 Apartments on Bentley Road on October 15, 1988. Her apartment was a ground level apartment she shared with another female. She was at home asleep during the morning hours about 04:39 when she was awakened by an intruder. She further testified:

"I was asleep on my right-hand side, and I was awakened by somebody putting their hand over my face and pulling me over to my back."

"What was the first thing that you heard or saw?"

"He told me just to be quiet and be still, and he would only be there for five minutes, five minutes only."

"All right. And did the subject have anything over part of his face?"

"He had a handkerchief from here down."

"You're indicating from the bridge of your nose down?"

"Right."

"Tell us what next happened."

"Then, after he said that, he backed away from the bed, and he unzipped his pants, and he masturbated, and then he came over to the bed and took my gown and my panties off."

"Did he have trouble getting an erection?"

"Uh-huh."

"And was he standing or in bed or what was he doing?"

"He was standing next to my bed."

"And did you make any attempt to run or do anything?"
"No, sir."
"Why not?"
"I couldn't really move."
"Were you in fear of your life?"
"Yes, I was."
"What made you in fear of your life?"
"Well, it's kind of scary when you wake up in the middle of the night, and somebody that you don't know is standing next to your bed."
"You said he removed your panties?"
"He removed my gown and the panties. Then he got on top of me, and he raped me. And then as he was, he got up and zipped his pants up. He came back over to the bed and lifted his handkerchief up and tried to kiss me, and I pushed him away, and then he left through the front door."
"Ms. Hightower, I need to ask you a few questions, personal, now. But if you would just listen to me. Did this subject that interrupted your sleep have sexual intercourse with you?"
"Yes, sir."
"Did his penis make penetration of your female vagina?"
"Yes, it did."
"And was that with or without your consent?"
"Without my consent."
"Was it forcible?"
"Yes, sir."
"And did you only submit in fear of your life?"
"Yes, sir."
[Those questions fulfill the requirements of the law for rape: carnal knowledge of the female, forcibly and against her will.]
"Can you say whether or not the subject ejaculated?"

"Yes."

"What next do you remember?"

"Then I just laid there, and he left the room, and like I said, I heard the front door close. And then I got up and went to see if he had gone for sure, and then I called the police department."

"And did you first get your gun?"

"Yes, sir, as soon as I got up out of bed. I had a .38 next to my bed, and I got that out, and I was carrying that when I walked through to see if he had left or not."

Lt. Sides of the police arrived, she said.

She further testified:

"I had bars put in my windows [...] because I was sleeping on the bottom floor, and the window was open, the right window. There [is] three windows, and the right window was open."

She and the police noticed that her stick was out of the window; they found it underneath the table. She had previously seen the stick in place in the window before going to bed.

Ms. Hightower described her intruder to be about 5'10" or so, with gray hair, wearing a gray jacket that zipped up and blue jeans. He had a blue bandanna over the lower part of his face. He was a white male, in the late 30s or early 40s, and talked with a southern drawl.

The victim was taken to Kennestone Hospital where she was seen by a doctor and examined.

I questioned the victim about later attempts by police to gain an identification of her attacker through photo lineups. This will show that this witness did not just jump at the first attempt to identify someone when given the opportunity, thereby giving credibility to her identification.

MALLARD: "Now, then [...] did Officer Grogan or some officer present to you a lineup of photographs in an attempt to get an identification?"

"Right."

"And did you see someone in that group of photographs that strongly resembled your perpetrator?"

"There was one person at one time, right, but I don't remember the name."

"Did you then come to meet Detective Smith in the early part of 1990, February 7th?"

"Yes, I did."

"And did he show you a group of photographs?"

"Yes, he did."

"And was the lower part of the faces of the photographs covered?" [To compensate for the perpetrator having covered the lower part of the face with a bandana.]

"Yes, they were."

"And were you able to identify anyone in that group of photographs?"

"Yes, I did."

"I show you State's Exhibit No. 48. Did you identify No. 2, the middle top photograph as being your assailant?" [Terry Greenway.]

"Yes, I did."

"Were you certain of that at the time you picked him out?"

"Yes, I was."

"And are you certain today that he was the one that raped you on the morning in question?"

"Yes, he was."

"Was there anything about the eyes of the subject that raped you that you noted? Was it anything that stood out in your mind that you recall him to you when you saw the photograph?"

"The eyes are the only thing I really remembered and the salt and pepper hair, but the eyes, I remember the eyes."

"At the time, how far did his face ever get to you?"

"Well, I mean he was right here. Then, like I said, that one time he tried to kiss me before he left."

"Did you also have a chance with Detective Smith to listen to a tape recording of an interview with another person?"

"Yes."

"And were you able to identify the person that was being interviewed?" [Greenway.]

"Yes."

"I'll ask you whether or not the voice you heard in the tape recording is the same voice you heard on the night you were raped?"

"Yes, it is."

"Were you later met by Detective Smith on March 20, 1990, at Kennestone Hospital?"

"Uh-huh, yes."

"And was some blood drawn from your arm?"

"Yes, it was."

The witness then identified State's Exhibit 33 as the bed sheeting taken from her bed after the rape and sent to the Crime Laboratory.

"Ms. Hightower, I know it's been a long time, and I'll ask you whether or not you can identify anyone in the courtroom that you saw on the night that you were raped on the 15th day of October 1988?"

"Yes, I can."

"Would you look around and see if you see that person that raped you here in the courtroom."

"It was that gentleman right over there with the blue suit on and the glasses."

"And is that, which one … "[and then something happened you very seldom see in a courtroom when the defendant interrupted].

"THE DEFENDANT: **Tell me again. Tell me again. Because I think it's a lie.**"

"THE COURT: **Excuse me just a moment. I'll have him bound and gagged if he cannot sit and control himself.**"

"THE DEFENDANT: **I APOLOGIZE.**"

"Ms. Hightower, was it the person that just spoke up at counsel table?"

"Yes, it was."

"MR. MALLARD: Let the record reflect that the witness has identified the Defendant on trial."

"THE COURT: Let the record so reflect."

"MR. MALLARD: Counsel may cross-examine."

CROSS-EXAMINATION
BY MR. CELLA:

Mr. Cella introduced himself and asked her if she needed a break. The witness confirmed she arrived home from a Cheers restaurant on (highway) #41 about 01:00 a.m.

"And what time did you get to Cheers […]?"

"It was around 7:00, 7:30."

"Did you go there for dinner?"

"Went there to dinner, and met some friends."

The witness identified the friends as being people she had met where she previously worked at "Popper's" and "Cork and Cleaver." She had been a bartender at Popper's, across the street from where she lived at the time. She was questioned extensively as to the time she was at Cheers, when she left, and that she left Cheers to go home.

"And on the way out of Cheers, you saw somebody that you knew coming into Cheers, didn't you?"

"Right."

"And was that Mr. DeGregorio?"

"Right."

"Okay. You had some alcohol to drink that night at Cheers, didn't you?"

"Yes, I did."

"Can you recall how much you had to drink?"

"I had two Scotch and waters."

"Now, are you sure about that?

"It's been three years ago, I mean - - "

"So are you sure or not?"

"Yes."

"Okay. Sure you didn't drink anything else other than Scotch and water?"

"Not that I can recall, no."

Mr. Cella questioned her about what she drank, how much, and referred her to her police statement years before and then asked her:

"Okay. And if you told them (police) that you had three vodkas and two Jagermeisters that night, does that refresh your memory about how much you had to drink that evening?"

"I don't think it was vodka. I still think it was Scotch."

"And what about the two Jagermeisters?"

"I don't usually drink very many shooters. I might have had one. My mother was in the hospital with breast cancer. It was a very rough day for me."

Cella questioned the witness about Xanax.

"What is Xanax?"

"It's a relaxer."

"And had you taken Xanas that night before you went to bed?"

"I had taken a 12 milligram Xanas before I went to bed that night so I could sleep."

"When you went to bed at 1:00 o'clock, then, you had taken Xanas and drank three vodkas and two Jagermeisters?"

"Yeah."

"Ms. Hightower, in view of the stress that was on you that day from your mother's operation and all, would you say that's more than you're accustomed to drinking?"

"Yes."

"Okay. Now, if you told the police on your taped statement that that's about normal for you, would that be more reliable, or would it be more reliable what you say today?"

"What I'm saying today."

"Okay. When you saw Mr. DeGregorio coming into Cheers as you went out, did y'all not make an arrangement for him to come by your place later that evening?"

"He lives right down the street from where I did, and he knew I was upset about my mother, and he wanted to make sure I was in the house and safe."

"In other words, you were expecting him to come by when you got home?"

"Yes."

"Okay. When you got home, what were you doing as you waited for Mr. DeGregorio to come by? Do you recall?"

"I got home, changed my clothes, and that's when I went and laid down on my bed."

"At the time you laid down on your bed, you passed out from the alcohol and drugs that you had taken, didn't you?"

"I fell asleep."

"Did you intend to go to sleep with the lights on?"

"Yes."

"Is that your normal habit?"

"Yes. I sleep with the lights on …"

"Okay. Now, you told Mr. Mallard that you had an opportunity to see this man in your apartment. Is that because the lights were on during this whole episode?"

"Right."

"And whatever lighting there was in the room, did that come from within the room?"

"Yes."

"How many lights did you have in your bedroom?"

"I had the bathroom light, I have a night light in there, and then the lamp beside my bed."

Mr. Cella inquired at length about how big the bulbs were, the amount of light in the room, and whether anyone touched the lights. She did not see any gloves, flashlight, or screwdriver in the perpetrator's possession.

"You did have some bruises on your arms after this incident though, didn't you?"

"I think that's where he turned me over, so I think that's where those came from." The witness further testified she worked with the police in preparing a "composite" drawing, and that she met with police frequently. She was questioned extensively about the composite and the descriptions she gave police, the opportunity she had for seeing her attacker, and how long it took for her to identify him.

Cella: "Ms. Hightower, one of the many reasons that you sued Concepts 21 is because of your belief that entry was gained with a passkey in this case, isn't that right?"

"Yes."

"Okay. Now, this stick that you put in your window, how long had that, well, first of all, you had sticks exactly like that in all your windows, didn't you?"

"Yes, I did."

"How many windows is that approximately? I don't expect you to remember exactly."

"About nine, I guess."

"And how long had those sticks been in your window?"

"Five or six months."

"Did you ever open your window at any time when you put those sticks in, and when you were attacked on October 15, 1988?"

"No. We never really, my roommate and I never really moved those sticks."

"Yet when you came out of your bedroom and went into your living room with your gun in your hand, you noticed that the window was open?"

"Right."

"And the stick had been taken out?"

"The stick was somewhere, right."

"And it was found later underneath a table somewhere, you said?"

"Table was right in front of the windows."

"Now, this table that you have described as being near the window, how close is it to the window that you saw open after you came out into your living room?"

"It was only pulled out maybe a foot."

"Okay. So there was about a foot clearance between the window and this table?"

"Right."

"Now, what kind of things did you keep on that table?"

"Plants, nick-nacks."

"Now, was any of that stuff disturbed on the table at the time that you went out into your living room right after this attack?"

"No."

"Can you imagine any way that someone could have come through your apartment, come into your apartment through that window without disturbing the contents of the table?"

"It wouldn't seem that way, no."

[Mr. Cella has raised a serious question as to whether entry was through the window, and suggests entry by use of a passkey by the front door; the victim's civil lawsuit against Concepts 21 would be strengthened if entry was made by passkeys—suggesting an employee may have been the perpetrator. I will return to this issue on redirect (later) and emphasize the open window.]

"Do you recall whether the police, in response to your 911 call, did they try to lift fingerprints off of the lamp in your bedroom?"

"Yes, they did."

"Okay. Did you have occasion to look at your window and notice some smudges on there that looked like they could have been fingerprints?"

"The window that was open?"

"Yes, ma'am."

"I saw the black stuff, you know, where they did the fingerprints."

"Okay. These smudges were something that were new to you? In other words, you hadn't ever seen them before that night, had you?"

"No."

"Leading you to believe that they had been left there by the man who raped you?"

"I guess, yes."

"... [H]ad you ever had occasion to make requests to the office at Concepts 21 to send maintenance people into your apartment?"

"A couple times, yes."

Mr. Cella showed the witness Defendant's Exhibit 5 which was a deposition the witness had given in the civil suit on January

15, 1990, wherein she was questioned regarding the weight of the perpetrator and her intoxication on the night in question. Cella referred her to an instance where she had estimated the weight of the rapist at 160 to 165; he then referred her to another page where she said she had ingested two Scotches and water rather than the three vodkas and two Jagermeisters as was reported to the police.

Mr. Cella finished, and I redirected her attention to those matters.

REDIRECT EXAMINATION
BY MR. MALLARD:

Mallard: "Quite a thick deposition. Looks like 91 pages. Is that what it appears to be?"

"Right."

"You saw the Defendant stand up earlier. Would you estimate his weight to be 160 to 180?" [I just wanted to draw the jurors' attention to his appearance to be in the range of what the witness had estimated his weight at 160 to 165.]

"I think I asked you, but I want to make sure. Did you tell us that before going to bed the night in question that the stick was in the window?"

"Yes, it was."

"And when you got up, did you notice the stick out of the window and the window raised?"

"Right."

"And was that before the police found it?"

"Right."

[Presto, the perpetrator forced the window and moved the table away from the wall, being careful not to knock over the nick-knacks on the table which would awaken the occupant.]

The witness was excused. At this point in the trial, Judge Brantley recessed the trial for lunch, and told the jurors that he had caused the court administration to issue payment for jurors' service through this day, saying, "It's not what you're worth, but it is the maximum per day the law authorizes us to pay, which is $25. So in your case, you each will receive a check for $125."

Lieutenant D. W. Sides, Marietta Police Department, who had previously responded to an earlier rape and burglary complaint at Concepts 21 Apartments on April 10, 1988, was recalled to the stand for further testimony regarding his involvement in this incident.

He testified he responded on October 15, 1988, at about 4:39 a.m. He said he was the watch commander, and having monitored the call, he responded to the scene where Officers Bertolo and Rigo arrived about the same time. He made contact with the complainant, Ms. Donna Hightower, who filed the report.

"Would you tell us what you did while there?"

"I contacted the sheriff's office and requested a photographer be en-route as a crime scene technician, and I seized some items of clothing and bedding."

"I show you State's Exhibit 33. Have you seen that before?"

"Yes, sir. These are the items that I took custody of and subsequently turned over to Detective Christopher there at the apartment."

"Where did you obtain State's 33 from?" [Sheets and pillow cases.]

"The bedroom which Ms. Hightower indicated she was in at the time of the rape."

The witness said he proceeded to have photographs made of the apartment, and waited for Detective Christopher to return from the hospital with the victim.

"I show you what is marked State's Exhibit 50 through 54 inclusive. Would you tell me what those are?"

"No. 50 is an exterior view of the incident location. No. 51 is a table adjacent to a window. This particular photograph shows a plant and a dirt material which apparently was knocked from the plant. 52 is an exterior photograph of a window. You can see the table aforementioned on the interior. 53 is another exterior photograph of the same window, and 54 is an interior view from a different angle of the aforementioned table."

After having the witness testify the photographs truly and accurately portrayed the scenes therein, they were admitted in evidence. *Entry through the window is again proven.*

"Did you determine a point of entry of the apartment of Ms. Hightower."

"When looking through the crime scene, the only point of entry that we could determine was the window which is shown in these photographs. The table showed signs of being moved away from the wall. A plant showed dirt debris which apparently had been knocked from it. The window blind, instead of being all the way up, all the way down, was tilted at a very sharp angle. It's a double-window system, and one side was tilted high up. Also, the photograph shows you a white stick. This, apparently, Ms. Hightower has used sticks as bracing devices in order to hold the window closed, as an additional security measure."

"And where was this stick that you noted?"

"It's on the floor and partially covered up by the table."

[Now there should be no doubt that the rapist entered through the window and not the front door—as the defense would like the jury to believe.]

I turned the witness over for cross-examination.

CROSS-EXAMINATION
BY MR. CELLA:

"The stick was never broken in any way, was it?"

"No, sir. I don't believe that it was."

"Do you have a theory on how someone could have gotten through the window from the outside without breaking that stick?"

"These are metal windows. In previous testimony, I talked about how you can stress one of these windows by pressing on it. If you have a slim object similar to a slim jim, which is used to open a car door, or maybe even a coat hanger, if you can stress it, you can slip it between the two and pop the stick loose. Once that's done, you still have the opportunity to put stress on the window to raise it."

"Which would leave fingerprints all over the window, wouldn't it?"

"It has been my experience in investigating cases that fingerprints are rarely, if ever, left sufficient for identification. [And I have actually used an example of trying to], a homeowner will ask me, well, why can't you find fingerprints? And I'll take them to the laboratory window and have them put their hand on it real quickly. It doesn't necessarily leave a print."

"In this case, Deputy Lanyi did maintain prints that were taken from the crime [scene] after processing, didn't he?"

"He did maintain two."

"And also, you have noticed in those pictures that there was the blinds that are at an angle?"

"Yes, sir."

"Do you have a theory on how that could have been done from outside?"

"Well, if you've placed yourself in the position of first trying to enter into a window that you can't get into, then you have placed yourself in the position of stressing the window, forcing something in between the windows to knock the stick loose. Now you've got the window up, and now there is a table in the way. It would probably be no great feat once you've accomplished this by reaching in and gaining the controls if not to completely remove the blind from your path, to get enough of it out of the way so you can move this piece of furniture, which happens to be the table, out of your path of entry."

"What evidence is there that the table was moved out of the way by the perpetrator that did this?"

"The best evidence that's in the photographs is the disturbed plant with the debris or dirt knocked loose from it."

[This is a prime example of how a good witness can handle the cross-examination by an experienced trial lawyer.]

"Did you have a conversation with Ms. Hightower about how she believes the entry was accomplished?"

"At the scene, I asked her, like I say, we discussed whether the door had been locked. She was insistent that it had, that she had braced her windows closed, and prior to leaving, she told me she didn't know how someone got in."

"Do you not state in your report, reporting officer replaced the stick? Were you the one that replaced the stick? Don't you say in there that you replaced the stick and could not determine how the window had been opened with the stick in place?"

"You asked how it could have been done, and I told you how I think it could have been done."

The witness was excused.

I then called Detective M. A. Christopher to the stand as a chain-of-custody witness. He received the original rape call, and went to Concepts 21 where he made contact with Lieutenant Sides. He was directed to proceed to Kennestone, Windy Hill, Hospital, where he found the victim. She was being examined by Dr. Malcom. Detective Christopher furnished a rape kit for the examination. The witness maintained control and custody of the 'kit' after it was labeled, sealed and secured, until it was deposited in the evidence locker at police headquarters. It would be later delivered to the GBI headquarters.

Mr. Cella had no questions regarding his testimony.

Detective Scott Smith testified that on February 7, 1990, he presented his photo display to victim Donna Hightower at which time she immediately identified number two in the display of six as her attacker. Further, the tape recording of Greenway's interview was played in the victim's presence. She recognized his southern accent as the person who attacked her on October 15, 1988. Detective Smith further obtained samples of Ms. Hightower's blood on March 20, 1990, for DNA purposes.

At this time period, Terry Greenway was out on bond on the initial charges for which he was arrested. Based on this identification, Greenway was re-arrested on rape and related charges, followed by a search warrant for samples of his [Greenway's] blood and hair for DNA testing. The next day, February 8, 1990, Detective Smith made contact with the jail nurse who obtained the blood and hair samples from Terry Greenway. Detective Smith then delivered the samples to the State Crime Lab for DNA comparison by the FBI.

I called Connie C. Pickens, forensic serologist, Georgia Bureau of Investigation, Division of Forensic Sciences, to the stand. She had been employed in that capacity for 12 years in the identification of body fluids and dried stains from blood, semen, and saliva.

She testified to her formal education, and continuing in-house training programs, workshops, and seminars, as well as an advanced blood stain analysis program at the FBI Academy in Quantico, Virginia. I offered her as an expert witness in her field, to which Mr. Cella conceded.

The witness did certain work in two of the sexual assault cases for which she received the rape kits for victims Melissa Hilyard and Donna Hightower, both from Concepts 21 Apartments in 1988. The witness testified that she received the evidence rape kits in a secure, sealed, un-tampered condition. She assigned an item number to each item with a crime lab number affixed to each case.

Ms. Pickens testified that on April 29, 1988, she received from Officer W. B. Lunceford a crime lab sexual assault evidence collection kit containing vaginal and/or cervical swabs (cotton tip applicator) and two glass slides from victim, Melissa Hilyard.

From a microscopic examination of the glass slides, the witness testified she found the presence of spermatozoa. She said she placed the swabs from the victim in the freezer at the laboratory, and they were subsequently forwarded to the FBI DNA Unit.

"Why are they kept frozen?"

"To preserve the biological evidence that's on the swabs."

Ms. Pickens testified that on February 9, 1990, she received from Detective Scott Smith a crime lab sexual assault evidence collection kit, identified as coming from victim, Donna Hightower.

From that kit, she identified two cotton-tipped applicators and two glass slides. Those swabs were placed in the aforementioned freezer within the serology section for DNA testing.

"And did you do any testing on the slides?"

"I made a microscopic examination of those slides."

"And did you find anything therein?"

"Yes. My microscopic examination revealed the presence of spermatozoa."

Ms. Pickens further testified to having received State's Exhibit 49, containing certain items: two glass test tubes (of blood) that were labeled Terry Thaddeus Greenway, and a sealed envelope containing the known pubic, head, and arm hairs of Terry Thaddeus Greenway. Ms. Pickens took possession of the blood sample, and another scientist (microanalyst) took possession of the hair samples for comparison with any questioned hair found at the crime scenes.

"With regard to the blood sample, what did you do with it?"

"I typed the blood sample, and also I prepared a dried stain from that blood sample."

"And would you tell us why you did that?"

"The dried stain is being prepared so that the blood can be kept in a suitable condition, and the typing is being done to determine the international blood group classification of that blood sample."

"And why are you making this blood stain?"

"We find that the blood is better preserved in a dried condition, frozen, than a liquid blood sample would be.... [T]he blood stain was then placed in a freezer in the serology section. The blood stain was subsequently forwarded to the FBI DNA unit for genetic testing."

"Would you tell us how you do that, how you go about making a blood stain?"

"The blood sample, of course, that we received is in a liquid state. We simply removed some of the blood and place several drops onto a clean piece of white cotton fabric that's attached to an index card. This is allowed to air dry, and once it's dried, the sample is frozen, and we freeze these samples to best preserve the biological sample, the blood sample."

"Was that the extent of your involvement in the Hilyard and Hightower cases?"

"Yes, sir."

[This witness received and prepared the DNA specimen samples from the rape kits and the known blood specimen of the defendant, to be shipped to the FBI for DNA analysis, as well as identifying spermatozoa in the samples from the rape kits.]

CROSS-EXAMINATION
BY MR. CELLA:

"You have indicated that you looked at two items in these rape kits that first would be the swabs from the cervical swabbing?"

"Those are the items that I received."

"And the other thing you took out was these containers that hold two slides that have blood stains in them?"

"No. The slides have a vaginal and/or cervical smears on them."

"Now, would those smears have come from the Q-tips?"

"Yes, sir."

"Is there any way that you have of knowing that the Q-tips that are in the rape kit were the ones that were used to smear the glass slides with?" [Actually, the doctor doing the examination of the victim at the hospital testified he prepared the slides, and visualized spermatozoa.]

"The swabs are labeled with the victim's name, and the slides are also labeled with the victim's name."

"Okay. But there is no scientific test you can do to determine if everybody that did the rape kit did their job right?"

"No. Not in my lab, no."

"Is your examination for the presence of spermatozoa strictly a visual determination?"

"It's strictly a microscopic examination, yes, visual through a microscope, yes."

"Now, do you do anything as far as quantifying the amount of spermatozoa present?"

"We grade or affix a number value to the amount of sperm that we observe, and this is purely an estimation of the number of sperm that we observe."

Mr. Cella continued for four pages of Q & A in how the numbering system works for determining the number of sperm present.

The witness: "In both cases, I reported the presence of spermatozoa, which would indicate that there were more than just a few. I can refer to my notes to see what I noted about that. On the Hightower case, I noted that there were 3 plus intact spermatozoa, and on the Hilyard case, my notes indicate that there were 4 plus intact spermatozoas."

"What do you mean by activity of the victim?"

"Well, a victim that is very active in perhaps moving around, there would have been some normal drainage of the seminal fluid from the body, so it's possible that you would see fewer sperm from a victim as opposed to one that was not moving around."

"Have you ever heard of a process called cloning of DNA?"

"Cloning?"

"That's right."

"Yes, I've heard of it."

"Could you tell the jury what that means."

"Cloning is merely the reproduction of DNA, in this, to answer his (Mr. Cella's) question, the reproduction of one piece of DNA from another."

"Okay. So in other words, if we start out with a very small sample of DNA from a crime scene, it's possible to clone it and reproduce it into a larger ... "

"Into a larger sample. That's correct."

Mr. Cella finished his cross-examination at that point, possibly leaving the jury with the inference that perhaps we should have proceeded with that technology. I needed to clear it up.

REDIRECT EXAMINATION
BY MR. MALLARD:

"But that process has not gained so much national recognition as the standard profiling of DNA by the Georgia Lab, the FBI, Life Codes, and so forth?"

"I think that the proper term for this technology is PCR or [Preliminary] Chain Reaction, rather than cloning, as opposed to the normal or the usual DNA procedure that's being used in the Georgia State Crime Laboratory. PCR is and has been used in criminal cases in the United States and in Georgia." [Subsequent to our submission of the present cases to the FBI—in this instance of less than a year—DNA laboratories and testing of DNA had become pretty much commonplace.]

"And you wouldn't usually use that process unless you had such a small sample that you wouldn't use the other."

"That is correct."

The witness was excused, and I called my next witness from the Georgia Crime Laboratory.

Mary Elizabeth (Beth) Horton, a laboratory technician, was sworn and testified as to the collection of certain trace evidence from State's Exhibit 33 (bed sheets) which was received at the lab. The witness worked under the direct supervision of Janet Gettings, the scientist of the trace evidence section of the crime laboratory, and examined the bed sheets for items of evidentiary value.

Preparatory to later forensic analysis of items found, the witness collected hairs which she mounted in slides for visual review and testing by the microanalyist, Janet Gettings. These hairs are listed as "Questioned" hairs to be examined against "Known" hair of the victim and any suspects developed: in this case, Terry Thaddeus Greenway.

"And would you tell me whether you found anything, and as a result, did you do anything with it?"

"Yes. I found some hairs on the, actually on all of the items that are in this bag, and I mounted those hairs on separate slides each, the hairs that were taken from each sheet were mounted on slides separately."

"And did you also mount hairs from the pubic combings in this case?"

"Yes, I did."

"Why do you mount hairs on slides as you've done in this case?"

"To be given to the chemist to look at under microscopes."

Items reviewed and mounted on slides for examination:

S-33 = (bed sheets)   Donna Hightower—victim

S-57 = Item 2A -   Slides: Questioned hair from fitted sheet
Item 3D - Slides: Questioned hair from Victim's Pubic combing

S-58 = Items 4B, 4C, 4D – Slides: Known Pubic, Head and Arm hair from Terry Thaddeus Greenway

S-59 = Item 3E - Slides: Known Pubic hair of victim
Item 3F - Slides: Known Head hair of victim

S-60 = Item 2B - Slides: Questioned hair from flat sheet

S-61 = Item 2C - Slides: Questioned hair from pillow cases
Item 2D - Slides: Questioned hair from pillow case

"Now, are all of these that you've just testified about mounted in the same case, that is involving the same victim?"

"Yes, sir, it is."

"And who's that?"

"Donna Hightower."

At that point, I turned the witness over for cross-examination, when Mr. Cella announced, "No questions, Your Honor." Then, however, he asked Judge Brantley to allow him to reconsider; that he had one question. However, after six pages, he finished. He was meticulously trying to find a defect in the witness's handling of the evidence—without luck.

CROSS-EXAMINATION
BY MR. CELLA:
"Could you tell us with respect to each individual hair that you have on there, which item that you found it on?"

"Which item I found it on, yes, sir."

"I found hair on each of the items that I mentioned. The mauve fitted sheet, which is our item 2A. I also found hair on Item 2B, which is a mauve flat sheet. I also found hair on Item 2C, which is two mauve pillow cases, and I also found hair on Item 2D, which is one blue pillow case."

Mr. Cella continued peppering the witness with how many hairs seen on each item, or the total number she found.

"And are these hairs on these slides so numerous that you couldn't count them by the naked eye?"

"No, sir. It's not. I just don't keep a record of how many hairs I collect off of each item."

"... [J]ust give me an approximation. How many hairs are we talking about here? Is it less than ten?"

"On some of the slides, on one or two, there may be less than ten. On others there is more than ten."

The witness was excused.

Janet Gettings, a microanalyist from the Georgia Crime Laboratory was then called to the stand.

DIRECT EXAMINATION
BY MR. MALLARD:
Ms. Gettings testified to her formal education (college degree) and training experience including an internship with the U.S. Treasury Department followed by six years in her present employment with the Georgia Crime Laboratory, qualifying her as a microanalyst in the analysis of items such as hairs, fibers, and glass.

"And would you tell us generally what procedures you use as a microanalyst in comparing, for example, hair."

"What we do is when the evidence comes into the laboratory, it's taken into what is termed a clean room, if you will. That's where the technician processes the evidence. The evidence is put on the glass microscope slides, and then I receive those microscope slides from the technician.

"At that point, what we are doing is we are looking at what is called 'question hair.' We are comparing question hair against known. The question hair, we don't know the source of it. At the time we start looking at it, we don't know where it came from. A known hair sample, we know, it came from a particular individual. We know that it was pulled from the head or the pubic region, what have you. That is known. So we are comparing a question hair against a known to determine whether or not the question hair could have originated from that same known person sample.

"We are looking at microscopic characteristics in the hair. What we do is we first start off with what is called is stereo microscopic examination. We are looking at things like the length of the hair, the color, the curl, real general characteristics. Then, what we do is we go to what is called a comparison microscope, and what it is is two microscopes that are side by side, but they're mounted together with an optical grid, so I can look at both the question and the known at the same time. That way, I don't have to take the slide off and put another one on to try to remember in my head what it looked like, but I can look at them at the same time. And what we are doing is looking at the internal characteristics of the hair.

"A good analogy is if you can think of a common wooden pencil. Say the sharpened pencil could be a hair that has a natural taper on the tip, and the eraser end of the pencil would be equivalent to the root of the hair, the part that's in your skin. Then the paint around the outside of the pencil is equivalent to what we call the cuticle. That's the layer of scales that surrounds the outside of the hair. Then, if you go into the wooden part of the pencil, that's equivalent to what is called the cortex, that's the meat of the hair, if you will, that makes up about 80 percent of the hair. In there, you have the pigment granules that give the hair its color. They are going to vary in size and distribution and such. And then we go into what is called the medulla. That would be equivalent to the lead running through the center of the pencil. Some people may have medulla in their hair; some people may not. It may be fragmented; it may be continuous.

"They're all different characteristics that we are looking at in comparing between the question and the known, and if, at any time, there is differences between the question and the known, we stop the comparison, and there is no point in going any further. If the characteristics are the same, we continue on. If we can find no differences between the microscopic characteristics of a question hair and a known hair, we determine that they could have had a common origin."

Mallard: "Is the way you compare it with dual microscopes, is that similar to what they use with comparing one bullet against another bullet in firearms examination?"

"In theory, the general comparison is the same. They're looking at a question bullet and a known bullet at the same time. We use transmitted light. We are looking all the way through the hair rather than just at the top of the hair. We are looking all the way through, three dimensionally, through the hair."

At that time, I submitted the witness as an expert microanalyst to the court, for cross-examination by opposing counsel—if he wished. That is, opposing counsel may agree or stipulate that the witness is qualified in the endeavor for which the witness is offered, or counsel may cross-examine the witness as to her qualifications to give an expert opinion.

VOIR DIRE EXAMINATION
BY MR. CELLA:

"Ms. Gettings, what disciplines or fields of science are you required to be an expert at in order to become an expert in your field?"

"I believe the general job description calls for bachelor's degree in a natural science."

"Okay. And what natural science is your degree in?"

"Forensic science."

"How do you define the field that you're an expert in? What word do you use to describe it?"

"My particular area of expertise is microanalysis."

For five more pages, Mr. Cella continued his probing cross-examination, hoping to find some deficiency in her qualifications. She testified most of her work is done with hairs and fibers; that her expertise is based upon her degree, experience, and exposure to numerous on-the-job actual cases in the laboratory. She had previously testified in courts where she was admitted as an expert witness in approximately 45 cases. She said she is exposed to random proficiency testing by the laboratory—two or three tests in the past year.

"Okay. And do they come and tell you your grade after every one?"

"It's a pass/fail. I would imagine they would tell me if I had failed it. I've seen the results, and they've always been correct."

At that point, Mr. Cella stated he had no objection to the witness testifying as an expert microanalyst. This cross-examination before the jury just re-emphasized her credibility, and ability, as a witness.

DIRECT EXAMINATION
BY MR. MALLARD (Continuing)

I had the witness go through the chain of custody of all the items she received in the laboratory from Detective Scott Smith, including State's Exhibit 33 (Hightower's bed sheets), as well as exhibits 55; 57; 58; 60; 61:

Questioned Hair mounted on slides –

No. 2A: questioned hair from the fitted sheet;

No. 2B: questioned hair from the flat sheet;

No. 2C, 2D: questioned hair from pillow cases;

No. 3D: questioned hair from pubic combing of Donna Hightower.

Known Hair of Donna Hightower mounted on slides –

No. 3E: the known pubic hair of the victim Hightower; and

No. 3F: the known head hair of the victim Hightower.

Known Hair of Terry Greenway mounted on slides –

4B: defendant's known pubic hair;

4C: defendant's known head hair;

4D: defendant's known arm hair.

"I show you now State's Exhibit 57. Could you tell me what that is?"

"Okay. There are three slides in State's Exhibit 57. One is from the pubic combings of the victim, which is State's 55, and two other slides are from a fitted sheet which were in State's Exhibit 33."

"All right. Now, did you make any comparisons between the Defendant Terry Greenway's known pubic hair and any hair contained in the slides that came from Ms. Hightower's fitted sheet?"

"Yes, I did."

"And what was your findings?"

"In comparison of the question hairs that were on the fitted sheet, several were consistent with the victim's own hair, and there was one pubic hair that matched the Defendant Terry Greenway."

"Before we leave that now, what is the fitted sheet to you?"

"One that has elastic around the corners."

"Is that the one you sleep on?"

"Yes."

"And you say other hair there was consistent with the victim's?"

"That's correct."

"And did you make a comparison with any hair from your Item 3D, which is Ms. Hightower's pubic combings, with Terry Greenway's known pubic hair?"

"Yes, I did."

"What was your findings?"

"There was two hairs present in a sample. One hair was consistent with the victim's own pubic hair, and one pubic hair match Terry Greenway."

SUMMARY OF COMPARISONS:

   (1) Questioned hair from victim Hightower's *fitted sheet,* versus Greenway's known pubic hair and victim's known hair:

      = Several hairs on sheet—consistent with victim's own hair;

      = 1 pubic hair matches Defendant Greenway.

   (2) Questioned hair from (victim) Donna Hightower's *pubic combings,* versus Greenway's known pubic hair and victim's known pubic hair:

      = 1 pubic hair matches defendant Greenway;

      = 1 hair consistent with victim's known pubic hair.

"Tell us what that means to a microanalyst when you say that it's consistent with the Defendant's known pubic hair?"

"Okay. Let me emphasize that hairs are not like fingerprints. It's not an absolute positive identification. The reason for that is that hairs are growing biological specimens, and no two are exactly the same, but what we do is determine a range of variation of characteristics that are in a person's hair, and when we make the comparisons, we are determining whether the question hair is in that range of variation, whether the characteristics are the same or not."

"*All right.* So what is your conclusion, then, with regard to the one hair from the pubic combings and one hair from the fitted sheet that matches the defendant's pubic hair?"

"The conclusion is that those two pubic hairs could have had a common origin with the known sample from Terry Greenway."

"And were those inconsistent with the victim's hair?"

"Yes, they were."

"Did you also compare some of the other hair recovered from the sheets and items submitted to you with the victim's known hair?"

"Yes, I did."

"And would you tell us what those conclusions were."

"There were numerous hairs that were consistent with the victim's own hair. There were two head hairs that were compared against both Terry Greenway and the victim that did not match either."

CROSS-EXAMINATION

BY MR. CELLA:

"Ms. Gettings, did you indicate that the pubic combing of the victim, the slide that contained the pubic combing of the victim, only had two hairs altogether?"

"I have two noted in my notes, yes."

"Now, looking at those from the naked eye, can you detect a difference in them?"

"I don't know that the layperson could. I don't know that I could with the naked eye."

"Okay. Now, you used the word match a couple of times during your direct testimony. In fact, I found myself writing it down, but that's an incorrect terminology in this field of endeavor, is it not?"

"No. I use it quite regularly."

"Does a match to you just, and I'm talking about just a common everyday usage in the English language, does match to you mean the same thing as sufficient similarities to conclude they could have had a common origin?"

"In terms of hair comparisons, it does to me."

"So a match, in terms of hair comparisons, doesn't really mean what we normally think of when we use the word match?"

"To me, a match means that all the microscopic characteristics were the same between the question and the known samples."

"You don't think that's misleading speaking as a scientist to call it a match in this particular field?"

"I don't believe so."

"Are you telling this jury that that hair matches? Are you telling us that that hair is, as a scientific fact, Terry Greenway's hair?"

"No. As I stated, it's not an absolute identification."

"So we don't have any idea, then, as far as the statistical significance, then, of what this match means?"

"As far as a number, I can't give you a number."

"How many different similarities did you detect in concluding that this was a match?"

"I don't keep track of the number of characteristics that I'm looking at. Really, what I'm looking for is dissimilarities. There were none."

Cella: "Well, your report states sufficient similarities. What is sufficient? Does that refer to a number?"

Witness: "No. There is no specific number. It's based on the experience of the examiner. If I might, if you can consider, for example, a mother who looks at two twins every day. The average layperson is not going to be able to tell those identical twins apart, but somebody who looks at those twins every single day will be able to tell a difference. It's the same with hair comparisons. If I'm doing this every single day, I'm going to be able to notice differences between hairs."

"Would you define for me, as well as you can, the characteristics that you're looking at, to conclude that two hair samples could have had a common origin?"

"There are numerous characteristics. Just to name a few, we'll start off with looking at the scale structure on the outside of the hair, the cuticle, how thick those scales are, is it the same between the question and the known. Looking at the pigmentation, we are looking at the size, the distribution, the shape, the density, the location of pigmentation, those kind of things, and the medulla, is it present, is it opaque, is it translucent, and so on."

Mr. Cella continued to do battle with the witness for six pages, in efforts to weaken her testimony concerning specifically, diseased hair, strength of similarities, and pigmentation.

"Have you ever come across the term DNA profiling in your field of expertise?"

"As far as hairs are concerned?"

"Yes, ma'am."

"To my knowledge, it's not to the point of being used in courts yet."

"Georgia State Crime Lab, then, has never done any DNA comparisons of hair up to now [1992]?"

"Not that I know of."

"You indicated that on the head hairs, there were some head hairs found that didn't match either of Mr. Greenway's known hairs or the victim's known hairs."

"That's correct."

"Okay. Did your examination reveal any pubic hairs that didn't match either the victim or the known sample from Mr. Greenway?"

"No."

The witness was excused. The court excused the jury for the weekend, to return on Monday, and gave them instructions admonishing them not to discuss the case among themselves or with anyone else during their time away from Court.

Woodknoll Apartments, March 23, 1989— Burglary; Aggravated Assault –

I called victim, Lisa Depetro to the stand. She had been a teacher for the past three years before being victimized on March 23, 1989, while living at the Woodknoll Apartments located just off the Marietta Loop and Roswell Street near I-75 in Cobb County. At the time, she lived with her sister in a ground level apartment—somewhat isolated at the back of the complex. She said her sister worked the late shift at U.P.S. and had left home at 03:00 a.m. for work.

Mallard: "At about 3:54 a.m. in the morning hours, did something happen in your apartment there?"

Witness: "I woke up. I had someone standing over me with the bed covers pulled back and a flashlight on me."

"Have you ever seen this person before?"

"No, not at all."

"And would you tell me whether it was raining that night?"

"Yes, it was raining pretty heavily at the time." [It was raining on several of Greenway's incidents, including his earlier peeping tom. Rain may be relevant to this type of endeavor.]

"Tell us, when you were awakened, what's the first thing you did?"

"I sat straight up in the bed and scooted back up against the headboard and said, 'Who are you? Get out of my apartment'."

"Were you forceful, stern about it?"

"Uh-huh."

"What happened then?"

"Well, at that time, the person said, 'Just lay there. It will just take a few minutes. Just lay there.' And that was basically repeated over and over again over the course of the next, I guess, 12 to 20 minutes."

"All right. What happened then?"

"I kept saying, 'Just get out of my apartment. I don't know [what] you are.' And tried to keep my voice calm, and then he reached forward and pushed me by the sternum back into the bed, trying to push me down. And I reached up to push him away, and when I did that, I felt something against my thumb, but I didn't think about what it was at the time.

"And finally, I looked and tried to get, I was on the, here I am on the left-hand side of the bed. The right-hand side of the bed was empty and open, so I scooted over and tried to run to the door to get out, and he beat me to the door and turned around and pushed me the other direction back into the room and pushed me into a bookcase. And at that time, we were at the foot of the bed, and we got into a fight. I was pushing him by the shoulders, and he was pushing me back, and I reached up and grabbed his shirt and ripped a button off of his shirt. And at that time, he stopped and he said, 'You ain't the one he said you was'."

"Would you repeat?"

"You ain't the one he said you was, exactly."

"Did he indicate in any way who 'he' was?"

"Not at all, and I stopped at that time, and I said, 'Sir, I don't know anybody that you would know, and I want you to get out of my apartment'."

"Did you note any particular odor about this intruder?"

"There was a real strange musty odor, and I didn't know what it was, and I'm not real familiar with the smell of alcohol. I didn't know if it was that, and it was real rainy. But it was a real permeating smell, and it was all in my room, and afterwards, I could smell it in the apartment."

"You think it would be the type of odor you'd get from being in a brick warehouse?" [Defendant Greenway worked for a brick company. The seed was planted.]

MR. CELLA: "Objection. That calls for speculation."

MR. MALLARD: "I'll withdraw it. What happened then?"

WITNESS: "After I told him that, he turned around and opened the door to the bedroom. He had closed the door. He opened the door to the bedroom and proceeded down the hall and walked out the same way he had come in. The sliding glass door was open, and I followed him out to make sure he had gone. I guess that was stupid to do, but I made sure he had left."

"Then what did you notice about yourself?"

"Well, I reached down. There was a phone in the living room, and I was going to call 911, and the phone wouldn't work, and so I was afraid that he had done something to the phone. And I looked at the phone after I had put it back down. There was blood on it, and I looked at myself, and I had blood all over me, too, and I didn't know where I was hurt. So I went into my bedroom, and there was blood everywhere there, too. But I picked up that phone and called 911 and realized after looking in the mirror and everything that I had cut my thumb, and I determined it was when I pushed up and felt that against my thumb. I think it occurred when he reached down and pushed me into the bed, and I reached up to push him back. At that time, he had something in his hand."

"Did you ever see a knife?"

"I didn't see it, no."

"All right. About how big a cut was it?"

"It was about two inches long, and it wasn't very thick. In fact, the paramedics came because when I was on the phone with 911, I told her that I was bleeding, so paramedics came. They didn't even do anything. I just got hydrogen peroxide out of my bedroom and cleaned it and put a bandage on it."

"Did you get a look at this man that attacked you in your apartment?"

"Yes, I did."

"And where did you get a look at him at?"

"Well, when he was in the bedroom I was able to see his face because the light was just on me. It wasn't blinding me or anything, so there was light enough to see his face. And when I was push fighting with him, we were close enough to be able to identify the person."

"Were you real close to his face while you were fighting with him?"

"Uh-huh."

"Were you looking directly at him?"

"Uh-huh."

"Did he have any bandana over his face?"

"None."

"And could you see his face and his features?"

"Uh-huh."

"Now, did he have anything else on him that you noted?"

"When he was standing over me in the bed, when he had the flashlight on me, sticking out of his back pocket, which would be his left side, there was something that was sticking up that was tall, I mean long, and it was metal. But I couldn't tell what it was, maybe like a screwdriver or a slim jim or something."

"Would you tell us what you noted about the sliding glass doors, how the entry had to have been made?"

"We always check to make sure the doors were locked when we went to bed, and I didn't think of this before, but the screen was on the inside of the door, which I thought was strange. Therefore, the glass part was on the outside, and so he had gotten in there somehow by jamming that door open from the outside."

After calling 911, Ms. DePetro said the police arrived within two and one-half minutes—she was still on the phone when they were at the door.

"And after this event, sometime later back in early 1990, specifically February 26, did you call the police department in Marietta and talk to Officer Smith?"

"Yes, sir."

"Why did you call them?"

"Well, I had been contacted to say that I was going to see a line-up, another line-up to try to pick out a person, and so I had Detective Smith's phone number. He wasn't the original detective on my case. And then I was at home one day after school, cooking supper in the kitchen, and we have a pass through that you could see into the living room, and I had the television on, and the sound was down [...]. There was a picture of the man on there that was the person who had broken into my apartment. So I ran into the living room to turn the volume up so I could see what was going on and what this person was arrested for. And then I called Detective Smith to let him know that that was the person who had broken into my apartment."

"So when you first saw the picture on TV, there was no sound that you could hear?"

"Right."

"So you didn't know why that person was arrested?"

"Not at all."

"Did you immediately recognize the person as being your attacker?"

"Yes."

"And I take it over the time since 1989, you've watched TV, have you not?"

"Oh, yes."

"Have you ever picked anyone before this that you saw on TV as being your attacker?" [I knew Mr. Cella would attack the identification as being suggestive, so I wanted to show that it was a random view, and the witness had had many opportunities to see people in public, on TV, etc., over the years since the event and had not identified anyone.

"Oh, yes."

"Have you ever picked anyone before this that you saw on TV as being your attacker?"

"No."

"I take it you have seen plenty of men on TV before?"

"Yeah, and especially right after it happened. As you walk anywhere, you're looking because you know that person's out there somewhere. So you're real aware of looking for that, and I never saw anybody that appeared close to looking like this person."

She went on to testify that she met with Detective Smith at the school where she worked. She was presented a photographic display of six pictures, State's Exhibit 48. She explained she picked out No. 2 (Terry Greenway) as her attacker.

"Ms. DePetro, would you look around the courtroom and tell us if you can identify the person that you saw as your attacker back on March 23, 1989, at about 3:54 in the morning?"

"Uh-huh. That man right there in the blue and the gray tie."

"Right side of counsel table?"

"Uh-huh."

MR. MALLARD: "I'd like the record, Your Honor, to indicate she has pointed out and recognized the defendant on trial."

THE COURT: "Let the record so reflect."

I turned the witness over for cross-examination. She made an excellent witness, and Cella will have to make a serious effort to discredit her and the identification, which for 31 pages, he did his best.

CROSS-EXAMINATION
BY MR. CELLA

Mr. Cella immediately began the inquiry with questions about her earlier contacts shortly after the incident, and the recent photo lineup, how and when it came about, the words spoken, etc., in an effort to catch the witness in a conflict. She said police had her view a lineup shortly after the assault (before Greenway's arrest) and she was unable to pick anyone from that lineup.

Cella: "And you didn't hear from them for a year?"

Witness: "Well, I moved and failed to give them my new address, and I moved I think about two times in the course of that 15 months."

"And then the police officer showed that you called them on the 26th to talk about this. What happened in those intervening six days? In other words, why did you wait so long to make the phone call?"

"I really don't remember. I don't remember there being a specific reason. I was very upset at that time when I saw it, but I can't remember any reason, you know, having waited six days. It wasn't a magical number or anything like that."

"Do you recall seeing any man or woman on-the-street interviews with people acting just shocked that Mr. Greenway was allowed out on bond?"

"No. I tried not to watch the TV because I didn't want to put anything more into it until I had to. That's what I'm doing now. I'm not watching the TV as far as how this is being covered."

"But you were exposed to some more publicity during those six days, weren't you?"

"The only thing I can remember is there was something in the newspaper about where the bail had been taken away, and that was, that's all that I can remember as far as news coverage from that point."

"So basically, on the day that you went in to look at the photographic line-up, weren't you basically looking for the man's picture that you'd seen on TV?"

"I was honestly trying to look at the pictures to see if I could find the person who had been in my apartment. I would never want to pick anyone out just to have the answer. I can't pick someone out of this for sure, so I would never want to accuse someone falsely."

"Isn't it possible, though, that try as you might, you weren't really able to erase the image of this man's picture being on your TV screen in your living room, were you?"

"Well, also try as I might, I couldn't erase the image of him in my bedroom either, so that's something that you don't forget."

Mr. Cella went back over the witness' testimony without any surprises. She said she wore glasses or extended-wear contacts. She further testified she was near-sighted, and wore corrective lenses to see far away.

Cella: "Did you have your contacts in at the time of this incident in your bedroom on March 23rd of 1989?"

Witness: "At that time, I was wearing extended-wear contacts, so I would assume I did."

"If Officer McGriff's report indicates you told him you weren't wearing your glasses— would that indicate to you that your vision was not corrected at the time of this incident?"

"Probably so because I wouldn't have mentioned my glasses otherwise."

"So does that indicate to you that you didn't have your contacts in?"

"Probably so."

"Just to make sure we haven't lost anybody during that little dialogue, your vision was uncorrected then?"

"Yes."

"And you don't know how bad your vision is, uncorrected?"

"No, but I am near-sighted."

"What ever happened to this, you said that you ripped a button off of a shirt. Whatever happened to that button?"

"The detectives found it underneath my bed."

The witness testified the intruder was wearing a white Oxford shirt, and it was a small, round, white button.

She continued: "I felt it rip when I pulled on his shirt, so it was right here. His shirt was unbuttoned to that point because he had on a white T-shirt beneath the shirt."

Cella: "Now, you said blood was all over the apartment, and it sounded pretty gruesome."

Witness: "Not gross, no, just where you could see it had splattered like when you have a cut on your hand and you move. There are splatters on the wall, and when I was standing still in my room, it was dripping, you know, pretty heavily. There is one of my pillows that was ruined from it because it got all over, but it wasn't gross just from my thumb."

Mr. Cella questioned the witness about the long metal object she described as a "slim jim" type instrument.

"Okay. The phrase slim jim, what does that mean to you?"

"That means to me something that people use to get in. I know that policemen use that to get into [people who have locked their keys in their car]. I've never done that before. I've never seen one, but in my mind, I was trying to figure out how he got into the apartment. I think I even said that when I gave my whatever, not testimony, but description."

Mr. Cella went into a long Q&A with the witness about an attempt to do a composite of her attacker.

"Okay. And when you walked out of the police station, did you have a copy of it in your hand?"

"No."

"Did you ask for one?"

"No."

"Did you want one?"

"No."

"Have you ever heard of it or seen it since?"

"No, not at all."

"This composite that you put together after 20 minutes of looking at the various overlays, did it resemble the man who attacked you?"

"Resemble, yeah, not an exact likeness. I don't guess you can ever get an exact likeness, but it did resemble the person."

"Did the composite look like he does when you looked at him in court today?"

"Somewhat."

"Does it change his appearance in any way?"

"The hair seems lighter to me now that it did at that time."

"Okay. Would you attribute that to natural graying process from growing older?"

"I don't know, possibly."

Cella asked about the source of any light at the time of the attack.

Witness: "My bed was against a wall, and there were windows on either side of the bed. My room was at the back of the apartment, and there are blinds, so there would be light coming through the blinds. From the outside natural light, and I think, you can go check, I'm not sure. I think that there is an outside light on the apartment complex back there, too."

REDIRECT EXAMINATION
BY MR. MALLARD:

"Ms. DePetro, just one thing. I believe you said you're nearsighted? Which means you need correction at a distance?"

"Right."

"And, for instance, driving?"

"Right."

"But as far as up close, you don't need correction?"

"Right. I can read or tell what someone looks like up close."

"Somebody that's in your face, you don't need your glasses on?"

"Right."

The victim has established all the elements of the crimes of burglary of her residence and an aggravated assault upon her person.

Detective Scott Smith testified that he was contacted on February 26, 1990, by victim Lisa DePetro regarding a burglary and aggravated assault at the Woodknoll Apartments on March 23, 1989. The victim had been cooking supper and said she had seen the man who attacked her on the TV screen. At that time, Smith was putting together the photo line-up to show victims, and the next day he met with the victim at her place of employment where he presented the line-up to her.

She identified position number two in the line-up (Greenway) as her attacker.

Detective Smith testified that in the cases where the attacker was wearing a bandana over the lower part of his face, he used a strip to cover the same portion of the faces of the six persons in the photo line-up so the witnesses would be seeing only the same portion of the faces of each of the persons in the line-up photo.

CONCEPTS 21 APARTMENTS, August 10, 1989—Rape; Burglary
DIRECT EXAMINATION
BY JACK MALLARD

Ms. Frances Stanford was very nervous as she took the stand and testified. I cautioned her to relax, and proceeded to establish that she lived alone in her ground level apartment at Concepts 21 on August 10, 1989, at about 04:00 in the morning. She said she had gone to bed at about 11:30 p.m.

"... [D]id someone interrupt your sleep?"

"Yes."

"And would you tell me what caused you to awaken?"

"I woke up, and there was a man standing over me with his hand over my mouth."

"When you say he was standing over you, was he up on the bed?"

"I was laying in the bed, and he was standing over the bed with his hand on my mouth."

"Would you tell me what you did and what he did, then, after that?"

"He told me that to do what he told me to do and that he wasn't going to hurt me. I promise. And then, he told me that a couple of times. I'll only be here a few minutes, and I'll be gone."

"And what did he do then?"

"He took off my underwear, and he raped me."

"Did he unzip his pants?"

"Yes, he did."

"And would you tell us whether or not you were in fear of your life?"

"Yes, I was, because after he raped me, he told me to roll over on my stomach, and I was afraid that I was going to be killed."

"Is that the only reason that you gave in to him, in fear of your safety?"

"Yes, because he was bigger than me."

"And was this done without your consent?"

"No, I did not consent."

"And was it forcibly?"

"Yes."

"I need to ask you a couple of questions, a few personal questions. Okay? During the intercourse, did he, in fact, make penetration of your female organ with his male organ?"

"Yes, he did."

"All right. Before he raped you, Ms. Stanford, did he have any trouble getting an erection?"

"Yes. When he unzipped his pants, he had to play with himself for a couple of minutes, and then he did."

"All right. Do you know whether or not he ejaculated in you?"

"Yes, he did."

"And was this period of intercourse, was it quick, long, can you estimate?"

"It seemed like it only took just a few minutes."

The witness further said the man made her roll over on her stomach. She then heard the chain lock on the front door slide, and the door opened and closed. She said the chain lock had been on when she went to bed, and the man opened it as he left by the front door.

"What did you do then?"

"I got up. I laid there for a minute, and then I got up, and the door to my patio door was open, and I closed it, and then I went back into my bedroom, and I called 911."

She testified that the police arrived. She showed them the screen to the sliding glass door to the screened-in porch had been cut like an "L", and the patio door was open. She said the door had been closed before she went to bed.

"Could you tell me whether or not the intruder had anything over part of his face?"

"Yes, he did. He had on something covering from probably here down wrapped around his face."

"All right. You're indicating across the bridge of your nose."

"Somewhere in there."

"And did he have anything on his hands?"

"Yes, he did. He had on some white gloves."

"Did you discover later whether or not anything was done with your phone cord?"

"Yes, sir. The phone in the living room that was on a table, the phone cord had been cut, and I had to use the phone in my bedroom."

"All right. I show you what is from State's Exhibit 37, what appears to be some white gloves. Can you say whether or not these are even similar to the ones that the subject had on in your apartment that night?"

"All I know is they were white gloves."

The witness further testified she was transported to Kennestone Hospital where she was examined by a doctor.

Mallard: "All right. Ms. Stanford, during the course of this assault on you, did the subject lose anything in the bed?"

"Yes. There was a cigarette that was in my bed that obviously he had lost, because it wasn't in there before, and it wasn't mine."

"Do you remember what kind of cigarette it was?"

"I think it was a Winston. It was a, one of the longer cigarettes."

"Ms. Stanford, if we can move forward in time to February 26, 1990. Did you call Detective Smith after seeing a broadcast on TV about this case?"

"Yes, I did."

"And why did you call Detective Smith?"

"Because I knew when they showed the picture that that was the man who raped me."

"Did you, in seeing the picture on TV, did you recognize him before you heard anything about the case?"

"As soon as they showed the picture on TV, I recognized him."

The witness further said she met with Detective Smith at her home where she was shown a picture line-up. The photo was identified as State's Exhibit 48, and she identified number two in the group of men in the photo.

"Do you know who you identified?"

"That man over there."

"You're pointing toward the Defendant, Terry Greenway, on trial. Do you see him in the courtroom?"

"Yes, I do."

"Is that the same man that was in your apartment on the night in question?"

"Yes, sir. He's the one that broke into my apartment and raped me."

"Is there any doubt in your mind today [...] that Terry Greenway [...] is the one that broke in and raped you on August 10th of 1989?"

"No."

"Did you have a light on in your apartment that night?"

"Yes, I did. I had the bathroom light on which was right across the hall from my bedroom."

"Were you getting some light into your bedroom from it?"

"I always slept with a light on."

"All right. Do you recall after this time, later in March, March 19 of 1990, were you asked by Detective Smith to go with [you] to Kenmed where some blood was [drawn] from you?

"Yes."

She then identified State's Exhibits 63, 64, and 66, photographs showing the cut phone cord in her apartment, her bed, and the cut screen to her patio. I then turned her over for cross-examination.

CROSS-EXAMINATION
BY MR. CELLA:
Mr. Cella re-visited the witness's testimony regarding the point of entry through the screened-in patio, and the statements made by the intruder, without any new revelations.

CELLA: "Did you ever see a weapon on this man?"

WITNESS: "No, sir."

"Did you ever see a screwdriver?"

"No."

"Ever see a knife?"

"No."

"Did this man ever take off those white gloves that you saw?"

"No."

"Did he ever touch you with his hands during this episode?"

"Yes. When he had his hands over my mouth, when he removed my underwear."

"Are those the only times he touched you?"

"Yes."

"Were you able to feel the texture of those gloves at that time, as the man's glove was over your face?"

"I don't recall that. I just had just the creeps all over."

"Do you remember telling the police that they were latex gloves?"

"Uh-huh."

"Now, what does the term latex mean to you? Could you describe that using some other words to describe what you mean by latex."

"Like a plastic, rubber type."

"Now, these gloves that Mr. Mallard showed you, these gloves are nothing like those gloves that you're talking about, are they?"

"Those gloves are not latex."

Mr. Cella established from the witness that she gave a description of her assailant a few days later as about 6'2" tall and his age in the mid-30s with a medium build. He also questioned her identification, though there was no light on in the bedroom. The witness insisted the bathroom light across the hall illuminated the bedroom. Cella asked the witness about efforts to assist the police in preparing a composite shortly after the attack.

WITNESS: "They just showed me pictures of things like the eyebrows, the nose, farther apart, closer together, just a lot of different things."

CELLA: "Well, wasn't it as far as, did the composite that you made have a handkerchief over its face?"

"They asked me about it."

"Okay. You weren't able to identify this man's face at all while you were trying to do a composite, isn't that true?"

"It was very difficult to do a composite."

"It was impossible to do it when you were trying to describe a man who had a handkerchief over his face, wasn't it?"

"Yes."

"Okay. Did you, during the time that you were in Concepts 21, ever have occasion to ask for a maintenance, assistance to fix anything in the apartment ...?"

"I don't remember if I ever had a problem where they had to come in or not."

"Do you ever remember an exterminator or anybody coming in to spray your apartment?"

[Mr. Cella is doing his best to shift suspicion to some person with authority and keys to enter the apartments, but this doesn't account for the forcible entry through the patio, a cut screen, and a sliding glass door having been forced open.]

"I know that they had exterminators that came in and sprayed because I came home one day and smelled the bug spray."

"Do you remember when that was in relation to the day you were raped? How many days before or weeks?"

"I have no idea."

"Do you recall the detectives looking over your bed sheets and pillow cases?"

"Yes."

"Looking for hairs?"

"Yes."

"Do you recall them looking around your apartment for fingerprints?"

"Uh-huh."

"Okay. Did you see any fingerprints that might have been left by this person?" [But the assailant wore white gloves.]

"No."

"Okay. Do you have any close friends who are black people?"

"No."

"Have there ever been any black people in your apartment?"

"No."

"If the crime lab found a Negroid hair in those hair samples that they picked, that wouldn't come from anybody who had ever been in your apartment, would it?"

"No."

"Because you're sure there has never been a black man in your apartment or a woman?"

MR. MALLARD: "Your Honor, I object to that accusatory-type question. The question is whether or not the subject who raped her was black or white." [I thought the implication was clear.]

THE COURT: "Do you insist on the question?"

MR. CELLA: "No, Sir."

THE COURT: "All right. Next question."

"But you are certain, though, that if there was a black pubic hair found in your bed, that it didn't come from a man who attacked you because you're 100 percent sure that this was a white man?" [There's no evidence it was a (black man's) pubic hair.]

"Yes. I know it was a white man that attacked me."

Mr. Cella returned to the photo line-up the witness was shown at her house some six months after the attack.

"Now, did you call the police or did they call you?"

"I called them."

"Now, before you saw the TV news, had there been any contact between you and the police going all the way back to when you had done the composite?"

"I don't know. Like I said, I had talked to them several times. I don't know."

"Do you remember ever looking at any other photo line-ups besides this one?"

"Yeah. There was a lot of photo books and things that I had to look at."

"How many times did you see the news before you called the police?"

"That one time."

"Now, did you listen to the whole news story before you called the police?"

"No. I just called them when I saw the thing, because it was like where they show the thing, and they say this is coming up at such-and-such time. I called them then."

"Okay. What did you hear on the news story before you called the police?"

"That they had someone that they believed it was a serial rapist."

"Okay. What else?"

"I think that he was caught outside of another apartment complex trying to break in."

"Now, what was it, Ms. Stanford, about Mr. Greenway's picture on the TV news that you recognized?"

"From the minute that they showed it, the way that, it was like I went back as to what happened to me, and I could see him standing there with the handkerchief or scarf or whatever covering his face. But it was the hair, because I kept remembering his hair."

"So basically, then, you didn't recognize the man's face, you recognized his hair on the news when you saw it on TV?"

"Yes. And I knew that from the scarf being over the face, that it just it looked, I mean, almost positively like him." [I'm glad we have DNA connecting Greenway to the crime].

"Now, after you looked at this photo line-up, well, how long did you take to look at the photo line-up before you picked the man out?"

"I immediately picked him out."

The witness was excused, and the court took a break.

I briefly recalled Marietta Police Officer John S. Biggers to the stand. He previously testified that he responded to the Cinnamon Ridge Apartments on January 7, 1990, in response to a 911 call where he arrested the defendant, Greenway, trying to break into the front door of Jeannine McClean's apartment.

Officer Biggers testified that he was on duty during the morning hours of August 10, 1989, and responded to a 911 call (Sexual Assault) to the Concepts 21 Apartments about 04:01 a.m. The complainant was Frances Stanford, who was present when he arrived.

Officer Biggers received a description of the assailant being in his mid-30's, 6'2" tall and weighing about 185 pounds. The subject reportedly was wearing white gloves and had a white scarf over his face just below the eyes. He was also wearing a dark shirt and blue jeans.

"Was there any indication whether or not the gloves were cotton or latex or anything else?"

"No, sir. She was very upset at the time. She couldn't tell me that information."

"Did you observe the point of entry into the apartment of Ms. Stanford?"

"It was at the rear of her apartment. There was a screened-in porch that leads to a patio. The patio screen windows had a vertical and horizontal cut in the L-shape form, about the size of a window, further entry into the living room through the sliding glass door, forced entry marks below the latch on the sliding glass door into the apartment."

"Now, you say the forced entry marks on the sliding glass door. Are these two glass doors?"

"Yes, sir."

"Do they slide on runners?"

"Yes, sir. It's one door, and it slides. The other one is permanent."

Officer Biggers proceeded to identify State's Exhibit (Photograph) 67 showing the forced entry marks just below the latch, and State's Exhibit (Photograph) 66 showing the screen was cut open in an L-shape. [This should remove any doubt of the suggestion by the defense that entry may have been made by someone with keys.]

Officer Biggers transported the victim to the hospital where she was examined by Dr. Morris.

Mr. Cella had only a few questions of no consequence.

I next called Dr. Jonathon Morris, an emergency medicine physician at Kennestone Hospital as a witness. He testified he saw Ms. Frances Stanford as an emergency patient at 4:54 in the morning. It was a reported sexual assault. He did the vaginal swabbings of the patient, and samples of hair and pubic combings were obtained by the nurse for the rape kit.

Dr. Morris testified to preparing a rape kit (which was provided by the officer), and returning it completed along with a chain of evidence and medical report to the officer.

Mallard: "Would you tell me what you did then with regard to the evaluation of the patient before examination?"

Dr. Morris: "Basically, we do a complete general external examination, use a Woods Lamp, an ultraviolet light, to detect the presence of florescent material on the patient, and then do a standard pelvic examination and obtain specimens from the vaginal and cervical area."

"And was there sperm noted in this case?"

"Yes, sir."

Mr. Cella only had a few questions of no consequence, and the witness was excused.

Detective Scott Smith testified about the reported rape and burglary of Ms. Frances Stanford on August 10, 1989, at Concepts 21 complex. He said he arrived at the scene about 4:00 a.m. and took photographs. He also took charge of the evidence: one night shirt, two bed sheets, two pillow cases, one female white slip, one female's panties, two pieces of cut phone cord, and one Winston cigarette and toothpick. The cigarette was un-smoked, and was found in the victim's bed sheets. All items were delivered to the State Crime Lab. He subsequently went to the hospital, where he obtained the sexual assault kit from Dr. Morris for delivery to the Crime Laboratory.

Smith testified that during the subsequent interview with Terry Greenway after his arrest, Greenway admitted that he smoked Winston Lights cigarettes.

Ms. Stanford called Detective Smith after the Greenway arrest. "Al right. What was the nature of her contact to you?"

"She stated that she had seen the news broadcast of Mr. Greenway's arrest and that she was extremely upset about it at the time, and she wanted to know what she needed to do."

"Did she tell you whether she had identified, recognized him?"

"She told me that that was the gentleman that attacked her the night of her incident."

"And did you, in fact, meet with her for that purpose?"

"Yes, sir, I did."

"And would you tell us whether or not you displayed the same photographic spread you identified earlier [...]?"

He went on to say he had presented the photo display with Greenway in position no. 2, at which time, the witness picked out Greenway as her attacker.

I had Detective Smith to step down before the jury and display an official City of Marietta map and referred him to the east side of the city showing Interstate 75 through the city. The witness further explained that the four apartment complexes where the rapes occurred are located within the same general area of I-75, Roswell Road, and the 120 Loop, all accessible from I-75.

I next called John G. Wegel, Jr., employed by the Georgia Bureau of Investigation, Division of Forensic Sciences Laboratory.

DIRECT EXAMINATION
BY JACK MALLARD

Mr. Wegel testified about his formal education and work experience in the laboratory. He graduated from Georgia Tech in 1972 with a Bachelor of Science in Chemistry, and a Master of Science in Forensic Chemistry from the University of Pittsburgh in 1975. He initially was employed in the drug identification section, after which he began working in the forensic serology section. Wegel began working under the supervision of Ms. Elizabeth T. Quarles for six months, after which he began working his own cases. Over the years, he attended many workshops and seminars dealing with forensic serology and blood typing throughout the United States for some 15 years. He handled about 40 cases a month on average.

Wegel said he did some work in this case regarding victims Frances Stanford, Donna Hightower, Melissa Hilyard, and Linda Linnard (the rape victims).

I asked: "Before we get to that, what kind of cigarettes do you smoke"?

"Winston Lights." [The same type cigarette (victim) Frances Stanford found in her bed-sheets after her rape.]

"And do you have a pack that you opened new at lunchtime?"
"Yes, sir."

I had the witness take one of the Winston lights from his pack, and a Winston non-light (regular) from another packet that I had procured.

"Do you note any difference in the regular and the Winston Light?"

"Yes, sir, there is."

He went on to describe the differences. Both are printed with the brand name Winston. The Lights have it in gold. The regular Winston is in black letters. There are two small gold bands around the filter of the "Lights" whereas the regular has a single very thick gold band around the filter.

Of course, one may question the significance of this finding, but it is just one more circumstance the jury can consider. We have established that Terry Greenway smokes Winston Lights and one such cigarette was recovered from the victim's bed after the attack. *This one additional circumstance fails to exclude Terry Greenway as a suspect.*

As to Mr. Wegel's analysis in this case, he testified that as a serologist he examines for identification the individualization of biological fluids, primarily blood and semen. When evidence of this sort is received into the lab, whether on slides or vaginal swabs from a rape kit, the evidence is labeled and stored for later examination. He testified that upon removing all the items from the freezer where they had been stored until further use was necessary, he examined each exhibit—finding there was no indication of tampering, and in a sealed condition.

We first took up the case of (victim) Frances Stanford. Microscopic examination of the vaginal or cervical swabs from the rape kit revealed the presence of spermatozoa. Mr. Wegel then testified that he had received a vile of blood belonging to the same victim for which he prepared a dried stain of the blood on white cotton cloth and then stored it in the freezer for use at a later date.

"And did you make a stain from the blood of Frances Stanford for use later by the DNA lab?"

"Yes, sir, I did."

Next, we took up the cases of the other rape victims: Donna Hightower, Melissa Hilyard, and Linda Linnard. As in the previous case, the witness identified the vaginal/cervical swabs and blood stains from known blood samples from each victim which had been stored in the freezer.

"Now, in summary, if I can ask you whether or not you, on or about March 28, 1990, sent a package of the items you've identified to the DNA unit of the Federal Bureau of Investigation, Washington?"

"Yes, sir, I did."

"And pulling all of these items from the freezer, how did you package and send them?"

"The vaginal swabs, of course, they're labeled on the white envelope that they come in from the sexual assault kit. All the bloods I placed into small white envelopes, and labeled the outside of the envelope so the scientists in the FBI would not have to handle the stains directly. They could handle the envelope. So I put the item number and the case number, and put the index card inside the envelope, and these were then placed into a Fed-Ex envelope along with a request letter, and then I took it to the Federal Express office that evening on the way home."

"Was a transmittal letter included as to the items you were transmitting to the FBI?"

"Yes, sir. There was a cover letter included and the envelope."

"And did the package contain a sample of each of the four alleged victims' known blood?"

"Yes, sir."

"Did the package contain, from all four rape kits of the four victims, the vaginal swabs?"

"It did."

"And did the package contain a separate sample, dried blood stain of the Defendant's known blood?"

"It did."

CROSS-EXAMINATION
BY MR. CELLA:

The cross examination re-established that the witness had not examined the swabs from the rape kits for spermatozoa on two of the victims, Melissa Hilyard and Donna Hightower. He had examined the slides on the other two victims under the microscope.

"And the Hilyard and Hightower cases?"

"I did not look at those slides."

"Okay. Was there another person with a similar job description as yours who looked at the Hilyard and Hightower cases?"

"I believe the Hilyard and Hightower, Ms. Pickens, who testified Friday, I believe."

[Yes, indeed, Ms. Connie Pickens had testified extensively as to how such exhibits are received, prepared and examined. And, she had identified spermatozoa from those (victims) rape kits. I do not find it necessary to go back over the details of such testimony in these two cases].

REDIRECT EXAMINATION
BY MR. MALLARD:

"Just a question or two to clear up and make clear the fact that the slides which you examined on the two cases that you examined, you said you used a dye in the Stanford and Linnard cases. Now, these are the slides made by the examining doctor you said, is that correct?"

"That is correct. These are the two slides that come in the kit."

"These do not go to the FBI lab in Washington?"

"They do not, only the swabs do."

VI

THE DNA EVIDENCE

I was now at the point in the trial where I needed to "educate the jury" on the principles upon which DNA testing is founded and the stage of its development, before the testimony of the scientist who performed the tests would be introduced. The jurors knew nothing of DNA testing or the power of such tests in identifying a person, and expert witnesses at times can be boring testimony. I will try to make it simple as I can for the jurors. In doing so, I will first call the DNA Unit Supervisor at the Georgia State Crime Laboratory, who is presently in the process of establishing a DNA unit there. This witness did no work or testing in this case, but will hopefully simplify the processes involved which will enable the jurors to better understand the testimony of the witnesses who will follow, and establish that the testing procedures are reliable and generally accepted in the scientific community.

This witness' testimony would be spread over 105 pages of court transcript, and hours of verbal warfare between me and Mr. Cella, each eliciting the main points and counter-points.

I presented Dr. George Herrin, Jr., who testified he started building the Georgia DNA unit in January (1992). Dr. Herrin testified to his formal education including a Ph.D. in Biochemistry received in 1985 from Rice University where his research was in molecular biology, the study of DNA. He then completed two and one-half years of post-doctoral research in molecular biology at Texas A & M University, after which he worked two years for Cellmark Diagnostics, one of the first two private labs doing DNA testing in the country. He was a staff scientist at Cellmark where about half of their business was criminal cases—the other half being paternity—and his duties included testifying in court. He said he had testified about 30-35 times in court as an expert witness while with Cellmark and several times since he was with the Georgia Laboratory. He had published many papers, abstracts, and documents regarding DNA procedures.

Dr. Herrin testified that the Georgia laboratory primarily uses the RFLP testing procedures for the most part, but may use the PCR-based system occasionally—if the case so merits it. The PCR test is slow and costly, and it has much less power to identify a person than the RFLP method—which is used by the other two private labs and the FBI in this case. The PCR may be used where the sample to test is too small for the RFLP test; with PCR, you actually multiply the DNA by taking one single copy and making copies from that.

Mallard: "When would you use that (PCR)? Would you use it only when you don't have enough sample (for the RFLP)?"

"That is, yes, definitely, that is our secondary method of analysis and certainly not my most preferred method of analysis because as I said, it is primarily an exclusionary technique. It has much less power to identify someone than the RFLP."

At that point, I offered the witness as an expert in his field of DNA profiling and molecular genetics. Mr. Cella took the opportunity to question him regarding his expertise.

VOIR DIRE EXAMINATION
BY MR. CELLA:
"Dr. Herrin, could you detail for us your experience in the field of human genetics, please."

"Well, I have never claimed to be a human geneticist. I have no research other than what I have done at Cellmark Diagnostics and the GBI in the field of human genetics."

Mr. Cella then asked if he participated in the formulation of Cellmark's database, which he had, testifying:

"A database is simply a collection of information. You could have a database of how tall everyone in this room is, a database of how many people are female and how many people are male. When you're talking about DNA typing, you make a database of what each person's DNA type is that you have run through your system."

"Okay. And when you say what a person's DNA type is, are you talking about an autoradiograph?"

"Well, I'm talking about the molecular weight in base pairs, or kilobases of each of the DNA fragments recognized from each of the individuals at each of the loci tested in this particular laboratory."

"And that's information that y'all gather off of an autoradiograph and then put it into the computer database?"

"Yes, sir."

"Have you had any training in statistics?"

"I've had some very limited training during course work, but I never took a full-length course named statistics."

"Is that an area that comes into play in your work in the lab?"

"Only in a limited fashion. I'm very familiar with the methodologies and the equations used in analyzing the data that we gather during our testing. I would certainly never claim to be a statistician and go try to earn my living doing that."

"Do you have to be licensed in your business?"

"No, sir."

"There is no licensing agency for the DNA labs?"

"No, sir."

"And there is no such thing as personal accreditations in this field?"

"Again, that would be called certification, and those standards are being developed, but they're not yet in place."

The court admitted the witness as an expert in his field, as offered by the State.

FURTHER DIRECT EXAMINATION
BY MR. MALLARD:

I asked the witness to explain the RFLP methodology which was used in the present case.

"RFLP stands for Restriction Fragment Length Polymorphism, which just means that we look at different size fragments."

"Has that system been recognized as reliable and have gained general acceptance in the scientific community?"

"Yes, it has."

"Is testing done daily in laboratories around the country using this system, the RFLP system?"

"Yes, it is."

"And would you tell us how this system was applied to forensics criminal cases."

"Well, it's basically the same type of system that is used in research and diagnostic laboratories. You obtain a DNA sample, you cut that DNA sample into fragments of varying length, and then you separate those fragments, and then you look at one or two of the fragments with a, of the fragments that you have obtained to see how many building units are present in each of those fragments."

I then had the witness give a short history of DNA, how it got started by Dr. Jeffries in England in the mid-1980s, then came into use in laboratories in criminal cases in this country. With the use of slides, the witness educated the jurors on the testing procedures through application of the RFLP methodology. The witness explained how the research began in the 1950s with the structure of DNA being discovered, then evolved through the 1960s - 1970s with restriction enzymes which enabled researchers to cut the DNA into fragments, and the transfer of DNA to a membrane by blotting.

Mallard: "Tell us in just a few words what is DNA."

"DNA stands for deoxyribonucleic acid, and it's the basic genetic material of each of our, of your body. It tells your body what it will be, how big you're going to be, what color hair, what color eyes, how long your arms will be, everything physical about you."

"Has it been related to, for example, a blueprint of a human being?"

"Yeah. The blueprint or a story of your body."

For admission of a novel scientific technology in a court of law, I must prove that the technology has been generally accepted in the scientific community as reliable. Although the judge can consider the previous one DNA prosecution in Georgia and other cases around the country where the use of DNA was admitted and upheld by the courts, the court and jury may also hear expert witness testimony which is being presented for consideration by the court, as well as for the benefit of the jurors in arriving at their verdict.

Mallard: "Is it (DNA testing) generally accepted, an accepted fact that every-one except identical twins have different and identifying DNA?"

"Yes, sir, it is."

"Is there anyone in the scientific community that disputes that?"

"Not to my knowledge."

"In other words, unless you have an identical twin, you're going to have different DNA than anyone else?"

"Yes, sir."

"And where is DNA found in humans?"

"DNA is found within the, the DNA that we are looking at here is found within the nucleus of the cell ... [I]t would be in a nucleating cell within the body, which would be like a white blood cell, a sperm cell, the root of the hair which has cells attached to it, bone fragment, organ fragment, teeth."

"And so anywhere you found cells with a nucleus, you would expect to find DNA?"

"Yes, sir."

Following the test itself, the witness explained the development of a final work product, the "autoradiograph," which is a piece of x-ray film with black bands on it (similar to bar codes on products in grocery stores). Once the film is developed, the examiner applies a set of mathematical criteria to the bands to see whether or not they match. Different bands represent a suspect, a victim, controls, etc. The film is viewed visually for interpretation.

"Have you ever seen any subsequent machine-assisted interpretation that was different from your visual?"

"Well, yes. Different in the fact that it couldn't see everything that I could see. I would say that there is not a machine out there, well, at least not a machine that I've seen out there, that can visually analyze the film as well as I can visually."

"So you consider the visual interpretation extremely important?"

"Extremely important, yes."

"Once that is done, what is your next procedure?"

"Well, the next procedure is to actually calculate mathematically the length of each of the DNA fragments which we have visualized on that film and apply a formula to those fragment lengths to see if they're close enough to be declared a match, according to our protocol."

For storing the data on a computer, the witness explained that he then uses a video camera, as did the FBI, where a picture of the x-ray film is taken and stored on the computer and analyzed. Thus, the calculations can be done much faster on the computer than by hand. He explained:

"That's how we arrive at the length of DNA fragments. Once we have arrived at how long each of the fragments and the pattern is, then we can look at our database and see how often [have we] seen this particular pattern of fragments before in our database."

The witness explained how the DNA fragments were cut up into different fragment lengths by probes (enzymes), and that the use of several probes will further discriminate persons apart.

"How would you characterize the use of three probes in a DNA case as far as rareness?"

"I would say it would be very unlikely to find two people randomly matching in three probes."

"Since you have said already that everybody has different DNA, then why can't you say that, what would you need in order to say that to the exclusion of every other person on earth, that you've identified a particular person?"

"Well, generally, we would like to see at least four to five probes, data from four to five probes."

"And even based on a database of a few hundred?"

"Yes, sir."

"Okay. Speaking of databases, do you consider a database approximately 225 sufficient?"

"It's sufficient to give you a good estimation or approximation of the result as if you had had a larger database."

Mallard: "Have you done a study on databases regarding small versus large databases?"

Dr. Herrin: *"Yes, sir, I have. I presented this data at a meeting last fall. What I did is I took our databases that we have here in the State of Georgia, and I used the whole database, which is approximately 450 to 500 individuals, and I calculated what the rareness of a pattern or an average rareness of a pattern would be. Then I split that database and said, let's only use 250 people out of it, and I calculated the average pattern, what we call a pattern frequency. And it turned out that the smaller the database, actually turned out to give a more common occurrence of the pattern."*

Dr. Herrin continues, *"In other words, the larger the database was the more rare the average pattern becomes. That's simply because the patterns are so rare to begin with that with a small database, you're really conservatively estimating the frequencies."*

[This comports with what the FBI testing expert will testify to regarding the FBI database which the defense expert criticized in pre-trial hearings as being too small, and no doubt will do so again when he is presented in rebuttal later in the trial; Dr. Herrin will hopefully pre-empt this issue in the state's favor.]

Mallard: "Then another way of putting it, let me ask you. Does the small database, then, from your studies, benefit the accused?"

"Well, I guess you could say that, yes, sir."

"In other words, puts him in a more common pool as opposed to a more rare pool with a larger database?"

"Yes, sir, because the larger the database, the more likely you are to have seen very, very rare events, and therefore, you're able to push those rare events out into their proper perspective rather than grouping them into a more common event."

Dr. Herrin said that he (in the Georgia Laboratory) does use the same overall system as the FBI laboratory (which did the testing in this case), and that Georgia did adopt the FBI protocols with minor variations for use in Georgia.

"If any of the steps during, the testing steps don't work properly, you note any problems, what happens?"

"You have two very likely results. One is that you will get no result whatsoever, and you just won't make any conclusion regarding the evidence. And the second one is that you would get, and it's a little bit less likely, is that you would get a false exclusion. In other words, you would falsely exclude someone from donating a particular biological specimen when, in fact, they did donate that biological specimen."

"And then that could be to the benefit of the accused?"

"Yes, sir."

"Is DNA the same in plants, animals, and humans?"

"Well, the basic building blocks of DNA are the same, but the sequences of those buildings blocks is not the same."

"Does DNA ever change in the body?"

"No, sir, not in any general sense."

"Do you know of any scientific test available that is more accurate than and useful for excluding an innocent person?"

"No, sir. That is the great benefit of DNA testing is that it will exclude a person who was not or who could not have been excluded by methods which were previously available to the forensics serologists."

"You indicated you were familiar with the FBI protocols and procedures. I ask you whether or not if followed, do they produce, in your opinion, reliable results?"

"I believe so, yes, sir."

At this time, the court recessed for the day. This appeared to be a good place to recess, with the jurors going home to think about the *process* by which testing is done, the value of DNA testing, and bolstering of the FBI laboratory which did the testing.

Upon the case being called to resume the morning of February 18, 1992, Judge Brantley inquired again as to the status of the case (whether we were on schedule). It's always hard to estimate the length of witnesses, especially scientific expert witnesses as the cross-examination is somewhat a guess. I had gotten good at dodging the question, and did so again.

FURTHER DIRECT EXAMINATION
BY MR. MALLARD (Continuing)

I continued with the jury being fresh and alert this morning by having my expert, Dr. Herrin, present a slide show with narration to the jury about the "process" by which a generic DNA case would be conducted and interpreted.

Dr. Herrin narrated, and I would guide him with a question at times as follows:

"The first slide I would like to talk about is what is DNA and how [is it] organized in the cell. DNA, as I said yesterday, is the story of your body, and all living organisms on this planet contain DNA: plants, animals, humans, everything [and], at some point during their life cycles, viruses. And all organisms are made up of a basic component known as a cell. And, for our purposes here, we can realize that a cell can be broken into two component parts.

"The white circle here represents the cytoplasm of the cell which is where all the proteins would be found in a cell, where on the outside of that cytoplasm is where all the ABO blood group antigens and proteins would be found. Inside the cytoplasm, there is another part of the cell, at least in plants and animals, which is called the nucleus, and this is represented here by the red circle. And the nucleus is where the DNA, as we are testing with the RFLP procedure, is found. And in humans, which is what I'm going to be talking about, there are 23 pairs of chromosomes.

"Now, a chromosome is just the structure or the biological structure that DNA is found in. You get one chromosome in each pair from your mother, and one chromosome in each pair from your father, and each one of these chromosomes is set at the time you're conceived. So from the moment of your conception until the moment that you die, the organization of your DNA in these chromosomes remains essentially constant, unless you're exposed to a great deal of ionizing radiation or some other substance which will cause the DNA to mutate, and you have to get pretty sick for that to happen.

"But anyway, these 23 chromosome pairs comprise the entire human genome, the collection of DNA in a human, and each and every cell within your body that has a nucleus contains all 23 of the chromosomes that you have. Your sperm cells or your X cells, if you're a woman, will only contain 23 chromosomes. They wouldn't be paired, but they'll contain all 23. One of the chromosome pairs is the sex chromosome, the X and Y, and that determines your sex. The chromosomes that we are looking at for RFLP typing don't have anything whatsoever to do with any physical attribute that you might have. We do not test for sex. We do not test for hair color, racial origin, any physical attribute whatsoever, or mental attribute."

Mallard: "And is this the part of the DNA that is different in every human being?"

Herrin: "Yes. And that's the reason that we test those. If we tested, for instance, if we could find the area of the DNA that coded for your right leg, say, almost everybody's DNA would be pretty much the same. Almost everybody has a right leg that has a knee and an ankle and a calf muscle and everything else that goes into making up a right leg. So it wouldn't do you any good to try and say how is this person different from this person. But on the other hand, there is a lot of DNA within these 23 chromosomes which is different, and that's what we look at is the areas which are different.

"Now, this slide represents a very simplistic schematic of a very short section of DNA. There is just really two or three major points I want to make from this slide. The first is that DNA is a double-stranded molecule. You can think of it as a ladder or a zipper. Just like a zipper, you can take it apart and put it back together, unzip and zip it up. The other thing is that the DNA is made up of only four basic building blocks. They're known as adenine, thymine, guanine, and cytosine which we abbreviate ATGC.

"Now, the crucial thing about the fact that there is only four building blocks means that the genetic code, or how you would make a sequence of these things, can be fairly simple. There is only four things you have to work with. It's not like you have the 26 letters of the alphabet. But the sequence of these bases, and these are known as bases or nucleotides, the sequence of these along any one strand determine the sequence or what will come from that strand of DNA. Now, each one of the strands of DNA can produce a protein which might be, for instance, your hair, it might be your eye, it might be your blood group gene, it might be anything. But whatever that sequence *is*, can be anything on one strand. But whatever that one strand *is* determines what the other strand will be.

"For instance, if you have a C on one strand, you will always have a G, or a guanine, on the other strands. This is known as a complementary base pair. These two things are now paired, always. If you have a C on one strand, you will have a G on the other strand. Likewise, if you have a T on one strand, you will have an A on the other strand. The important thing is, because like I said, if it's double-stranded, and it's like a zipper, and we can take it apart, and we can put it back together, how does it go back together? Well, when you take it apart and you put another piece of single-stranded DNA in a solution, two pieces of single-stranded DNA in a solution, they find each other, and they mate along these bases so that the Gs will find the Cs, and the As will find the Ts, and that's an extremely important issue in how we do our testing because if that feature of DNA was not present, we could not do the testing that we do today.

"Now, just to go back again real quickly, where you can get DNA from (in) humans is blood and blood stains, semen or semen stains which contain sperm, pulled hair root, and this does not mean like a hair root that you've gotten out of a cap or something. This means that if somebody has really forcibly pulled a hair out of your head or eyebrow or your arm or something like that, organs, tissues, bone. And then sometimes from saliva, some people you can get it from, and some people you can't, and it just depends on how much of their inside of their cheek lining is being shed at any one particular time. Some of my associates, I can't get anything from their saliva ever, so they're not shedding anything.

"Now, this slide is going to be, is really the crux of the whole issue, because this goes through all of the various steps that we use in doing the testing, and I'm going to try to explain them. Clearly, the first thing that you do is get a biological sample, and this could be anything, could be a blood sample, it could be a swab which has been collected in a sexual assault kit which has been submitted to the laboratory. The first thing that you do is isolate the DNA from any cells which are present in that biological material. Now, when you get the DNA out of the cells, those 23 chromosome pairs represent three billion, with a B, base pairs of information. That's a lot of information. It's like a big story. It would be like trying to read Warren Peaks [*sic*][War and Peace] in an hour, and you couldn't do it unless you're the best speed reader that's ever lived. It's just too much information.

"So what do we need to do? We've got all this information in a tube. We can't get anything out of it. We can't tell you that this person could or could not have contributed a particular stain at this point. The next thing that we want to do is fragment or cut the DNA using the restriction enzyme that I talked about yesterday a little bit. All this is is a protein which acts like a pair of scissors, and it goes down the DNA, and it finds a particular sequence of those bases, and it cuts both strands of the DNA at that sequence. If you think of a pair of scissors and you've got a newspaper story, and you've got a pair of scissors that will only cut that story if you can find the word win, that would be exactly like the restriction enzyme. The restriction enzyme looks for a sequence of bases and, for instance, the one that the FBI uses, and the one we use looks for the sequence G.G.C.C., and whenever it finds that sequence, it cuts right after that second G, both strands of the DNA right there every time."

Mallard: "Now, this is a chemical. It's not physically like scissors we know. It's molecular scissors?"

Herrin: "You can't see it unless you looked under an electron microscope. But anyway, now we've got a test tube full of thousands and thousands of DNA fragments, and some of these fragments are a few hundred base pairs long now, and some of them are a few tens of thousands of base pairs long, and we still can't tell you anything at all about what this story is. It's like we've taken that newspaper story, and we've cut it up at the paragraph mark, and we've jumbled it all together, and we're asking you to read it without doing anything else to it.

"Well, the next thing you might want to do if you had done that would be to sort the paragraphs out into some sort of order. And what we do is we sort the DNA fragments into an order by length. How many base pairs are there in a DNA fragment? And we do this on a piece of agarose gel, which we call an analytical gel, and we do this because DNA has a net negative electrical charge, so that when you apply an electrical charge to it, it pushes the DNA through that gel.

"We've separated the DNA fragments out. You might say, well, how does it know how to separate them? Well, let's assume that my pointer here which is about six inches long when it's compressed is a short DNA fragment, and I'm pushing this pointer through a tub of water, and it would be very easy to push it through when it's compressed like this, or a tub of oil, say. Now, let's say that I pulled it all the way out to its full extension and I'm holding it like this, and it's now representing a DNA fragment, which the pointer now is about two feet long. It's representing a fragment which is about two feet long. It's representing a fragment which is 20,000 base pairs long, and I try to push it through that same tub of oil, it would be a lot harder to push it through that tub of oil. So the short fragments go through the gel much quicker, and migrate or move to the bottom of the gel, and the long fragments stay up here at the top.

"Well, now we've got all the DNA fragments separated according to length, and they're in this gel which is like jello. And I don't know if any of you have ever tried to carry a piece of Jello around your house for about six weeks, but it would be a little bit difficult. So what we do is we do this procedure which is known as a Southern Blot, which was developed in 1975 in England, and it's really a very simple concept. It's nothing in the world but blotting up a spill. If you have ever spilled coffee, and you blotted it up with paper towels, you have done essentially what we do with a Southern Blot."

Mallard: "Before you go back to that step, go back to the analytical gel. Why do we use that? Is that so we can determine the size of the DNA fragments?"

Herrin: "Yes, sir. That's so that we can actually separate the DNA fragments. The different people have different lengths of DNA fragments at specific locations in their DNA, and this is what separates those fragments out."

Mallard: "And in other words, the size of the fragments are determined by how far it is pushed by the electrical charge through the gel?"

Herrin: "Exactly."

Mallard: "And they'll be spread out according to length?"

Herrin: "According to their length. And in between here, I didn't really say it, but what we do before we do the Southern Blot is we treat the gel with a chemical to break the two strands of DNA apart so that we now have single-stranded DNA.

"But going on to the Southern Blot, it's just a sponge which has been soaked in a chemical solution. You place your gel on top of that, and then on top of that you place a nylon membrane, which just looks like a piece of white typewriter paper, but it's got a little bit tougher physical characteristics. And the DNA binds to it so that when you sit the membrane on top of the gel, and the DNA comes out of the gel, it sticks to that nylon membrane. And the important thing about this is that it sticks exactly in the same position it was in the gel, so you have a permanent record now of what you had in that gel. So if you had fragments down here at the bottom, you will now have fragments at the bottom of your nylon membrane, and then on top of that, you place the paper towels and weight to prevent everything from blowing away and to help the blotting procedure.

"Now, once we've gotten a permanent record of what we had in the gel, and remember we've started up here with the sample, so now we've got a permanent record of what DNA we got out of this biological sample up here. We now want to find some specific fragments. Now, we only test a few of those 23 chromosome pairs. The FBI, I believe, tests chromosome number 1, 2, 4, and 17 routinely. I don't know which ones they've got in this particular case, but those are the ones they routinely test, and we test those same four plus one additional.

"But anyway, what you do is you take your nylon membrane, and you place it into a plastic Tupperware or Rubbermaid container which contains a solution into which you place here another single-stranded DNA molecule, which is a DNA probe. And these are the probes that we kept talking about. I kept saying probe, probe, probe yesterday. All that is is a single-stranded piece of DNA which has been tagged so we can figure out where it goes.

"If you have ever been to the doctor or somebody that you know has been to the doctor, and they wanted to do a thyroid exam on them, they might have injected them with radioactive iodine so they can find out where the iodine was going inside their body and what it was doing. That's the same sort of thing we do with our DNA probe. We put it into the solution. It finds its complementary base pairs, the A's match up with T's, the G's match up with C's, and you now have some radiation bound to this membrane.

"Once we've done that, the radiation which is bound to the membrane will expose a piece of film. So we place the membrane in contact with a piece of x-ray film, and the radiation exposes the film just like light exposes normal camera film, and we can get a record of where that DNA probe bound or which fragments it found on the membrane, and we'll get either one or two bands.

"Now, depending upon whether or not your mother and your father gave you the same DNA, we'll get one or two bands. If they've got the same DNA fragment or the same length of DNA fragment from your mother and your father, you'll see one band. But if you got different length DNA fragments, you'll get two different-sized fragments to visualize on the x-ray film."

Mallard: "Dr. Herrin, that last step, is the only reason that you unzip the DNA and reattach the manmade radioactive DNA is [...] so that you can locate it on the film?"

Herrin: "Exactly. We could do the same thing. We could put the DNA probe in there if it wasn't tagged with the radiation, but it really wouldn't do us any good. We wouldn't be able to figure out where it went.

"Now, this procedure that I just talked about 15 minutes there, I guess 10 or 15 minutes, really takes quite awhile to do in a laboratory. To do the DNA extraction, cutting the DNA with a restriction enzyme, separating the DNA fragments, and then blotting onto the nylon membrane takes anywhere from one or two weeks, usually about two weeks of working days. The probing, or the scientific term for that is hybridization, it takes two days per probe, so if you do four or five probes, that's at least ten days that you have spent doing that. And then you have to expose the x-ray film anywhere from a day to three weeks. The average exposure time is four to seven days. And then you have to interpret the results you get, usually takes you a day or so, somewhat less than a day, maybe. So you can see that quickly. If you do four or five probes, you might have spent a couple of months, at least, doing that one particular case.

"Now, this is just sort of to try and bring home the hybridization again. This blue line here represents one single DNA fragment that is bound to the nylon membrane, and remember there is thousands of these DNA fragments. The red represents radioactive DNA probe which was placed in the solution. And what happens is the redness goes down here, and it finds, let's say, that each of these red segments represents 50 G residue or 50 G nucleotides. Down here, you would be looking for 50 C nucleotides, or bases, so that it would match up. And that's how it works.

"Now, just to show you what some of the equipment and the stuff really looks like, this is an agarose gel. It's sort of clearish, opaque thing right here. This plastic is the tray that we pour it in. This is known as a comb, and it's because it looks like a comb. It's got wider and flatter teeth than a comb that you use for your hair. We put that in the gel while it's still liquid, and we do that to form wells, which are the little holes in the gel like just a hole in the ground is a well. And we do that because that's where we load the sample. Each individual well receives one and only one DNA sample.

"So in other words, you do not load, if you're doing, let's say we are doing a blood stain case in which we have been asked to identify or determine whether or not a blood stain found on someone's clothing could have come from one of two people. You do not load all three of these DNA samples into one well. We load each one into a separate individual well, and the way that we know that they're loaded individually is that we place a blue dye into the DNA sample, and it doesn't do anything to the DNA. It's just a tracking dye. And if there is a blue dye in the well, that lets us know that we've loaded a sample in that well, so we don't accidentally load two samples into the same well. This is just showing the whole apparatus that is used for the electrophoresis, which is the passage of electrical current through the gel.

"Here's the Southern Blot. As I said, it's a very simple setup. We have a plastic tray to contain any liquid, sponge, couple of pieces of blotting paper, the gel, the paper towels, and the nylon membrane is right on top of here, you can't see it, and then the plastic weight on top. So it's a very simple setup. You could make one in your house for about $5 if you can get the membrane, which is a little more expensive than that."

Dr. Herrin continued:

"You always have some kind of DNA standard marker which lets you size, construct a standard curve so you can calculate the size of the DNA fragments in your unknown lanes. There is also always a known DNA not associated with the case for which you know the DNA banding pattern, so that you can determine that everything is working correctly in the case. And then there will be the various samples that were associated with the case. From a sexual assault sample, that would usually entail a DNA sample from the alleged victim and the alleged suspect, and female DNA from the swabs which were collected, and then male DNA from any sperm which might have been on those swabs. So there will be a total of, I think, seven lanes loaded beside the DNA mark."

Dr. Herrin explained that in some 98% of the cases of sexual assault where vaginal cells are collected on the swab taken from the victim by the examining physician or nurse at the hospital (and placed in the rape kit) will contain the victim's own DNA, and "is a great internal control because it allows you to know that the swabbings that you're testing did, in fact, come from the victim."

Thus, not only would the test in such case identify the perpetrator's DNA, but also that of the victim herself.

CROSS EXAMINATION
BY DEFENSE ATTORNEY CELLA:

For forty pages, Marc Cella cross-examined Dr. Herrin in an effort to find any weaknesses or contradictions in his testimony. The thrust of this questioning was to attack the methodology as used in forensics rather than in paternity cases—that the population data bases utilized by laboratories were insufficient, and further that the power of any match between a defendant's DNA and that of the accuser is greatly exaggerated, he claims.

Mr. Cella: "In forensics like you're talking about here, you're comparing DNA autorad from a suspect against a population database that purports to represent every individual of that person's race, isn't that right?"

Dr. Herrin: "I'm not really sure if I understand the gist of your question."

Cella: "Okay. Let me see if I can make it a little clearer then. The last step, what is the purpose of the last step of your procedure where you compare it in the database?"

"I simply give an approximation of how frequently you would expect to see any particular banding pattern in the general population, not an absolute number but an approximation."

"Now, if that approximation is going to be valid at all, your database has to meet a certain set of standards as representativeness, doesn't it?"

"Well, as I stated yesterday, I don't know of any standards that have been established for developing a database for RFLP methodologies."

"Okay. When you're setting up your lab with the Georgia Bureau of Investigation, are you comparing your tests to a similar database that's intended to represent the entire Caucasian population of the United States?"

"Well, my database, after comparison with other databases, is very similar to those collected in other states and other regions of the country, but my primary concern was to get a database of Georgia residents because I felt like those would be the people who would be most likely to be needed to be compared against, not Georgia natives but Georgia residents."

Mr. Cella questioned the existence of different percentages of certain DNA profiles in the country due to the term "population substructure."

Dr. Herrin: "That's what it's referring to with respect to RFLP methodologies, but again, I have not seen any data that show a significant difference between populations from various states or regions of the country."

"How many people do you use to represent the Caucasian population of Georgia in your database?"

"We have between 280 something and 290 something people, depending on which probe you're looking at."

Cella: "Are you telling us, then, that it is commonly accepted among the people who work in this area, that is, human geneticists, that you can get an accurate database using 280 individuals to represent six and a half million?"

Witness: "There are a great many human geneticists who agree that the databases are adequate, that have been collected by the various laboratories, are adequate to produce the approximations and figures that we are giving at this time, and then there again, there are some who disagree with that contention."

Mr. Cella questioned Dr. Herrin about some minor differences in the Georgia laboratory procedures and that of the FBI.

"Okay. You testified yesterday that, at least the way I interpreted it was that there is no such thing as a false-positive in this business. Do you really believe that?"

"I believe there is no technical way to get a false-positive, yes, sir."

The witness explained:

"False-positive in this setting would mean the incorrect matching of two samples. In other words, saying that a biological sample of specimen came from a particular individual when it, in fact, did not."

"When you were at Cellmark, weren't there two false-positives that were discovered by use of proficiency testing?"

"Well, there was one discovered while I was at Cellmark, and then one that was discovered after I left Cellmark." The witness went on to say that was in 1987 to 1989.

Mr. Cella continued with other inquiries. I would come back on re-direct examination later to emphasize the matter of the false-positives as being not with the technology itself, but human error, the labeling system on the tubes. He had never heard of a false-positive as far as the technology is concerned.

⌘ ⌘ ⌘

Fast forward to 2012—twenty years after the foregoing testimony—and Dr. Herrin is now the Director of the GBI Crime Lab System. He tells me nothing much has changed with the defense experts attacking the testing, whether it is chain of custody (technicalities) or frequency estimates. He says that the frequency estimates from a full DNA profile are usually expressed as one in trillions or higher, although they have gotten away from reporting numbers when they are that high and use a different statement when higher than one in 10 billion. As to the databases, the Georgia unit still uses about 300 persons in its database for each DNA marker. During this period, the Georgia DNA unit has increased its testing from 400 to 500 cases per year to 1500 to 2000 per year. At the same time, the backlog of cases is still almost six months behind, though a high priority case may be completed in two to three days.

I have noted there are few experts who hire themselves out to take issue with the technology used in DNA profiling. Generally, they attempt to find some technicality due to human error which can be proven. At the same time, the evolution and use of DNA testing in criminal prosecutions have proven itself to be the answer to clearing a large percentage of violent crime; cold cases are still being solved every day which would not otherwise have been cleared. In most cases, when the Defense learns of the DNA test results, they plead guilty.

⌘ ⌘ ⌘

I then called Special Agent Audrey Lynch, of the Federal Bureau of Investigation, to the stand to testify regarding the DNA tests done in the case.

Ms. Lynch testified to her qualifications as an expert witness. She received a Bachelor's degree in biology from the University of New Hampshire, a Master's degree in cell biology from the

University of Connecticut, and while attending graduate school, was on a national institute of health pre-doctoral fellowship. She then worked for about 13 years in various disciplines of scientific research. She had worked for the FBI for about 11 years, and at present, was in the DNA unit.

The witness had previously testified as an expert in DNA profiling in criminal cases about 18 times, though she had tested in excess of 300 cases. Most cases do not go to trial—they plead guilty. She routinely receives proficiency testing—known as quality control—in house on a quarterly basis, and has never made any mistakes in proficiency testing.

I then offered the witness as an expert in the field of molecular biology, specifically in DNA profiling. Defense Counsel Cella decided he would cross-examine her on her expertise or qualifications to give an opinion as an expert in her field of endeavor.

VOIR DIRE EXAMINATION
BY DEFENSE COUNSEL MARC CELLA:

"Ms. Lynch, are there a set of standards among the scientific community that you must meet in order to be considered an expert in DNA profiling?"

"At this present date, throughout the country, no, there is no set of standards that every laboratory must adhere to."

"And is there any sort of board certification that you hold, certifying by any group that you are an expert in DNA profiling?"

"Again, at this date, I am not. There is no certification that I am taking part in. The FBI Laboratory to date does not take part in a certification program. And actually, in the area of DNA profiling, I can't think of any organization that, at this time, is giving that type of an accreditation in that field."

Likewise, there was no relevant body for which the FBI laboratory had been certified in the field of DNA profiling.

Counsel obviously wanted to show there was no certification boards for which DNA profiling had been recognized, and that the methodology for DNA testing was somewhat of a recent technology as used in forensics—although testing had been done in most states by this time and admitted in evidence in many states in criminal cases. [The law does not require that laboratories or experts (in general) must be certified by "boards," only that experts be qualified by education and training.]

"How long have y'all been doing DNA profiling in the FBI?"

"It's been approximately three years. The FBI Laboratory began to actually accept forensic cases in December of 1988."

Judge Brantley ruled the witness would be received as an expert witness. He then sent the jury to lunch, to return at the appropriate hour, advising them of interruptions which would have him busy at certain times for which he would release them early that evening. Judge Brantley, throughout the trial, kept the jurors advised of potential interruptions and of a time-line of the trial for which he and the lawyers were trying to keep. He had been pushing me and Mr. Cella about holding to the time line, while telling the jurors a trial was somewhat like that of an "unrehearsed play" and hard to predict how long it would take.

FURTHER DIRECT EXAMINATION
BY MR. MALLARD:

I now would have the witness go through an introduction to the jury about DNA. While her preliminary testimony will be essentially the same as Dr. Herrin, it will overlap somewhat; however, I want to show the jury that both the Georgia and FBI labs adhere to basically the same procedures, and their expert opinions about DNA profiling in general are the same.

"Ms. Lynch, would you first tell us very briefly what is DNA and where do you find it in the body?"

As did Dr. Herrin, the witness recounted the introduction to DNA, its makeup, where it is found, and its value in forensics.

"Is this technology, the RFLP technology utilized in DNA profiling, is it used solely by the FBI laboratory?"

"No. This procedure is utilized by forensic laboratories both private and state forensic laboratories throughout the United States, Canada, European countries, England. It's also utilized in other disciplines such as paternity testing laboratories and also for medical diagnostic purposes."

Without repeating, I then had Special Agent Lynch go through the testing procedures with the jury—as did Dr. Herrin—with some illustrations and overheads, depicting each step of the RFLP process.

She continued:

"Everything that I do as far as drawing any type of conclusion or interpretation is based on a side-by-side comparison. It's based on the DNA profile that I obtain in a body fluid stain, such as a semen stain on an item of evidence, with the DNA profile that I see in a known blood sample from an individual."

The witness explained the numbering system, that an item of evidence from a crime scene will have "Q" (for questioned) numbers and "K" (for known) numbers designated as known samples from certain individuals, and that a comparison is based on a side-by-side examination to determine a "match."

She continued: "So my first conclusion that I can make is called, we call it a match. A match means that the DNA profile that I observe on an item of evidence matches that of the known blood sample from an individual, and that means that individual could be the source of that body fluid.

"In looking at this, I will also explain a little bit more of it. This is just an illustration, but it's an illustration of what is known as an autoradiogram, and those are the final products which I will base my conclusions on. On all those, and here you see lanes with multiple bands in them. These are called size marker lanes, but they can be thought of as a ruler. It's a ruler that I lay down on my gel that will allow me, using a computer-assisted program, to actually measure the size of the various bands that I observe in the DNA profiles.

"On every autorad, I'll call it that for short, you will also see in this lane over here, its designated CL. That stands for a cell control. It's a known source of human DNA which we know the results of it. We run that on every test to ensure, and so that we will be sure that the results we are getting are accurate and a valid result. Here, also on the Q1, will represent a vaginal swab on which a semen stain has been identified. With DNA, we have the ability through a procedure known as differential extraction to separate the DNA from the female from the DNA from the male.

"What I mean here is whenever you're dealing with semen stain, especially on a vaginal swab, you're going to have a mixture of body fluid from two sources, semen from the male donor, and epithelial cells, these are just cells from the vaginal vault of the female. With DNA, through this procedure, you can separate the female DNA. This is the DNA that comes from her own cells and would be expected to match the known blood sample from the female, or victim in the case, from the male DNA, which would represent the DNA that came from the sperm cells in the semen that was deposited in the vaginal vault of the victim.

"So looking at Q1, which the M meaning the male fraction representing the DNA from the semen on the swab, we want to make a comparison to our known samples. In this case, K1 was a known sample this is still just an illustration, but a known sample from the victim, the female. K2 represents a known sample from a Defendant or suspect in a case.

"So what I will do is just simply do my side-by-side comparison. I look at the positions of the bands in the male fraction of the item of evidence and compare it to my known samples. These two line up. They're in the same position and line up as the two bands in the known sample from the Defendant in this illustration. That would be called a match, and that would mean that this individual could be the source of the semen on that vaginal swab. And the male fraction lines up and matches the known sample of the victim, which that's what we expect, and that's what we always see because the swab came from that victim and has her DNA on it. So this is one conclusion I can make, a match.

"Number two conclusion is everything in the same setup. Here again, we have the known samples from the victim, from a defendant or suspect in a case, and here we have questioned items. In this case, you can see that the DNA profiles in the question items do not match either of these samples. That is a no match, and that's an absolute exclusion. When I have a no match, it means that the body fluid on this item, the semen or the blood, could not have come from either of those individuals, and that's absolute exclusion.

"The third conclusion is just an inconclusive, meaning I have insufficient information to make a determination one way or the other, whether it's a match or a no match. It's just an inconclusive result."

The witness explained that an "inconclusive" result may arise from an insufficient amount of DNA or degradation of the sample.

With that programming of the jury on the process, I moved the witness into the actual receipt of the evidence from the Georgia

Bureau of Investigation Crime Laboratory, and the testing done in each of the four rape cases.

Special Agent Lynch identified the exhibits received. She went over the markings, her initials, and numbers given each item so there would be no issues about quality control of the products after receipt into the FBI Laboratory. Agent Lynch testified that when received, the Federal Express envelope containing the items was sealed and showed no signs of tampering. She identified all four cases:

State's Exhibit 2A was marked Q1 & Q2 = vaginal swabs from Linda Linnard

State's Exhibit 2B was marked K1 = known blood from Linda Linnard

State's Exhibit 3A was marked Q1 = vaginal swabs from Melissa Hilyard

State's Exhibit 3B was marked K1 = known blood from Melissa Hilyard

State's Exhibit 4A was marked Q1 & Q2 = vaginal swabs from Frances Stanford

State's Exhibit 4B was marked K1 = known blood from Frances Stanford

State's Exhibit 5A was marked Q1 & Q2 = vaginal swabs from Donna Hightower

State's Exhibit 5B was marked K1 = known blood from Donna Hightower

State's Exhibit 5C was marked K2 = known blood of defendant, Terry Greenway

I asked the witness whether she followed the procedures and steps which she had illustrated to the jury earlier in her testimony.

"Yes, I did. The procedure that I previously described is a standard procedure or protocol that's followed in every case that we work in the laboratory."

She testified that [she] will run four probes in every case tested in the laboratory, meaning that she is looking at four different places within a person's DNA.

"And with regard to the Linnard case, would you tell us what your conclusions you reached are in that case."

"Based on my side-by-side comparison of again, the DNA in the male fraction from the vaginal swab with the known samples that were submitted to me, I determined that the DNA in the male fraction on the vaginal swabs matched that of the K2 sample which was the known blood sample from the Defendant, Mr. Greenway." [Greenway was identified as leaving his DNA in the vaginal swabs of the victim, Ms. Linnard.]

The witness explained it was a three-probe match. Although the fourth probe was a visual match, she did not use it in her calculations—as a conservative approach—because she could not determine whether it was a one-banded or a two-banded pattern with a 100 percent certainty, explaining there could have been two bands so close together that they appeared as one.

"And what was your interpretation as far as frequency of occurrence with regard to the case of Ms. Linnard on the three bands that you used in your statistical analysis?"

After an objection by Mr. Cella on technical grounds as to whether her probability statistics were based on sufficient and reliable data, and the court overruling the objection, the testimony continued. These issues had been determined in pre-trial hearings.

Ms. Lynch: "Based on the Caucasian database that we were utilizing at the time [C2] I did my analysis in this case, I determined that the probability of selecting at random an unrelated individual from the Caucasian population who would have a profile that matched that of the K2 sample from Mr. Greenway, the Defendant, was approximately one in 80,000."

The witness explained that the data in Ms. Linnard's case was later ran on another database the FBI was using, the C3 database which had been enlarged from the C2, and arrived at different results. Mr. Cella again vigorously objected, complaining of a lack of notice. After lengthy arguments, pointing out that at the pretrial hearings, the C3 database was acknowledged by the defense expert (who testified).

Mallard: "Ms. Lynch, you were about to tell us in comparing the Linnard statistics to the C3 database, what did you come up with at that point?"

Ms. Lynch: "Using the C3 database, the probability of randomly selecting an unrelated individual from the Caucasian population who would have a profile that would match the K2 sample from the Defendant, Mr. Greenway, would be approximately one in 140,000."

"So it had changed from one in approximately 80,000 to one in approximately 140,000. What is the difference in the C2 and the C3 database?"

"The difference is the number of individuals. The C2 database had approximately 225 individuals, whereas the C3 had approximately 750 Caucasian individuals."

The C2 database was selected from individuals who were in training to be special agents at Quantico, Virginia. The C3 database was comprised of the C2 individuals as well as known blood samples from Caucasians in Florida, Texas, and California. Persons within the C2 database were agents in training from all over the United States, and not centralized in one area. *The witness testified, as did Dr. Herrin, that small databases favor the defendant as indicated by the foregoing.*

We then moved to the second case victim, Melissa Hilyard, where Agent Lynch, based on a side-by-side comparison of the

DNA profile, found the semen on the vaginal swab from Melissa Hilyard matched the profile from the K2 sample which was the known blood sample from defendant, Terry Greenway. There was only one swab provided and tested from the rape kit of this victim, but two swabs were provided and tested from the other three victims.

Based on the C2 database being utilized at the time of testing, the probability in this case of selecting an unrelated individual from the Caucasian population who would have a profile that matched the K2 sample from the defendant was approximately one out of 7,000, utilizing only three of four probes.

In the case of the third victim, Frances Stanford, a comparison of the male fraction of the semen identified on the swabs coming from the victim to the known sample from Defendant Greenway was a match between the DNA from the semen on the swabs with the K2 sample from the defendant's known blood. For the same reasons, only three of the four probes were utilized in the calculations which resulted in approximately one in 80,000 using the C2 database and approximately one in 140,000 using the C3 database.

In the fourth case (victim Donna Hightower), Agent Lynch found a match between the DNA profile from the male fraction taken from the vaginal swabs of Donna Hightower with the DNA profile of the K2 sample from the known blood sample of the Defendant, Terry Greenway. The frequency of occurrence was the same as number one and number three, hereinbefore, one in 80,000.

Mallard: "Were any of these autoradiographs or probes run, was there in any way any indication of an exclusion of the Defendant as a suspect in this case?"

"No. There was nothing at all that would have excluded the Defendant in this case."

Agent Lynch testified that in each case, she first did a visual interpretation of the auto-rads for a match, which was followed by a "computer-assisted" program to verify the match. She explained the power of the match:

"We've been talking in terms of the possibilities in terms of numbers such as one in 80,000, meaning the probability of selecting an unrelated individual in the population who would have a profile that would match that of the K2 sample from Mr. Greenway, it would be approximately one in 80,000. Another way of looking at it is to look at percent of the population. Based on these results, I can either include individuals as potential source of the body fluid on the swabs, or I can exclude them.

"An exclusion would be an absolute exclusion. It could not have come from that person. An inclusion means that person could be the source. Looking at it this way, you can look at the percent of the population based on my results. Using the C2 database [...] approximately .0011 percent of the Caucasian population are included. That means approximately .0011 percent could be the source of the semen found on the vaginal swabs.

"Based on my analyses of the K2 sample from Mr. Greenway, he is included in this .0011 percent, but that also means that 99.9989 percent of the population could not have left that semen stain on that swab. This is an absolute exclusion of this percent of the population.

"Then, going to the C3 database in which we were talking about one in 140,000, in this case, .0007 percent of the population are included as potential sources of the semen on those swabs. Again, by analyzing Mr. Greenway's known blood sample, the K2 sample, he is included in this .0007 percent that could have left that stain. But that means that 99.9993 percent of, again, we are speaking of the Caucasian population are excluded. This percent could not have left that stain because they just do not have the DNA profile that I observed in my analyses."

While the jury is no doubt having some difficulty with understanding "population genetics," I am sure that Mr. Cella on cross examination will emphasize the number of others in the Caucasian population which could have the same DNA profile as the Defendant. I will deal with that on a re-direct of the witness after Mr. Cella finishes his cross-examination.

CROSS-EXAMINATION
BY MR. CELLA:

"Ms. Lynch, you testified in a motions hearing in this case that these probability estimates are only valid if we assume that the database that y'all use is representative of the Caucasian population of the United States. And that is still your testimony, isn't it, that these results are invalid if the database is not fairly representative of the Caucasian population of the United States?

"Correct. The databases are representative of the U. S. population, Caucasian population in this case, and so it's valid, in my opinion, to certainly utilize."

A colloquy followed between the witness and Mr. Cella regarding whether it would be more appropriate to have a southern or Georgia database, with the witness contending that the FBI database of special agents were sufficient, with the witness continuing:

"We also have compared our database with databases from various crime laboratories, approximately a dozen throughout the country, and in doing those comparisons in the Caucasian population have seen, again, no significant differences. So the database is representative of the U. S. population, regardless of which geographical region you are in."

Cella: "You said all the scientists who have reviewed the FBI's various databases agree that it's representative of what it purports to represent?"

"If I said all, I did not mean all. I meant to say it has been reviewed by scientists outside the FBI."

"Yes, ma'am. And some agree that it's representative, and some don't agree that it's representative; isn't that right?"

"Yes. There are individuals that do not agree."

"Okay. Now don't you feel a little bit uncomfortable assuming that 225 individuals fairly represent the entire Caucasian population of the United States in view of the fact that we've only been using these probes since 1987?"

"No, I do not for several reasons. There has been; you can find it in basic genetic texts. You can find it in numerous scientific peer-reviewed articles where populations of as low as 150 individuals are adequate for the operational purposes that we are using. Also, again, that's another reason that the fixed-bin approach is used by the FBI laboratory. The statistical method we used was intentionally designed to also compensate for smaller population sizes, but there are numerous individuals that say that a database of 100, 200, or several hundred is certainly adequate for what we are doing."

The thorough and sifting cross-examination for some 60 pages continued with Mr. Cella probing the witness's testimony in efforts to show weaknesses regarding disagreements between experts in the scientific community concerning databases being used by the FBI, statistical calculations, power of the match with probability estimates, rarity of the DNA profile in the population, probes used, and every aspect of the testing process including band match window criteria (the maximum variation, plus or minus, of a determined match).

"So this means that 2,000 people's banding patterns on your autoradiograms would fall within the same bin and therefore be suspects in this case according to the technology as it exists today?"

"Yes. That means that approximately 2,000 individuals in the Caucasian population of the United States would be expected to have this same composite DNA profile that I observed on the three probes that I did the match calculations."

Mr. Cella: "Nobody knows where those 2,000 people are. They could all be here in Marietta, couldn't they?"

Ms. Lynch: "That's possible. I think that's extremely unlikely, but it's possible."

[This point seems to undercut the force of the 'match' as I had anticipated, and I will return on re-direct and offer a more practical view of the probabilities.]

"Because your database is only looking at a couple of hundred people instead of all 200 million, right?"

"Correct. But it's still a rare event, and based on the calculations, we've already said that based on probabilities, which are estimates, you could approximate that there may be approximately 2,000 people in the total United States that would have that profile."

Upon Mr. Cella completing his cross-examination, I asked for a re-direct examination.

REDIRECT EXAMINATION
BY MR. MALLARD:

"Were all measurements in these four cases well within the matching rule of the FBI?"

"Yes. As a matter of fact, they were very tight. I previously told you that the match criteria is plus or minus 2.5 percent. Within each one of these cases, the bands between the DNA profile on a male fraction of the swab and that of the known blood sample from the Defendant, Mr. Greenway, were within plus or minus 1 percent. That's much tighter than 2.5."

"So it wasn't even close to the outside bounds then?" I asked.

"No, not at all."

"You did some calculations for Mr. Cella, and if I can go over that, I believe you indicated [200] million, the estimated Caucasian population. Are you being very generous to the Defense with that figure?"

"Yes."

"And then we got down to approximately 2,000 persons in the population of the whole United States, they could have that profile; is that correct?"

"Yes, using the information from the C2 database, which was the figure one in 80,000."

[Now I will place the potential 2,000 suspects in proper perspective.]

"And does that include females?"

"Yes. That number reflects the general population Caucasian population which is male and female."

"Of course, over 50 percent of the population are females, aren't they?" [And, would be eliminated.]

"Yes."

"So then we would have, then, even by these generous figures, 1,000 males, white males, in the population; is that correct?"

"Yes."

"And these figures would include the 200 million, I believe included also perhaps Hispanics, did they not?"

"Correct."

"But you also have a separate Hispanic database do you not?"

"Yes. We have a black database, a Caucasian, as well as a Hispanic database."

Mallard: *"So using these gratuitous figures, then, let's see, 1,000 white males, let's say, in the whole United States. If you [got] 50 states, how many would you have in each state, or approximately in the State of Georgia?"*

Witness: *"If they were evenly distributed, you'd have 20."*

[By probability estimates, the 2000 figure has now been reduced to 20 in the State of Georgia. After all, we obviously have a local serial rapist over a period of years in a very small geographical area of Cobb County.]

"20. And assuming there [is] 159 counties in the State of Georgia, would you estimate approximately eight counties per profile?" Does that sound right?" [159 divided by 20. One such DNA profile to be found within an eight county area, statistically.]

"I see what you're saying, yes."

"And then, of course, even with this figure, we are not even talking about the age factor, are we?"

"Correct. That would represent males of all age from very young babies to elderly men." [And, we were looking for a rapist in his 30s or 40s.]

"Now, let's say we are looking at our suspect as being [...] a white male in his 30s or 40s. So this figure still represents the age from birth to death, does it not?"

"Correct."

"So in looking at the age group 30s or 40s, we would still reduce this figure, would we not?"

"Correct. Because there are going to be certain ages that would not be capable of ejaculation."

By now, hopefully, the jury could see that with probability statistics, we have identified the only person in North Georgia with the DNA profile who would be capable of raping the victims in this case.

Mr. Cella could not leave it alone and asked for re-cross examination.

RECROSS EXAMINATION
BY MR. CELLA:
"And that little numerical exercise you went through has absolutely no foundation in genetics, does it?"

Witness: "The foundation, it's only laying in probabilities, and that's what we are talking about was probabilities."

The witness was released.

While 16 autoradiographs were introduced into evidence—four probes for each of four rape cases—one below at random is being shown as an example of their appearance.

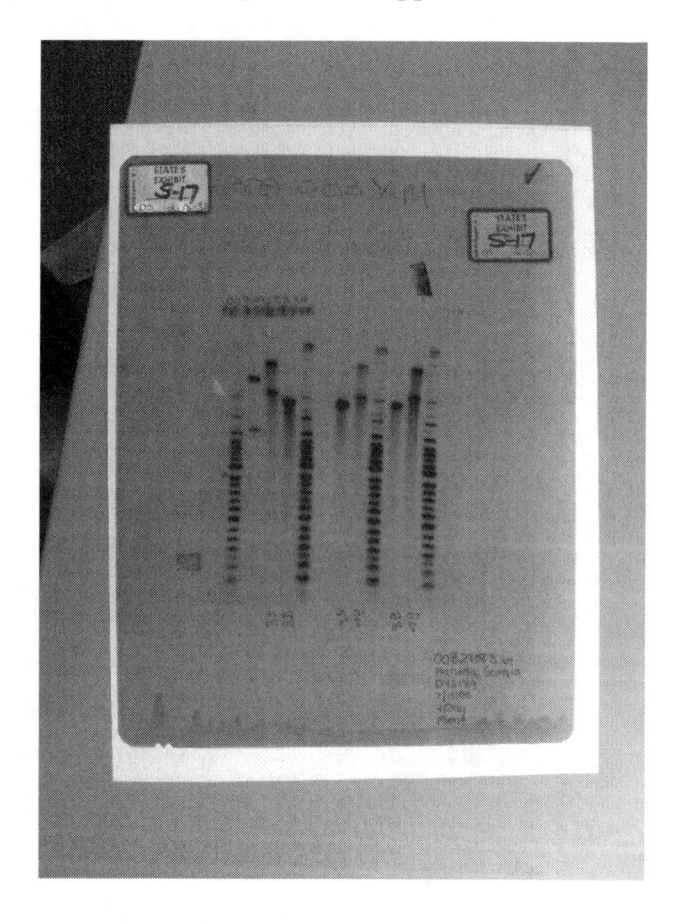

I next called to the stand, Dr. Wyatt Anderson, a professor in the genetics department at the University of Georgia, and former head of the department, for whom a research laboratory was named. Dr. Anderson participated in the formation of their genetics department 12 years before. Following his Doctorate at Rockefeller University, he taught at Yale University. While at the University of Georgia for 20 some years, he served in teaching, research, and laboratory work. His specialty was population genetics: the very issue upon which the defense had focused their attack. This was the reason I procured him as a witness. He was a member of the National Academy of Sciences, unlike the defense expert witness who would later testify.

"Dr. Anderson, is it a scientific fact that everyone, except identical twins, have different DNA that can be identified?"

"Yes. We expect almost everyone to have different DNA, except for identical twins who have copies of the same single fertilized egg."

"Do you have reason to know about identical twins?"

"Yes. I am an identical twin, and, in fact, I had just several months ago, I got a sample of blood from my brother and contributed some of my own, and the state crime lab did a DNA fingerprinting on us for five probes, and we turned out as we guessed we would to be identical."

Dr. Anderson testified that he was familiar with the FBI's protocols and methodology in DNA profiling, and that he had received the lab notes, autoradiographs and records in the cases now before the court involving the defendant, Terry Greenway.

"And have you had a chance to review and study the results and conclusions reached by the FBI lab in those four cases?"

"Yes, I have. I have gone carefully over each of the autoradiographic films and checked for matching of all the bands which are part of it. And I have also taken some time to study the FBI's method for calculating probabilities of these patterns, DNA patterns, in the population, and I believe that they are accurate."

I asked the witness if he was aware of the issues that have been raised (by the defense) in the case, which he was.

Mallard: "And would you first tell me whether or not there is any objection to using the multiplication rule in your statistical analysis."

Dr. Anderson: "Some biologists have raised objections, but I do not feel that they are valid. I believe it's perfectly reasonable to multiply across loci, across the probes, to obtain an estimate of the overall frequency or probability of a DNA pattern. There have been a number of studies of these human data sets, and they indicate there is no departure from statistical independence which would require that you treat them separately. They can, in fact, be multiplied. In my opinion, it's a perfectly valid procedure. It's based on one of the basic principles of genetics."

I asked Dr. Anderson about the sufficiency of the FBI's two databases, i.e., 225 and 750.

"The smaller database, the C2, I believe, is adequate although it is smaller than you would like. 750 is much better. The bigger the database, the better the information you can hope to get. But the database of 225 is, I believe, still adequate. *And for statistical reasons, a small database will actually favor the Defense.* A larger database may not, but, of course [...] you'll have an opportunity to estimate frequencies better. And in this case, both databases have been utilized with, I gather, the same results."

"Do you, in this case involving the four tests, do you consider this to be a rare, a very rare event from the estimates reached by the FBI?"

"Yes." [He goes on to use the figures from each of the four cases.]

Dr. Anderson commented on the sub-structuring of the population issue raised by the defense, as well as the FBI's conservative binning procedures, and found no problems.

"Finally, let me just ask you this. Do you consider the evidence in the Greenway case and all four of these matches to be valid and conclusive?"

"Yes. I believe the match is very clear, and the probability calculations are arrived at correctly."

With that, I yielded the witness for cross-examination. I knew the witness could with-stand a vigorous cross examination by defense counsel.

CROSS-EXAMINATION
BY MR. CELLA:

Mr. Cella pounced on the witness immediately by asking him whether he knew three other named experts around the country.

"And you're also familiar that all three of those gentlemen have leveled severe criticism at the use of these databases in calculating frequencies in the general population; is that not true?"

"Yes, that is true."

"And you disagree with every one of them?"

"I disagree with every one of them. I, and actually a very large number of other people who you've not named, do, in fact, disagree strongly."

"When you testified in the Caldwell case, did you not determine that using the product rule in that case was inappropriate?" [The prior Georgia case in which I had utilized the witness.]

"No. I did use the product rule in that case."

"When you testified in the Caldwell case, was there some question about whether the probes used by Lifecodes were in Hardy-Weinberg equilibrium?"

"In order to avoid any problems with Hardy-Weinberg equilibrium, I had the Lifecodes Company do a different kind of calculation. It was more conservative. Since that time, evidence has accumulated assuming Hardy-Weinberg is a reasonable thing to do. So in this particular case, the calculations which the FBI has used do assume this Hardy-Weinberg equilibrium, and I believe it is reasonable. It is a matter of accumulating evidence. It's not changed my mind, but it seems to me more reasonable to do now. I was more cautious then at the onset of DNA fingerprinting in trials."

Mr. Cella continued with his probing inquiries in an attempt to find some difference of opinion of the witness with other experts and those who had testified in the case, with minimal, if any, success.

"Is there not a substantial body of evidence that the probes D1S7 and D17S79 are not in Hardy-Weinberg equilibrium?"

"I do not believe so. There was some early formulations by Eric Lander which suggested there were, but subsequent to that, a group at Yale University have shown that, in fact, his calculations were biased and that Hardy-Weinberg equilibrium seems to account quite well for the data."

They continued with their verbal combat over articles published on the matter for some time, with the witness concluding:

"It's a matter of some controversy, but I believe that the evidence is very strong that DNA fingerprinting is validly applied and that both Hardy-Weinberg and linkage equilibrium are not problems in the calculations of the probabilities with which these fragment patterns in individuals occur. They are reasonable estimates of how many people in the population might have these patterns in common, and, in fact, the conclusion from this paper, as you know, says that therefore, in the forensics setting, we conclude that an innocent suspect has little to fear from DNA evidence unless he or she has an identical twin, which, of course, made me wonder about my brother. But I believe *that* conclusion is valid."

After some further lengthy cross examination over several hours, Mr. Cella completed his cross-examination without appearing to place a dent in the witness' testimony.

At that time, I arose and told the court that
THE STATE OF GEORGIA RESTS ITS CASE!

VII

THE DEFENSE EVIDENCE

The Defense DNA Testimony

Mr. Cella did not surprise me by calling his DNA expert witness, Dr. Ronald T. Acton, a professor in the Departments of Microbiology and Epidemiology, School of Public Health at the University of Alabama. He recited his education which included his doctorate degree at the University of Alabama, post-doctorate fellow training in immunogenetics at California Institute of Technology and one year at Oxford University in England. His experience and education were impressive. He testified he had experience in utilizing the restriction fragment length polymorphism (RFLP) technology (as was in use at the present DNA profiling) in 4,000 cases.

Dr. Acton was critical of the FBI databases (as being more national) as compared to his own Alabama databases, which he said was more representative of the people of Alabama. He discussed the settlements of French, Spanish, English, and Indians, in his state's early history, and thought there was an issue of population substructure. It was interesting, and he said that "Alabama differs from the frequency in certain genes compared to these other areas with regard to certain of these genes."

The witness was generally critical of the FBI's method of collecting the individuals in their databases, as well as the size of it. He further testified that he thought there was a problem with population substructure: that the FBI database is not representative of the frequencies in the relevant population, and you would be unable to draw the conclusions which they had drawn as to the probability estimates and, further, that the "fixed-bin paper that two of the three probes used are not what we call in Hardy-Weinberg equilibrium."

Dr. Acton suggested, "The best way, most scientific, valid way to answer that question, which we do all the time in genetics, is to collect a large enough sample where you can go through the population. And you're talking about needing thousands of people. Now it's been calculated you may need 20,000 ..." [although his own database has nothing like that.] The day was long, and the testimony was boring. Judge Brantley took a recess for the day. I was concerned that the jury was not able to reconcile between the differences in this technical language. The witness was throwing up objections and concerns he had with the testing technology, as well as the FBI's work in the case. Of course, I had heard the same objections a year before against the testing done by Lifecodes Lab (one of the big two labs in the country doing DNA testing).

At one point, Mr. Cella asked his expert witness about the consensus among experts in the field of DNA profiling, and he stated:

"Well, I won't say it's a consensus because this whole issue of the application, all the issues we've been talking about, the lack of standards, no uniform match criteria, all labs use a different match criteria, and the population genetic issue are all subjects of very heated controversy within the scientific community."

[What! If he has such disdain for the validity of DNA profiling in general, why has he done 4,000 cases as he claimed. I'll also note this for cross-examination.]

[Could it be that he is the only one who does it right? And, almost all states, the FBI, and the independent labs, are all doing it wrong? Or, could it be that he is making a good living going around the country as an expert witness and 'bashing' other labs' work—when it suits him to do so. I knew from the previous *Caldwell* case that Dr. Acton was one of the *Defense Expert Witnesses* in DNA cases who was being used as a 'so-called' hired gun. More later.]

Proceedings resumed on February 20, 1992.

Dr. Acton continued with comparing the way he does things in his lab, with the FBI, and going over the same issues in an effort to show the probability estimates testified to by the State's witnesses (which he claimed had no basis for their opinions).

Finally, Mr. Cella turned the witness over for cross-examination.

CROSS EXAMINATION
BY MR. MALLARD:

I immediately recalled to him that we had met before: in June (of last year) during pre-trial hearings in this case, and a year before that in the *Caldwell* case. I then asked him if he had changed his mind about anything he had previously testified about in court. He said not that he could recall. I had his testimony just in case. *I also had information from other cases he had testified in around the country. Networking among prosecutors comes in handy.*

I referred him to his earlier testimony on direct that he had tested 4,000 cases; however, in pressing him about the type cases he tested, it turns out that most of them were paternity, with only about ten cases being forensic cases—and only two being rape cases.

Dr. Acton said his lab was increasing the volume of business, the number of cases being tested.

"And you use this RFLP technology, do you?"

"Yes, sir, I do."

"Now, this RFLP technology, you have no problem with that, do you?"

"No. The technology, as in terms of the molecular biology of the technology, is sound within the limitations that I noted, that we have problems resolving it as a limit of the technology, of resolving discrete fragments that differ by certain size ranges, but that's something we have to live with."

Mallard: "And all labs don't use the same protocols, enzymes or probes, do they?"

Dr. Acton: "No. Your probe is dictated by the, obviously, by the question you're asking. I mean obviously, diagnostics you use a specific probe for the disease that you're attempting to learn about."

"And, in fact, you use the FBI protocols, don't you, with minor variations?"

"Right. We use the, basically, the FBI's protocol as modified by – ".

"And you use it for this identity testing in your lab?"

"That's correct."

"Do you use two probes in your paternity testing?"

Dr. Acton testified he previously only did two probes in his paternity testing, but had recently gone to three probes.

"And do you use the same enzymes as the FBI?"

"Yes, we do."

"Do these probes that you use, some of them are the same probes the FBI uses?"

"Three of the probes are the same as the FBI uses."

Dr. Acton testified he got 99.1 percent exclusion in his lab using [only] two probes for most cases, while the FBI are using four probes.

Mallard: "Now, let's talk about population sub-structuring. Is that something that applies only to the FBI, or does that apply to any lab?"

"That applies to any lab."

"And it applies to your lab, too, doesn't it?"

"That's correct."

"And, in fact, you said before, I believe, that's a common problem?"

"That's right. That is the major problem."

"And yet you still do testing, do you not?"

"Well, that's the reason we've invested all this time to get our database for our population that we actually perform testing for, and we have over a thousand blacks and a thousand whites just for Alabama."

"Are you a statistician?"

"No, sir."

"In fact, database study's outside your realm, isn't it?"

"Well, no, database studies aren't. It depends on, database studies include, you know, the sampling, the evaluation of the frequencies. We've actually published quite a number of papers in that arena. But I'm not a statistician, and I can, you know, I can interpret and understand some of the rudimentary statistics used by, I'm certainly, when it gets too far involved, I'm not qualified to do that." [Yet, he was being critical of three experts of the State: one in particular, Dr. Wyatt Anderson, who was highly qualified in this area.]

"In fact, when you were questioned in regard to the study of Lifecodes' database back last year, you brought to my attention the fact you are not a statistician. That's a highly statistical article in referring to databases."

I referred Dr. Acton to my previous inquiry the year before when he was asked about the Devlin article, and asked him whether it was outside his realm.

Dr. Acton: "The Devlin article was an article where they used very sophisticated statistics to ask the question about Hardy-Weinberg, and indeed, I am not qualified to critique those procedures used for that article."

[Yet, a great deal of the witness's testimony has dealt with his criticism of the FBI's probability estimates claiming a Hardy-Weinberg problem. And yes, he uses the same protocols, probes, enzymes as does the FBI and other labs. Notwithstanding his claims of all the common problems in doing DNA profiling, his own lab has increased DNA testing, and one might wonder 'why', if indeed, the technology has so many problems.]

I decided to inquire if he was making big money going around the country testifying.

"Now, you have testified many times, I take it - - ."

"Yes, I have."

He said he had testified in many rape and murder cases, 22 times outside of cases from his own lab. All of his testimonies, except for one for the prosecution, were for the Defendant. He testified against testing done by two of the big private labs, Lifecodes and Cellmark, and of tests done by the FBI.

Mallard: "So you've testified against the labs which do the bulk of forensic testing in criminal cases, have you not?" [Although, he has only done two rape cases in his lab.]

Witness: "Well, I've certainly testified against those. I don't know if they do the bulk of the testing because I don't know what the total numbers are in America or how many of those total numbers they do. But I've certainly testified against their work, yes."

"And you've no doubt testified in cases your own lab has done?"

"That's correct."

"Have you ever bad-mouthed the work that your lab did?"

"No, I don't get up and bad-mouth it."

"Let me ask you, has your procedures ever been recognized nationally as a standard to be followed in forensic testing?"

"Well, of course, there is no standard evaluation for forensic testing - - - and we use the same procedure for paternity as one uses for forensics."

"In view of, Dr. Acton, of all of these common problems which you say that all the labs have, including your own lab, [...] do you intend to stop DNA testing?"

"No."

"Well, don't you have an interest going around the country, knocking other labs?"

"No. I mean I don't have, why would I have an interest? I mean if anything, it would be better if, as scientists, we could all unite and say we all agree that this is the procedures that should be followed. As it turns out, now we are not united as the scientists, as a whole, that have been involved in this."

"Well, how much are you expecting to be paid in this case, including your pretrial testimony?"

"Well, my rate's $100 per hour for pretrial work and $150, and I don't know."

I asked him to estimate, and he said it would be $3,000 or $4,000.

Mallard: "You testified against Cellmark in 1990 in Vicksburg, Mississippi, did you not?"

He did, but didn't remember how much he got paid.

"And what about the Dale case in Maryland?"

Again he didn't know, but it would have been $4,000 or $5,000.

"What about the Alvera case in Florida?"

He said he thought about two to three thousand dollars because it was a smaller case.

He said he had testified in a recent case in Louisiana, and of the 10 or 12 criminal cases he was paid in all those cases.

"Then, of course, you testified in the Caldwell case, the criminal case where Caldwell was prosecuted for raping and murdering his 13-year-old daughter?"

"I testified in that case, yes."

"And you testified on behalf of Caldwell in that case?"

"That's correct."

"And your fees were more in that case, weren't they?" [I was guessing.]

"Yeah. I think over $4,000, a little over $4,000 ... that I recall."

"Did you do a written report of your work and your conclusions in this case, the Greenway case?"

"No."

"You've got nothing in writing?"

"No. I was not asked to generate a report."

"And neither did you do a report in the Caldwell [case] either, did you?"

"No. I was not asked to do a report there either." [It is a common defense trial strategy where defense experts are involved. They seldom put their work and findings in writing because it would need to be disclosed to the prosecution, as are our reports given to the defense. It's like ambushing the prosecution with unknown defense expert testimony at trial.]

Mallard: "So these cases with which you drew all of this money to work up and testify in, you made no report at all of what you did, of your conclusions or anything else?"

"Well, I made a verbal report both to an attorney that I've, of course, testified, but I was not asked to generate a written report." [A verbal report to Defense Attorney.]

"In other words, the Defendant's lawyer didn't ask you to do a written report."

"That's correct. Not a written, I did a verbal." [Without a written report, one may wonder how an expert witness would remember the details of his work in these cases.]

"Are you, by chance, a member of the National Academy of Sciences?"

"No." [But, the jury will remember that the State's expert, Dr. Wyatt Anderson, was.]

[I believe by now I have given the jury something to think about in deciding what credit, if any, to give this witness. Judge Brantley will, at the end, instruct the jury with guidelines on evaluating the credibility of witnesses.]

[But, there is one more curious matter I had noted during direct examination by Mr. Cella. Although I had introduced 16 autoradiographs (x-ray type film of the tests) for the four victims (four for each victim), Mr. Cella never did ask his expert, Dr. Acton, whether or not there was a visual or computer "match" between the DNA of the defendant and that of the DNA left by the rapist.]

Has Mr. Cella set a trap for me to ask the question to learn that Dr. Acton will testify there was *not* a match, in his opinion, and, of course, this witness had never put his opinions or findings in writing? There is a rule of thumb that you should never ask a question for which you do not know the answer. However, I don't always adhere to that rule. In this case, I will inquire. If he says "no" there was no match, I have lost very little, if anything, because with all his critical testimony about the tests—the jury probably thinks there was no match, in his view, or, the jury may not have realized the omission of this critical information.

I then asked the most important questions of the cross-examination:

"Have you viewed the autorads [autoradiographs] in this case?"

"Yes, I have."

"And you weren't asked, but I'll ask you. Is there a match between, a visual match between the sample of Greenway's DNA and that from the vaginal swabs?"

"In the autorads that I evaluated there was, yes."

[I can't believe it, but the importance of what the defense expert has just testified is the Defendant left his DNA in the swabs from the four female victims. There was a 'match.' Now, the only thing left from his testimony is his objections to the probability estimates – what the 'match' means.]

I thought, no doubt this would have a tremendous effect on the jury. This later proved to be true. During deliberations before the verdict, the jurors sent a note to Judge Brantley inquiring whether that was in fact the testimony they heard. Obviously, one or more jurors didn't hear it—but Judge Brantley would not answer the question. Judge Brantley told them it was a factual question he could not answer: they would have to remember the evidence in the case. I asked Judge Brantley to have the Court Reporter go back to the testimony and read the question and answer, but the Jury had not asked for a reading of the testimony, and the Judge refused.

⌘ ⌘ ⌘

Mr. Cella proceeded to call witnesses on behalf of the Defendant, Terry Greenway. Not unusually, he would call some State witnesses whom the Prosecution did not call to the stand, although they may have some minor role in the case. I normally do not call a witness who would not add something to the case—they may be duplicitous, immaterial, or seemingly unimportant to my theory of the case. I may even assume the defense will call the witness, and forego presenting the witness, knowing I will be able to cross-examine the witness for any tidbits of help the witness may have. I do not want to drag the case out with useless information. The defense may want to use the witness to add something to their theory about the case of which I don't share.

Mr. Cella called Sgt. (formerly Detective) William Grogan, Marietta Police Department, to the stand. Sgt. Grogan was asked about the reported rape case by Donna Hightower. Grogan was a Detective in 1988 when Detective Christopher, who responded to the scene, turned the case over to him for a follow-up with a taped interview the next day. I had not called the witness because what the victim told Grogan would be hearsay, but the defense was calling the witness to try to catch the victim in contradictions regarding descriptions, time-lines, how many drinks she had that evening, point of entry, whether another arrested suspect 'strongly resembled' the defendant, and the like. For 20 pages, Mr. Cella questioned Sgt. Grogan with little, if any, help. The victim's recorded statement was in substance consistent with her testimony: it just showed, in some respect, that her testimony was the product of the frailties of a memory (due to time), which goes to her credit. Had she at trial been perfect in all respects in her recollection, I would have been surprised.

On cross-examination, I went over the important aspects of her trial testimony showing her testimony was the same as her recorded statement.

Next, a friend of the Greenway family, Ms. Martha Simmons, was called. She had known the defendant through the Church of God of Prophesy for 21 years, and his wife longer. Mrs. Greenway's father was the pastor. Mr. Cella asked the witness to describe their social interaction in Church activities.

Witness: "We have always attended every state convention, every general assembly, which is in Cleveland, Tennessee. I have some pictures. Could I show these at this time?"

The witness displayed the photographs, including some taken in 1971 at their marriage in Dephilsda Woods. Mr. Cella asked her where that was.

"That is a place where scripture is cut into stone, and you just walk through the Bible. It's like the Commandments and just different things, and they have the largest cross in the world up on top of the mountain."

"Ms. Simmons, over the 21 years that you've known Mr. Greenway, have you come to be familiar with his general reputation in the community of the Church of God of Prophesy?"

"Yes, I have."

"And is that character good or bad?"

"I've only known good character. He has always had a reputation for being a gentleman, just easy to get along with, a very nice person."

Now that the defense has placed Greenway's character in evidence, this permits me to go into anything to the contrary—question the witness about any 'bad stuff.' I felt sure putting up good character witnesses was the decision of the Greenways, not Mr. Cella, for he would have known what I would do with it.

CROSS-EXAMINATION
BY MR. MALLARD:

I asked the witness a few preliminary questions leading up to the thrust of my inquiry, as to the extent of her knowledge of the family, finding that most of her exposure to the defendant was in church. Then, I pulled out the carving knife about defendant's good character.

"What do you think of the reputation and character of a person who admittedly goes down to the strip joints in Atlanta, the bars, the Tipsy Topsy bar and Tattletale's and drinks? Is that character good or bad?"

"I don't think that would be the best character, but then I'm not the judge of a person. That's out of my hands."

"Oh, I think you have judged him. You said he's got good character. Now, my question is what is the character, in your opinion, of a person who would do that?"

"Well, maybe they were not thinking or they were trying to find another outlet in their life to see what life was all about. I don't know, but the only times I have been around Mr. Greenway, he has been a perfect gentleman."

[Of course, I didn't know, or care, what her answer would be. The question and her answer is for the jury to consider. I will be able to disprove good character.]

"What do you think of the character of a person who would become a peeping tom in and about the premises of another person at night?"

"Why are you asking me to judge another person because - - "

"No. I'm asking you what is your opinion of a person, as far as his character, who would peep into other people's residence, apartments, become a peeping tom and invasion of privacy?"

"I don't know a person that's a peeping tom."

"Well, did you know about Mr. Greenway having been arrested and convicted up in Hall County, November 5, 1984, having been arrested at 32 minutes after midnight? You learned of that, did you not?"

"I've heard that, yes." She went on to say she learned about it from the newspapers and other acquaintances.

"And you didn't pray with him over the situation and try to get help for him?"

"No. We always pray about our membership, but I didn't pray with them over the situation, no."

She went on to admit she knew he had a drinking problem, and the church did not agree with that either. She had, likewise, heard about the second arrest in Hall County for peeping tom six months apart from the first arrest.

"Do you know the family so well? Did you know that he and his wife was not living together?"

"Yes, I did."

"And did you know that he was dating another woman prior to his arrest for several years?"

"That happens."

"And did you know that he told that woman that he was not married?"

"I wouldn't know that."

"What would you think of the character of a person, Ms. Simmons, who would at 5:00 o'clock in the morning, 5:11 I believe, to be exact, January 7, 1990, ... would be at the front door of a young lady who was alone with gloves on his hand and a screwdriver in his hand, trying to break in after he has disengaged a light to the apartment. Is the reputation and character of such a person good or bad?"

She said she really had no answer. I didn't expect her to agree with me. Friends who testify in such instances are doing so out of the goodness of their hearts, and do not want to be wrong in their assessment of someone they have befriended. However, the good character testimony has now been damaged beyond rehabilitation—no matter how many more witnesses they have coming. Mr. Cella may now limit the number of character witnesses, knowing what will happen.

The defense next called Ms. Suzanne Rhodes, Property Manager of River Ridge Office Building, who testified that she was responsible for obtaining security for the complex. She said that she knew Terry Greenway as a guard who worked for Future Security, who was responsible for the security at the office tower with eight floors. She said Terry usually worked weekends, from 12:30 to 8:30. Mr. Cella questioned her about Terry's good reputation:

"During the time that you were in this position, did you receive any complaints about Mr. Greenway's attitude toward women, men, or any of the tenants in the building?"

"No. I never received any complaints about anything that I recall about Terry."

The witness went on to testify she never had any problems with Terry's drinking on the job, and that his general reputation was "excellent."

On cross-examination, I went to the heart of her testimony.

"Let me ask you, in hiring a security guard, that's an important position in the sense of trust and so forth?"

"Yes, it is."

"So do you do any checkups on the person you hire as a security guard?"

"Yes, definitely. Of course, in my position, I contracted with another company to hire the security officers, and they were required, as part of my contract, to do a screening of their officers."

She testified that any checkups on applicants would go to their background, whether the person has got a criminal record.

"Did it come to your knowledge that in '84, he had been arrested twice for peeping tom in an apartment complex in Hall County?"

"That came to light after he was arrested, and we were told about it by the security company. We were naturally very upset with them because we felt they should have known that. Their explanation was it was no longer on his record." [Had it not been, I wouldn't have known about it.]

"Let me ask you. Assuming you had known about this, would you still have hired him?"

"No. I would not have been able to. I couldn't justify that." [So much for his excellent reputation.]

Mr. Cella next called Mr. Darryl Hunnicutt, who was Operations Manager at River Ridge Office Building, who testified he was over all property operations, including security. He testified that the defendant, Terry Greenway, was "one of our best guards, most conscientious, that everybody really liked him, and they never had any complaints against him."

Mr. Cella: "Now, did he wear a mustache the whole time he was employed with you?"

Witness: "Yes, sir."

The Defense contended that Greenway had a mustache during the time period of the rapes for which he was on trial, but some victims did not see mustaches. Of course, he had masks over his lower face in some cases.

Very little, if any, cross-examination was necessary. I elicited that he knew nothing about Greenway's frequenting bars in Atlanta, drinking, etc. We were moving through these witnesses fast. Obviously, the Defense must have something more than I had seen so far. The State's case was not threatened at this point.

Mr. Cella next called a relative of Greenway by marriage, who testified that Terry had married her niece 21 years ago. [I won't use her name.]

Cella: "Did you have occasion to get together with Mr. Greenway at a family function in early November of 1988?"

"Yes, I did." She said it was at her sister's golden wedding anniversary on November 12.

"Now, has Mr. Greenway had a mustache the whole time you've known him?"

"Yes, always." She then identified a photo made at the wedding anniversary on November 12 showing him with a mustache.

When presented for cross-examination, I responded:

"I have no questions of Ms. [...]."

Rather than give credence or importance of his having a mustache, I decided to not cross-examine the witness since several photos in evidence of Greenway shows him looking different, and the rape of victim Hightower was on October 15, 1988, not November 12. Furthermore, victim Hightower testified the perpetrator had a cloth over his nose and face.

Mr. Terry Schimmel, Chief Engineer for Bickerstaff Clay Products, Greenway's second employer, was called to the stand. He was asked by Mr. Cella how he knew the defendant.

"Well, Mr. Greenway worked under my direct supervision at our Smyrna, Georgia, location from June of 1985 until February of 1990."

The witness hired Greenway to supervise the manufacturing department, with job duties being in charge of the second shift operations of the forge department, a highly automated production line with about four people. The second shift started at 3:00 p.m. and would go to 11:00 p.m. As the other witnesses testified, Mr. Schimmel had no problems with intoxication or with Greenway otherwise. Further, Greenway had a good reputation: "Excellent."

Cella: "Okay. During the time that he was employed at Bickerstaff, did Terry ever have an accident that resulted in some lost time from work?"

[Suddenly, it hit me for the first time that they were setting up a possible injury related accident at work which would alibi for one of the crimes. The prosecution had no notice or information about the defense witnesses since the State had no right to discover their evidence at that time in history. I would have to see where it goes.]

"Yes, he did. He had an on-the-job injury in March [18th] of 1988." [Well, at least none of the crimes occurred in March of 1988, the next rape occurring on April 10, 1988.]

"What was the nature of the injury to Mr. Greenway on March 18 of 1988?"

"He had a near amputation of one of his index fingers."

"How did it happen?"

"He was helping reassemble a piece of equipment and got his finger in a pinch point."

"Was surgery required?"

"There were, there was some reconstructive surgery that was necessary, including a steel pin and sutures and this sort of thing."

The witness went on to explain Mr. Greenway was hospitalized for about three days, and then had to be off because of the risk of infection. He said Greenway was back to work on April 3rd, a Monday [one week before the April 10th rape]. He was placed on light duty.

CROSS-EXAMINATION
BY MR. MALLARD:

Since the witness had testified to Greenway's good character and lack of intoxication, I went over Mr. Greenway's bad traits as with the other witnesses. He was unaware that Mr. Greenway, after work, went to downtown Atlanta bars with fellow employees. He testified that Greenway's job performance and attendance were good.

Mallard: "But he was out a lot, wasn't he?"

Witness: "No, not necessarily. He wouldn't have been with us for five years if he was a problem. I can promise you that."

[I had known that Greenway worked for Bickerstaff, and had obtained the company records for whatever good they might be—not knowing what might come up.]

Mallard: "Well, other than the injury when he was out injured, he was out on, of course, routinely on vacation, but he was also, starting in '86, out a total of 19 days. Does that sound right?"

"Including vacation, he would have been eligible for ten days of vacation in that 19. I wouldn't say that was unreasonable."

"Well, when it (record) says 'notified plant personnel, he's out', what does that mean?"

"That meant that he called in, and for whatever reason, he was not able to be at work that day."

"And in 1987, did it increase to 23 days he's out? Does that sound unusual?"

"Without scrutinizing the record, I would say that was getting on the excessive side, but again, we wouldn't continue to keep him in our employment if he wasn't satisfactory."

"And then, of course, in '88 when, some of that was injury, but a total of 34 days out. Does that look unusually high?"

A long dissertation followed by the witness suggesting I was "pulling some stuff out of context here."

I responded: "No, I'm not. I said vacation. You mentioned that. I mentioned on-the-job injury. He was out then, and other reasons, tardy, excused tardy, excused, what is that? When he's late for work?"

"That would be when he was late for work."

"And in 1989, he was tardy quite a bit in '89, wasn't he? All personal business, tardy excuse, one, two, three, four, five, six, seven, eight times tardy. That's a little excessive, isn't it?"

[I was making a case for the jury that the records show he pretty much came and went at will, and any attempt to make an alibi for him was futile.]

I asked the witness if he was aware that Greenway had been arrested in 1984 before he went to work at Bickerstaff in 1985. He did not know about it.

"Mr. Greenway didn't tell you about it?"

"No, sir."

"And when he was employed, is there a requirement that applicants disclose this type of incident?"

"There is a place on the application where they are supposed to record it if they have had a problem."

"Apparently, he didn't. Otherwise, you would have known about it."

"That's correct."

Mr. Cella called to the stand, Dr. Michael J. Morrison, an orthopedic surgeon, who performed surgery on Greenway's finger. He testified that he saw Mr. Greenway in March [18, 1988].

Dr. Morrison: "He had suffered a, what we term a contusion laceration involving the outer joint of the right index finger.

There was an open injury into that joint. There was a fracture into the joint involving a bone, and the joint itself had actually been disrupted where the two bones in the progeny joint [were] actually altered to where the joint was unstable."

Cella: "What did you have to do to fix the finger?"

"Well, it was an open injury, and so, you know, he received anesthesia, and then the injury was cleaned up surgically, pieces of tissue that were dirty or dead were cleaned away. The area was explored to see if there were injuries to the arteries and nerves around that area, and then the joint itself was reconstructed by moving soft tissues, the ligaments and all to actually bring the bones together again. And also, the bones themselves which were fractured were brought together and held with, I believe, it was one major pin was used to hold the bones in alignment."

Mr. Cella was obviously trying to convince the jury that the defendant was not physically capable of committing a rape on April 10th, 1988, on Melissa Hilyard.

Cella: "And that pin would have been inserted in the tip of his finger, then, across that joint that we were just talking about, the DIP joint?"

Witness: "That's correct."

"Is there, in general, a loss of strength in the finger as a result of this kind of injury?"

"That's actually variable, but there can be."

Dr. Morrison further testified that this type injury requires rehabilitation by immobilizing and protecting it, and that the pin would typically stay in place for four to six weeks. He said that the pin was actually removed on April 26, 1988 (16 days after the rape).

Cella: "Could you tell us about Mr. Greenway's rehabilitation, where it was, and when it was, and how it progressed?"

"My recollection is that he was splinted, and the finger had a pin in it for approximately six weeks, and then he underwent, I believe, another six weeks, approximately, of physical therapy." The therapy was at another facility and he had no details. There was a partial disability because of the injury.

Although his testimony was straight forward, I needed to cross-examine Dr. Morrison. I would gently inquire into his treatment of Greenway to see if there was anywhere to go with it. The question is whether the defendant could have raped a woman during the time of his rehabilitation period.

"Dr. Morrison, I believe you said that was five percent disability of total body."

He affirmed it was, explaining that the same would be true if the tip of your finger is cut off, that it was an arbitrary standard that tries to say, anatomically, what you're missing in terms of your body function. He said that inserting the pin was to help hold both the two bones in relation to each other.

"When is the next time that you saw him after the 18th?"

He said he next saw him on April 14, 1988, at his office (4 days after the rape).

"And had he progressed okay?"

"A note here says, 'Terry is doing well, and no problems with the skin. Skin is clean, closed, and dry. X-rays show that the pin position was maintained,' and it says that the bone fragments were in the same position that they were placed in at the time of surgery."

It sounds as though rehabilitation and recovery went well.

Dr. Morrison further explained that the splint dressing ran from pretty much the tip of the fingers, and the thumb is free, but four fingers are together.

[No one has testified that Greenway could NOT have been in Ms. Hilyard's apartment on April 10, 1988, raping her—thus no alibi—but the jury, if sympathetic to Greenway, could have some concern over it. This is the only evidence in the case (for defendant) which is simple, and proven without question as to his injury. But, did it prevent him from committing the act of rape?]

Dr. Morrison explained: *"There is a splint over that which you can't see here, and what is over the whole thing is an ace wrap with tape holding it in place [...]"*

Now, I had what the jury would understand, that this was simply one of those temporary "ace wraps" which many athletes and others use in case of sprains, etc. They can be simply removed as necessary from time to time, taking showers, etc., or, when entering a person's apartment, threatening them into submission of rape. Victim Melissa Hilyard had testified she was surprised in bed with a light shining in her face. She made no resistance. The perpetrator commanded that she take off her underclothes. She was afraid for her life, and she could not identify anyone. She would not have seen the bandage in the dark, even if he had not removed it before the rape. I could explain that to the jury in closing argument. It would not raise a reasonable doubt as to his guilt with the overwhelming evidence against him.

After Dr. Morrison's testimony, Mr. Cella announced, "Defense rests, Your Honor."

Somewhat surprising, Mr. Cella did not call defendant's wife to the stand. He probably thought she was what we call a "loose cannon"—that is, someone who is not under control and might blurt out anything in light of how she had involved herself in her husband's defense before trial. Of course, Cella knew as well that I would go down the "primrose path" with her about her husband's past activities.

Judge Brantley informed the jury that all the evidence is before them, and that we would now move into the next phase of the trial.

Closing Arguments -

Judge Brantley then prompted counsel to present our arguments to the jury. **I gave a** preliminary (opening) argument regarding the law of which the court would instruct the jury, and applied those legal concepts to my evidence in the case.

Next, Mr. Cella made his usual detailed, well-presented, lengthy, closing argument emphasizing doubts the Jury should have because of inconsistencies, lack of identifications, and other issues, and because DNA, he says, is not yet at the stage in its development to be reliable.

I returned to the jury with my final closing argument on the evidence presented to the jury and reasons why they should convict on all 14 charges—making sure I covered all issues I felt the defense had raised any questions about. I wanted to ensure that I explained away anything that may have been of concern to the jury. I emphasized that the Defense expert, Dr. Acton, had testified there was a visual match of the autoradiographs in the rape cases, thus agreeing with the State's expert witnesses as to there being a "match" in the DNA test results.

We both utilized over an hour for each side to summarize our view of what had been proven, or not proven.

Greenway marked his 21st wedding anniversary on Thursday, in jail, awaiting a jury decision as to his future.

VIII

THE JURY, VERDICT, AND SENTENCE

Because of the voluminous nature of 14 felony charges, Judge Brantley was required to give lengthy legal instructions to the jury.

After two weeks of jury selection and trial, and having received the instructions, the jurors were sent to the jury room for deliberations. Because of the many charges, witnesses, exhibits, and the lengthy scientific evidence, we did not expect a quick verdict. After selection of the foreperson, Judge Brantley released the jurors under strict instructions about their conduct, to return the next morning to begin deliberations.

While awaiting the verdict—at the office, and then in the courtroom as the jury would deliberate—a prosecutor will always ponder over the case. Could I have done something more to ensure a guilty verdict? I could not think of a single thing I should have anticipated, but did not. I felt at peace about the case. The real tragedy of the whole case was not just the lasting injuries to the victims, but to Defendant Greenway's own family. They waited as well, hoping he would be going home with them!

And then it was over, after about 12 hours of deliberation over a period of about two days, it was reported that the jury of 10 men and two women had a verdict.

The courtroom was quiet while everyone sat impassively awaiting "justice" to be done. A packed courtroom of victims, families, and friends on one side behind the prosecutor, and on the other side behind defense counsel sat the Defendant's wife, family, and friends. *Which side of the courtroom would sigh in relief while the other cry out in anguish as the verdict is read?*

It didn't take long. Judge Brantley came on the bench and announced that the jury had a verdict on all 14 counts. Wow! It had to be guilty. They would not have acquitted in such short time on all counts. The jurors filed into the courtroom and sat in the jury box with the two alternates joining them. I watched each juror as they came through the door, seeking an answer from their eyes and body language. I had over the years seldom missed a "call" as to the verdict. It would be a guilty verdict, I thought.

Judge Brantley asked the Clerk of Court to announce the verdict.

The Clerk quickly read through all 14 counts—announcing "guilty" each time. Mr. Cella requested Judge Brantley to "poll" the jurors: that is, question each juror, individually, in order to ascertain whether this was their verdict in the jury room and that it was, indeed, freely and voluntarily given. I have known, during this process, of a juror having second thoughts, or hesitation, about his or her answer, which would result in the judge sending the jurors back to further deliberate until they thrashed out their problem. But, that was not the case here.

Judge Brantley scheduled sentencing for the next day, February 25, 1992, at 10:00 a.m.

The media was constant during the trial and especially during these last few days in reporting the activities of the day.

After the verdict was read, 'Mandy' Greenway, Defendant's wife, who had been in his corner from the time the charges were made and who had so aggressively fought for him, exclaimed in everyone's hearing, "It's not true. He's not the one who did that. It's not true." Her statement was reported in the local Marietta Daily Journal by Luke Johnson, as was her statement as she approached me shaking her finger in anger, saying to me, "God will take care of you. He'll have the last say in this." Without hesitation, I calmly replied, "He already has, ma'am." She left the courthouse with her teenage sons. She was further quoted as saying, "We've got generations to come who will fight this, if necessary, our grandchildren. It's not over, we're not going to quit fighting." **"The problem is who did this [...] Somebody needs to find out who the real rapist is. He's still out there."** She took me by surprise in getting in my face, shaking her finger at me, but she was acting out her sorrow and frustration.

Some jurors were interviewed and quoted in the paper. Several jurors said the DNA evidence was not the overwhelming factor in the guilty verdict, but just one piece of evidence considered along with everything presented. One victim, Jeannine McClean, who was awakened by her Himalayan cat, Precious, causing the arrest of Greenway, (and who was still nervous after the verdict), was quoted as saying, "He can't come back and get me. Hopefully, he won't hurt anyone else the rest of his life."

The next day at sentencing, Mr. Cella announced that Mr. Greenway's wife, Shermanda, wished to address the court before sentencing. Judge Brantley told her to come forward and was sworn. Mr. Cella asked her to tell the court anything that she would like before sentence is passed to which she responded in a lengthy statement that her husband was innocent, that they were both sorry that any of these women were attacked, but that it was not over. She said they would proceed with their life, and find other evidence. She predicted that the judge was going to give her husband four life sentences plus 155 years. She ended with asking Judge Brantley to look into his heart and into his conscience and let God be his guide. [Apparently, Mr. Cella warned her of what I was going to recommend in sentencing.]

Judge Brantley then asked if the Defendant had anything to say before sentencing, whereupon Greenway spoke for the first time on his behalf, reiterating what his wife had said, adding he was "sorry if anybody's hurt at me; ask, I ask forgiveness. I just ask forgiveness if anybody's hurt at me. I wish I could undo what has been done, but I can't undo it, and all we can do is change the future, and I plan on changing the future." He went on to say he had a drinking habit, and he planned on changing that. He then asked "forgiveness" again from his accusers "like the Bible says." He said he respected Judge Brantley, and the jury for their decision. [He failed to pay any respect to the Prosecutor.]

Judge Brantley then asked me for my recommendations as to sentence to be imposed. I had no reservations in recommending the maximum sentences on each count, as predicted. I pointed out to him that the victims had filed victim-impact statements for him to consider in that they had undergone counseling for years in an effort to overcome these events which would remain with them for their lives, and that there were seven victims and 14 counts—two counts per victim. I said this was not a short crime spree, but offenses which lasted for three years before he was caught—all spread out over a period of three to six months apart. I, then, asked the court to consider separate, distinct sentences as to each victim in the case.

On behalf of the defendant, Mr. Cella asked Judge Brantley to remember the other victims in the case: Mr. Greenway's three young sons and his family and friends.

Judge Brantley announced the sentence, prefacing it with, **"You have come from a county north of this county like a predator, and the women of this county have been your prey. The victims in the indictment have suffered untold misery. Your family, too, is a victim, but they're not one that the court has made, but rather one that you have made. I truly, truly believe that you should spend the rest of your natural life in prison, and I have framed the court's sentence accordingly. I have followed the State's recommendation as to the odd-numbered counts in the indictment. I have not followed their recommendation as to the even-numbered counts."**

He proceeded to sentence Defendant to 60 years total on counts 2, 4, and 6, concurrent with the sentences in the odd-numbered counts. On counts 8, 10, 12 and 14, he assessed 65 years on probation. In the four rape counts, 1, 3, 7, and 11, the sentences were life in prison on each, with 20 years for each of the burglary counts and ten years on the criminal attempt to commit burglary. Judge Brantley stated, "If you should serve it, you would be about 100 years old, further, I assess this 65-year period so that if for some reason the executive branch of government releases you from prison, you will at least be under some court supervision. If you should serve that probated sentence, you would be about 105 years old."

Judge Brantley announced the case was closed. But, nothing is necessarily over! There would be an appeal, but, that would fail, too. Greenway's wife, Mandy, would 'stand by her man'— but not for generations as she had promised when he was sentenced. She apparently gave up on those promises. A few years ago, she divorced her husband and remarried.

IX

THE EPILOGUE

Rape: the Crime

When I began writing this book, I knew I wanted to accurately portray the type of crime that "rape" is to the reader. Having prosecuted many rape cases over four decades, I thought that would be the easiest task I had, but my experience with victims of sexual assaults were, for the most part, limited to "pre-trial interviews," "prepping before trial," "leading them through their testimony" at trial, customarily talking to them after the verdict and explaining what the sentences meant, and explaining how appeals were handled. With hundreds of other cases assigned to my division of the court for trial and disposition, there was insufficient time for the special pre-trial consultation, care, and post-trial follow-up of these "special victims."

I call them "special victims" because I have learned something during recent months while writing and interviewing these victims—those who would still talk about their experiences:

that to this day, over 20 years after their attacks, they still suffer "fallout" from their experiences as a victim. The lasting impact from a sexual assault is so much different than any other crime, which makes it impossible to properly convey to one who has not seen first-hand, as do doctors who examine them after their attack, counselors, victim-advocates, and psychological professionals who see them one-on-one for years and decades later.

Victims of thefts, robberies, arson, you name it, all suffer in some way, other than a monetary loss. In addition, the victims and their families, who suffer from physical assaults and murders, are in a different category from that of women who suffer the invasion and assault of their privacy and person. The fear generated under such circumstances that they will be another statistic; that the intruder will not only rape but will murder (her) in order to prevent an identification; that she has perhaps minutes to live, and the frantic thought processes as how to best deal with the situation—should she fight, resist, scream, or should she submit under this scenario in the hope of living, are all victim considerations. Afterwards, there is the decision of whether to report the crime for fear of subjecting herself to the degrading, insulting, revelation of being a rape victim. Not only will she be the subject of law enforcement inquiries—having to reveal prior personal things she would rather not do, but also knowing that when the accused is arrested (if ever), she will be made to appear dirty by the rapist's attorney upon cross-examination.

So long as the people touched by a violent sexual offense lives, there is no end to the anguish!

I'm speaking of the victims, the victims' families—even the Defendant's own family. Oh, there are so many people decades later whose lives are still in turmoil and hurting from the actions of this perpetrator. I found this out as I spoke to these victims.

I wanted to chronicle the magnitude of people affected by Defendant Greenway's actions, but, at best, it's been hard to do. First, the people he directly victimized! Some, to this day agonized in telling me about how they have been traumatized; then, there are their families, children, and spouses, who were and are still affected. Their lives have been lived in a vacuum-like way, some still fearful of the possibility their predator will get out of prison and still cause them harm. One of the rape victims—who did not want to return to Georgia and testify at trial—would not speak with me, still unable to deal with her experience. Others were still reluctant to speak of (it), but supportive of the effort to touch those victims who refuse to report the crimes or cooperate with authorities.

Some victims' names were changed and other personal information omitted, to protect their privacy.

With that backdrop, I interviewed most of the victims and asked for some update of their lives: What they were willing to share. All had changed in many respects. Some turned to law enforcement, or married husbands who were in public safety while others became teachers. Some armed themselves for self-defense.

The Victims – in their words
Ms. Linda Linnard, who was a rape and burglary victim at her Powers Ferry Apartment on August 26, 1987, told me:

"After the rape, I was an emotional wreck for a long time. I was unable to stay in our apartment by myself nor could I go inside by myself. I either waited in my car until my husband came home or I asked my neighbor to walk me inside. In addition, I started carrying a hand-gun with me AT ALL times (work, grocery store, mall, etc.). I shudder to think what would have happened if someone had made a sudden move toward me. As a matter of fact, there was a situation about a year after the rape where I almost shot my husband when he came home earlier than I expected (that is when I decided to start counseling). I am getting ahead of myself a little. The day after the rape, life for everyone else was going on as usual but, for me, I lived in a fog of sorts; my husband and I took a couple of days off but we had bills to pay, and because we had just moved to Atlanta from Texas and had just started our jobs, we had very little money and no vacation or sick time built up. Going back to life as normal was a struggle but I did it (sort of). My husband had a job that required him to work two nights a week and being in that apartment alone (let alone at night alone) was more than I could handle, so I would go with him.

"One of his jobs was at Georgia Baptist Hospital as a security officer, so I would go and sleep in the women's bathroom then go home the next morning, take a shower and go to work. My husband worked side jobs as an electrician so there were some nights when he was working at a Burger King doing remolding, so I went with him and slept in the car and, again, went home the next morning took a shower and went to work. We did this for about three months. Then emotionally, I just couldn't handle being in that apartment or in that city anymore. I thought that by moving it would help and it did a little; however, evidentially it all came crashing down around me again. We moved to Savannah, which is where my husband and I were both from, so I felt comfortable with the surroundings. We both got jobs, and, after my insurance started, I [began] counseling, which was really the beginning of my healing. I went to counseling once a week for about a year. My counselor helped me little by little take control [of] my life again.

"Now, all of these years later, I still have emotional 'hang-ups' because of that one night. For example, I still have a very hard time staying by myself especially at night. Since my husband and I have been able to afford it, every home that we have owned has had a security system, not because we are wealthy people, but for my peace of mind. There was a time when my husband worked out of town a lot (this was 15 years after the rape), and my mother would have to come from Savannah to Macon to stay with me because I would go days and days with no sleep. This is just one way that this has affected me – there are so many more. I was unable to connect with my husband sexually; we had sexual relations, but I was always disconnected from him (I just went through the motions but was unable to really enjoy the experience). Then there are the nightmares; they do not happen nearly as often as after it first happen, but even now, they pop up and, when they do, it's like the day after all over again, and I work hard to remind myself of where I am now and how far I have come emotionally because I am pretty determined not to let what happened over-come me.

"Although I asked the Prosecutor, Jack Mallard, not to use my true name (for this book), I wish that my story of how I have dealt with the attack will be of some help to other victims of sexual assaults who have been unable to report it or come forward and assist the police and prosecutors in solving the crime. I cannot imagine how I would have been able to suppress what happened to me and lived with myself; it was only possible with the support of loved ones, the law enforcement community, victim advocates and psychological counseling, and being able to testify against my attacker in the courtroom where I was part of seeing that justice was done."

Ms. Melissa Hilyard, a rape and burglary victim on April 10, 1988, at the Concepts 21 Apartments declined to contact me for this book. However, she did reluctantly testify at trial and filed a "victim impact statement" which was available at the sentencing of the Defendant. Her statement provided an estimated financial loss for wages, moving costs from Georgia to her family home, doctor bills, counseling, etc. in an estimated amount of $15,150.00. This was, however, only financial; her written victim impact statement was as follows:

"You cannot begin to imagine the emotional damage a rape can have on a person: the threat of AIDS, pregnancy, possible abortion. I was on both nerve pills and sleeping pills for quite a while just to deal with life and to sleep. [Nightmares], crying and nervousness, insecurity, no self-confidence or value of self-worth are just a few of the emotional things you have to deal with. Even after three years, these feelings still come into play in everyday life. For a woman like myself, who wants a husband and family, this was devastating. I felt like I would never marry; I was not good enough or had nothing to offer. I was lucky two years after the rape - I did find a very kind and understanding man. But the rape and its repercussions are very much a part of our relationship. My family had a very hard time accepting the rape. My father died still very angry about it a year and one-half ago (statement dated 5/14/91). I am glad he does not have to see my pain if this goes to trial. My family fought hard for me and helped me to deal with the emotional pain. We are very close and they would not let me give up. These incidents could possibly put people away, but, due to my faith and my family, I was going to come back and be a useful member of society once again. As for my career, I was a manager of a store and, in order to get out of Georgia where I felt unsafe and after an attempted break-in at our second apartment where I felt the rapist was after me, I took a step down (to ass't), took a cut in pay, and my family moved me home to WI. There was great interest as to why I left my position to move home – the rape was my secret shame personally and professionally. "

Ms. Twila Pruitt was the victim of an aggravated sexual assault in her Concepts 21 apartment on July 15, 1988. She shared with me the following:

"I did go through counseling after the incident. I'm not sure for how long though. I could no longer live in the apartment. I stayed with friends and family until my roommate and I could find another place. I couldn't be alone for a long time afterwards. To this day, I won't take a shower unless someone else is in the house. [This victim was taking a shower when predator Greenway broke into her apartment.]

"My parents were embarrassed and my boyfriend broke up with me. They lived in a small town and I felt blame was put on me. I met my husband a few months after we moved into our new apartment. I needed to feel protected so I hooked on to him pretty quickly. It's not that I didn't love him, but I feel that if this, the incident, hadn't happened, I probably would have stayed single longer. We've been happily married for 21 years, so I guess it was meant to be.

"I am happy now living in California. I have 3 kids 17, 13 and 10. I have told them about what happened. I want them to ... never ... think it won't happen to them, because that's what I thought.

"I never mind sharing my story because I want people to know that a person can get through something like that and be stronger. My faith in God got me through it, and I am living for a reason."

Ms. Donna Hightower was the victim of a rape and burglary at her Concepts 21 apartment on October 15, 1988. She told me:

"That horrible experience has changed my life in more ways than can be told. Though I thought nothing could be worse at the time (with my mother in the hospital), then this predator invaded my personal 'safe place – my home' and left me with a changed outlook on life: that no place is really safe. I never hesitated in reporting this attack, cooperating with law enforcement, and going through the time-consuming investigation and trial—though it has the effect of stripping away a victim's privacy. To those victims who hesitate, or fail to cooperate in the investigation and prosecution of these type crimes because of the exposure and embarrassment, I encourage them to lay aside their fear and come forward and reclaim your life."

Ms. Lisa DePetro who was the victim of an aggravated assault and burglary at the Woodknoll Apartments on March 23, 1989, now lives outside Georgia, and shares the following:

"I was a first year teacher, sharing an apartment with my sister in a new state the first time I came face to face with evil. My sister worked the midnight shift at UPS and wasn't home when it happened. She was my first thought when I was awakened that night by my covers being lifted off me. I was confused and frightened to see a man standing there above me. I quickly scooted back to sit up against the headboard and my thoughts cleared. This monster was telling me to 'just lay there'! In seconds, my feelings went from terror to an indescribable peace and calm. I truly believe God provided this protection; not panic or stillness, just calmness. I needed to make sure my sister was OK. I remember telling him he must have made a mistake and jumped out of bed to try to beat him to the bedroom door. He got there first, closed it and backed me up toward the opposite wall. I again told him that he must have made a mistake and finally saw the knife when I reached forward to push him away. He pushed me and cut my hand. I repeated that he had made a mistake and he looked at me and said, 'You ain't the one I thought you was' and just turned around, opened the bedroom door and walked right back out the sliding glass door he had jimmied open earlier. I made sure my sister wasn't in her room, then, I called the police who stayed on the phone with me until they arrived a few short moments later. Little did I know at that moment how fortunate I was. I was spared the pain and heartbreak of a more violent attack that this man had wreaked upon many women. That knowledge came later when he was captured and convicted of numerous sex crimes. I am thankful, but my heart breaks every time I think back to seeing the other 'victims' who were much more brave than me who testified and helped keep this man from hurting anyone else for a very long time.

"Why did I fight? Why didn't I do what he told me to do? 'Just lay there. It will just take a minute?' I have no answer other than that still, small voice of God. I remember thinking that the intruder responded to my reassuring 'teacher' voice, so I used it. God had placed in me a desire to teach at a young age, and I have lived my life trying to honor Him by using that gift. Right after the attack, my sister and I moved to another community and I went back to the classroom. The next year I taught at a private, Christian school and began to move on with my life. The only lasting effect the attack held over me was a cautiousness about first floor apartments and hotel rooms as well as a wariness about strangers walking too closely behind me. I met my future husband that year. In fact, we were dating when I saw my attacker suddenly appear on the television screen. When I saw that he had been arrested and accused of being a serial rapist, I felt dead inside. I didn't feel worthy to have been spared when others hadn't. The reality of the extent of God's provision hit me like a ton of bricks. It is ironic to me that I was at my happiest when I finally was able to testify against this man. I had been married for 9 months and we had just found out that we were going to have our first child.

My husband and I have expanded our family and have been blessed to have lived in some very interesting, diverse places."

Ms. DePetro further shared with me many blessings from God for their expanded family of six children, the opening of a Christian child care center, and the 'life or death' decision they were able to make when, in the 'depths of despair' they were confronted with a decision whether to remove their seventh child from life support (with severe brain damage)—a decision made only with God's divine guidance.

Ms. Frances Stanford was the victim of a rape and burglary at the Concepts 21 Apartments on August 10, 1989. Her story as told to me:

"The night/early morning it happened I will never forget. Awakened by a stranger standing over my bed with his hand covering my mouth, telling me not to scream, he wasn't going to hurt me, 'I'll be finished in a minute and then I'll be gone'. While he was raping me, something kept telling me [to] focus on him. Every detail you can remember will help you. When his cigarette fell out of his front pocket of his tee shirt, I thought he was going to see it but, fortunately, he did not. When he finished and told me to roll over on my stomach and lay there, I thought he was going to shoot me. When I heard him slide the security chain and unlock the front door and close it, I did not know if he was really gone, so I just laid there for what seemed to be forever. Then I got up to check the front door and found the sliding glass door to the screened in back porch open, [so] I closed it. [I] went into my bedroom and dialed 911. When the police got there, I remember them asking me how did I make that call, [since] the phone line in my living room had been cut. When I showed them the phone in my bedroom, which was black and grey, they said he must not have seen that one.

"I was transported to Kennestone ER by police car. The exam seemed to take forever. They cut my finger nails in a plastic bag, careful not to let any of them fall onto the floor. The vaginal smear hurt, as I recall. Then they combed my pubic hair and also pulled some of it out, and the same with my hair on my head. I remember them telling me that I needed a prescription for some meds that I really needed. When I stated to them I had no money, some of the nurses in the ER pulled together enough money for me to buy the meds. The police officer took me to the pharmacy across the street from Kennestone to get them.

"The first time I went back into my apartment, I felt like I was in a morgue. The cold strange feeling I cannot put into words. It was an awful feeling, not only then, but every time until I got all of my belongings out.

"Meeting with Detective Grogan, I believe to do the sketches, was a difficult thing to do. However, he tried to make me as comfortable as possible. It was not easy. I told him every detail I could think of to make the composite sketch. I was told later it was almost an exact picture of him.

"I was terrified for a long time standing in lines in stores. I thought everyone was staring at me as if they knew I had been raped. I kept telling myself it was just a feeling and no one knew. I looked at strangers in [a] different way. I can't explain this; it was just a feeling. I felt like I wanted to stay inside and never go out again.

"The day I saw his picture on the news I knew right then it was him, no doubt about it. I called Scott Smith. He came over with a photo line-up and I immediately told him it was him, I was absolutely sure without a doubt in my mind. He said, 'OK, that's all I need to know. I'll get the proper paperwork and go get him.' Finally I thought the end is in sight, little did I know it was just begun.

"I went to counseling at the Rape Crisis Center at the Y. Those people were a God-send; they told me all the emotions I had been having were completely normal. I can't remember how long I attended the sessions, but they finally told me I was going to be OK and that I had completed all that they had to offer.

"The trial seemed to take forever; victim-witness people were very nice and polite and tried to do their best to comfort me while I was waiting to testify. However, I know that they cannot let you out of sight, but I just wanted to go to the bathroom to pee and have a melt-down in peace. The lady in charge of me went everywhere I did.

"I remember the victim who had moved out of state who wasn't going to come to the trial to testify, and I called her mother and spoke with her and explained to her that none of us wanted to do this but we had to and we had to do it as a team. We're all in this together and each one of us must do our part. I pleaded with her, 'Please ask your daughter to come.' She did; however, I did not get to see her after she testified. She took the next flight out to wherever she was from. I did call her mother when it was over and gave her the good news. She thanked me and politely asked me to never call again.

"When I took the stand to testify I was scared, real scared, I think I even raised my right hand instead of my left. I stared at him, answered the questions and when asked if that person was in the courtroom, I did not want to point and say 'yes, he's over there.' I wanted him and the entire courtroom to know what he did, broke into my apartment and raped me, and I wanted to give him the coldest 'go to hell you bastard' look he had ever seen; this was my time. I'm going to make you pay for a very long time for what you did to me. You raped me and put me through hell and I'm over it now. You no longer have any control over me. Game's over and I won. Who's in control now?

"When the news came on that night, I remember them saying something about one of the victims giving him a piercing cold look. I knew that they were talking about me: The smallest victim with the biggest mouth.

"I was born and raised in a small rural town in Alabama outside of Birmingham. Four brothers and no sisters, number four in line. My brothers always taught me to take up for myself for they would not always be around to protect me, so I needed to learn to defend myself and never ever let anyone run over you. Speak up for yourself – no one else will.

"I went through the entire trial alone; my mother didn't come because she couldn't bear to see me go through it. My father was in a nursing home dying. I remember her asking me, 'Why do you want to put yourself through this again? You will have to relive so much of this. Do you really want to do this?' My answer was, 'Yes, I have to do it for myself. If I don't, I never [will] really be over it.' I thank God that I did.

"When the letter came from the DA's office about news of the case they prosecuted several years ago, I thought he was up for parole. I was ready to go to the hearing and ask that he not be paroled. I will be his worst nightmare when his parole hearing comes up.

"I really feel sorry for his children. The boys—they will always have the title their father was a rapist. As for his wife, I often wonder if she really didn't know or if she was covering up for him."

About a year following the trial, Ms. Stanford married a Cobb County Sheriff's Deputy, now retired, and they celebrated their 18th anniversary during the period we conversed about this update in her life; they have no children.

Ms. Jeannine McClean was the victim of the attempted burglary of her apartment at Cinnamon Ridge Apartments, at 05:11 a.m. on January 7, 1990. Her Himalayan cat, Precious, is credited with awakening her and saving her from a worse fate; predator Greenway was arrested at her door. She now lives out of the state, and expresses concern for her safety if Greenway makes parole, fearing he will hold her responsible for his arrest. She adds:

"I still, after over 21 years later, do not sleep soundly at night—especially on the rare occasions I am in the house alone at night. I am now an expert marksman and have an abundance of firepower at my bedside if I need it. My 6 years as a Deputy at CCSO (Cobb County Sheriff's Office) provided additional defense training as well. That along with my wonderful husband and beautiful German shepherd at my side should make it easier, but at night, as I drift off to sleep, the demons don't rest."

She told me she went into law enforcement because of her experience with the criminal justice system following her attack.

INMATE TERRY GREENWAY – IN HIS OWN WORDS

TERRY GREENWAY, PRISON PHOTO

It was March 1, 2012, at the Central State Prison. Inmate Greenway confessed to me that he did, in fact, commit the crimes for which he was convicted. As he sat across a small triangle table from me in the medium security prison where he is now serving his sentences, he no longer blamed his "being where he is" on alcoholism and, for the first time when pressed by me that he can no longer use alcohol as a crutch, he admitted that he was guilty, and he had no problem with me for prosecuting him, the jury in convicting him, or the witnesses who testified against him. He only had a problem with the sentences imposed by Judge Brantley.

On September 19, 2011, I wrote inmate Greenway requesting an opportunity to interview him in prison for input for this book. After several months, I received his reply—a lengthy letter along with a religious card and Biblical quotes—wherein he agreed for a friendly visit. In his five-page handwritten letter, Greenway still blamed his troubles and incarceration on *alcoholism*, without reference to his crimes or his victims. It was a typical letter from a long term inmate glossing over his present predicament with excuses of "alcohol made me do it" and setting up his next parole hearing with his going to (prison) church, Bible study, and, "I serve the Lord Jesus each and every day, and if God will's for me to get paroled I will," while denying that he had jailhouse religion. He also works at the prison sewing plant—sewing boxer shorts for the prison industry. He also attends Alcoholics Anonymous. Greenway said his downfall in life was being an alcoholic. His entire written theme indicated he was preparing himself for being paroled in February, 2013—one year away.

In his letter written December 18, 2011, he even wrote: "P.S. *I hope our Falcon's (Atlanta's Pro Football Team) do good in the playoff and our Atlanta Braves (baseball) will be a much better team by leaning (sic) what happen (sic) to them last year.*" [The Falcons didn't do "good" in the playoffs, being knocked out in the first round.]

Notwithstanding Inmate Greenway's invitation to visit him, I was not his attorney or a family member and would need to obtain special permission from the Department of Corrections to interview him.

My application to the Georgia Department of Corrections for a special visit to Central State Prison to meet with Inmate Greenway was finally approved for 09:00 a.m., March 1, 2012. However, I was limited in my interview of Inmate Greenway to certain questions and issues, and *excluded from asking him if his victims have any reason to feel threatened. I thought that would be the most relevant and important issue to determine.*

I arrived at the prison—one I had not personally visited before as a prosecutor—and made my presence known at the guard's shack where I put myself and briefcase through the scanner. I was admitted to enter. The sounds of the two steel gates clanging shut behind me before I arrived at the main building just reminded me of sounds I heard numerous times before in the many prisons and jails around the state. For only a short time, I would be inside the locked, brick and steel "home" to hundreds of human beings who would be there for decades or life, a*nd, I questioned if it would deter others who visited such facility from crime and recidivism.*

Once inside, I was met by a young lady, Ms. Gwendolyn Hogan, from the Public Relations Division of the Corrections Department. I had not realized she would be present during my interview. I followed her to a small interview room where we waited for Inmate Greenway to be delivered. I only had a pen, notepad, and some notes for the interview. No electronic devices were allowed inside the prison—and I had an hour to do the interview.

Inmate Greenway entered the room. He was dressed in prison uniform with no restraints. This was not unusual under the circumstances. He smiled and acknowledged us, taking his seat in a metal chair. At least my chair had a soft cushion. We sat at a small table across from each other with Ms. Hogan sitting to my right. She would take a few notes as would I. I did have an outline of questions I would put to him. Immediately, I noted the "upbeat" in Greenway's demeanor. He was friendly, cordial, smiling, and actually appeared "chipper." He said to me that he saw me at Hays prison, a maximum security prison in north Georgia where he was assigned in the late 1990s, and that I apparently was touring the prison. I acknowledged I was visiting the prison during that period of time, but I did not see Greenway, or didn't recognize him. [I was there to see a (potential) witness inmate.]

Inmate Greenway's appearance as he faced me, compared to 20 years ago in the courtroom, showed a marked transformation of age. Now, his appearance at age 59 just emphasizes life in prison—as shown by his photograph above. It's only evidence of growing old in prison, and should be a deterrence to others should they follow his path. I hope it serves such deterrence because of the impact not only on his family and the victims, but upon the financial burden of the institution of Government. The ratio of prisoners to population is a statistic we as a people cannot long endure or tolerate.

I addressed him as "Terry." He first told me he had recently communicated with his "family," and decided to decline the interview; that he had written me a letter the day before telling me of that decision. [After returning home from the interview, I did in fact have his letter declining the interview in the mailbox.] However, after my arrival, he said he decided to conduct the interview. I told him it was up to him—that he could decline any or all questions.

I sized up Terry immediately. He was in a predicament wherein he wanted to put forth his case for parole, and if he refused the interview it would not look good for him. I had made it clear in my letter to him that I would not write of his "good stuff" he claimed without an opportunity to question him. [I wanted to see if he would admit for the first time his guilt.]

Initially, I let him (again) go over his preparations for the next parole hearing, which included a "Faith and Character-Based Initiative": A program where certain inmates are put in dormitories designed to provide an "environment for change" tending to "support the offender's successful transition from custody into the community ... "through the promotion of personal responsibility, integrity, accountability, and the building of one's faith." I knew the Parole Board would be deluged with all these things he was telling me about.

I had several issues which I would question him about.

I threw the soft ball questions first. One of the victims, Twila Pruitt, had recently told me in her follow-up interview that, at some time after her attack, her father (name omitted) had worked for a company, Air Treads, in the Atlanta area years prior to her attack; that while so employed he knew the Defendant Terry Greenway—who also worked there. So I told Terry I was interested in his employment prior to the time of trial; he started giving me several places such as "Shasta," "Ingles" and others. I asked him if he knew of "Air Treads," and after prompting him, he said he had worked there but many years earlier (1970s). I then asked him if he knew (naming Ms. Pruitt's father) to which he vaguely did recall the name. *Perhaps not important, but weird, that he would sexually attack a former fellow employee's daughter.*

I also asked him about his wife, Mandy, contacting my sister in Brunswick. He said he knew Mandy was acquainted with Gracie, but that he did not know of her contacting my sister about the case; neither did he know of Mandy writing the Chief Superior Court Judge prior to his trial about bond. He did tell me in his letter and in person that Mandy "did run my case" and that she "had everything done with my lawyer, Ha Ha." Terry further said that his wife "Mandy" had divorced him about five years ago and remarried, but that they were still friendly. He has nine grandchildren from his three sons and they live outside the state, he said.

I told Terry that he, in his lengthy letter, had blamed his being where he is on "alcohol" and that I didn't buy it, that he had never acknowledged his guilt of the crimes for which a jury convicted him—14 felony counts—and the testimony of eight women. I recited the crimes to him. I further pressed him that he claims to be "a man of God" and that I always felt that one who is a

Christian had gotten there by confessing their crimes and asking for forgiveness, something he has never done; that he couldn't be rehabilitated while blaming everything on alcohol. I questioned whether he was going to the Parole Board with that story. I suggested now was the time to decide which way he was going. He quickly acknowledged he was there (in prison) because of his own actions—not alcohol. He admitted he was the one who put himself in prison because of crimes he committed for which he was convicted, and he blamed no one but himself. He had no issue with me or the jury, nor his lawyer, but felt the Judge gave him too much time to serve, saying the "sentence was unfair." [Actually, I recommended more time—Judge Brantley probated part of the sentences; not that it really mattered since *one life sentence is sufficient to keep him in prison all of his remaining days in life.*]

I asked Terry if he had psychological counseling while in prison. It didn't surprise me when he said he had not. After observing and discussing the case with him, he showed no signs of any need for counseling: Though uneducated, he came across as very competent in his communication skills and thought processes. He showed no remorse for his victims, or indication he was seeking forgiveness from them, and no concern for their harm he had caused. In my view, he was only thinking of himself—and a "way out of prison."

With my hour long interview coming to an end, I had one last query I wanted to make of this convicted serial rapist. "What makes a person like you rape?" I asked. I asked him whether it was one of those sexual desires—a compelling and uncontrollable urge? He could only produce an answer of something to do with alcohol and [it] leading to other things. I thought: Which comes first, the alcohol or the compelling urge to rape? Does it really matter?

In the beginning of the interview, I told Terry that I was no longer a prosecutor, and as a writer, I needed to be able to be objective and consider both sides of the issue; otherwise, I wouldn't be there; further, that I had recently interviewed most of the victims, who wanted him where he was, and now I was giving him the opportunity to state to me anything he wished me to hear going forward to his parole hearing.

I hope I have been objective. I have related his 'good stuff' he claims should make him a good parolee, while the victims have had their say on the matter, and no doubt will continue to do so for his upcoming parole consideration.

My request under the Open Records Act to have declassified, and obtain internal records from the Department of Corrections and Pardons and Paroles Board pertaining to Inmate Greenway's incarceration, was denied. I wanted to determine if he had any disciplinary problems or conflicts in prison.

The Parole Board – the unspoken words

Terry Greenway, the convicted serial rapist, is incarcerated in the Central State Prison at Macon, Georgia. He is awaiting his next parole hearing in February, 2013. In 1992 after his trial and in response to Greenway's inquiry, the Parole Board informed him he would be considered for parole in February 1997—seven years after his arrest—which was the law at that time. By letter on April 17, 1997, the Board informed Greenway that his 1997 consideration was denied, advising him he would be again considered in February 2005. Again by letter, Greenway was notified on February 4, 2005, that he was *denied parole* because it *would not be compatible with the welfare of society due to the severe nature of the offense(s).*

Will he gain his freedom this time? Is his chance better than before? Will he present more compelling reasons than he has before? He has finally confessed his crimes, though at my urging, and admitted his guilt to horrendous crimes for which he was convicted. I have always understood that "confession" was good for the soul, and the first step in a person's rehabilitation—but not necessarily justifying release. *Punishment also serves a purpose.*

No doubt, at this time, there are internal forces working for inmate Greenway's release which was not so in the past: It's called *Budget Crisis and Prison Overcrowding!*

In 2011, the Governor appointed a Special Council on Criminal Justice Reform to address the budget-busting and incarceration rate of adults in Georgia prisons, noting that 1 in 70 adults in Georgia were behind bars at the end of 2007, compared to the national incarceration rate of 1 in 100 adults, and that Georgia had the fourth highest incarceration rate in the country.

In November, 2011, the Council released its findings and recommendations which did not (apparently) surprise anyone that nearly a half-million people under correctional control actually costs taxpayers more than $1 billion dollars per year, while the recidivism rates remain high. Recommendations included directing more resources towards community corrections, supervision, mental health, and treatment and intervention options.

As I write this, the General Assembly is considering a law to control growth in the State Prison population by sentencing *non-violent offenders* to alternative programs. Where this is going, anyone can guess—we must wait and see. The prisons are steadily filling up with "lifers," those under life sentences. I did my part in sending many of them there.

Thus, pressure exists on the Parole Board by internal and external forces. The cost/budget factor of maintaining older prisoners in a burgeoning prison system versus the need of maintaining integrity with the public in weighing its safety concerns, especially in such a case where the sentencing judge expressed his intent and wish that this prisoner be incarcerated until he was 100 years old, as well as the *legitimate interests* of the victims and the public in the decision of the Board, *to be compatible with the welfare of society due to the severe nature of the offense(s).*

The Georgia Pardons and Paroles Board [The Board] is part of the Executive Branch of State Government, having been created in 1943 following a period of public concerns about corruption in the parole process by former governors. The Board members, consisting of five, are now appointed by the Governor to seven year terms and confirmed by the State Senate.

The Board's website makes clear that the Board is independent, with many factors going into its discretionary decision to "parole" an offender including the "impact" of the crime on victims and their safety concerns, and "limited resources," commenting that a lack of bed space and overcrowding could result in "Federal" intervention and mass releases. Further, the Board has broad constitutional authority to parole *after the inmate has served an appropriate portion of a sentence.* What is "appropriate" is strictly in the Board's eyes, within confines of their rules.

The only trigger for release on a life sentence is that of "Parole." There is no "right" to parole, only consideration. The law in effect when Greenway was sentenced provided for consideration of parole after 7 years, but was changed in 2006 to 30 years. There is no "good," "gained," or "earned" time application to his prison sentence. An inmate paroled by the Board will have parole supervision.

The Board's website points out that their rate for paroles successfully completed is 69% compared to a national rate of only 49%. The cost of parole supervision was placed at $4.65 per day, miniscule if compared to the cost of incarceration—which I understand to be about $18,000 per year.

The website for the Board states: *Created by Constitutional amendment in 1943, the Georgia Parole Board is a national model for stable and professional leadership. The agency was well-constructed: It contains authority to carry out established needs of the criminal justice system, flexibility to address the unforeseen challenges, and protection to make decisions on paroles and policy free from political influence. What has made Georgia's Board such a leader, however, is the professionalism of its members. Their collective experience and commitment to criminal justice ideals keep Georgia's Board continually attuned to long-term as well as short-term public safety solutions.*

As a Prosecutor of four decades, and being familiar with decision-making of the Board and its reputation in carrying out its function, I believe the foregoing to be true. I know the Board has been tested many times with hard, controversial decisions, and [it] has generally risen above the fray.

The case is now in the hands of the "Board." Greenway wants out; his victims want him where he is now—no threat to those outside prison. I purposely did not contact the Board members for obvious reasons: they will be deciding Greenway's fate, and I helped to put him where he is.

ABOUT THE AUTHOR

Jack Mallard received his Law Degree from Woodrow Wilson College of Law, and was admitted to the Georgia State Bar in 1966. He began his career as an Assistant District Attorney in the Atlanta Office in 1967. He was a Prosecutor in Fulton, Cobb, and Forsyth counties during a 40 year span, and retired in 2007. During that period, he prosecuted hundreds of high profile and capital murder cases, including the first two DNA cases and two murders by anti-freeze. Mr. Mallard served on the Georgia Organized Crime Prevention Council (1972-1981); Board of Directors, National District Attorneys Association (1990-1998); and was selected by his peers as Assistant District Attorney of the Year (1995). He was recipient of the Governor's Public Safety Award (2001). After retirement, Mr. Mallard wrote and published his first book, *The Atlanta Child Murders: the Night Stalker* (2009), based upon his prosecution of Wayne B. Williams in 1982. Mr. Mallard was born and reared on a farm near Jesup, Georgia – one of eight children. He served four years in the U. S. Air Force. He and wife, Becky, now live north of Atlanta in retirement.

Made in the USA
Charleston, SC
22 December 2012